Ethics and Human Reproduction

Ethics and Human Reproduction:
A Feminist Analysis

Christine Overall

Boston
ALLEN & UNWIN
London   Sydney   Wellington

Allen & Unwin, Inc.
8 Winchester Place, Winchester, MA 01890, USA.

The U.S. Company of
Unwin Hyman Ltd,

P.O. Box 18, Park Lane, Hemel Hempstead, Herts HP2 4TE, UK
40 Museum Street, London WC1A 1LU, UK
37/39 Queen Elizabeth Street, London SE1 2QB, UK

Allen & Unwin Australia Pty Ltd,
8 Napier Street, North Sydney, NSW 2060, Australia

Allen & Unwin (New Zealand) Ltd,
in association with the Port Nicholson Press Ltd
60 Cambridge Terrace, Wellington, New Zealand

Library of Congress Cataloging-in-Publication Data

Overall, Christine, 1949–
Ethics and human reproduction.
Bibliography: p.

Includes index.
1. Human reproduction——Moral and ethical aspects.
2. Feminism.   I. Title.
QP251. 083   1987   174'.2   87–1107
ISBN 0–04–497009–9 (alk. paper)
ISBN 0–04–497010–2 (pbk. : alk. paper)

British Library Cataloguing in Publication Data

Overall, Christine
Ethics and human reproduction: a feminist
analysis.
1. Human reproduction——Moral and ethical
aspects
I. Title

176   QP251
ISBN 0–04–497009–9
ISBN 0–04–497010–2 PBK

Set in 10 on 12 point Palatino by Phoenix Photosetting, Chatham
Printed and bound in Great Britain
by Billing & Sons Limited, Worcester.

Contents

For Narnia, Melissa, and Dorothy,
to whom it matters

Acknowledgments

I am delighted to recognize and thank all of the people who contributed to the making of this book. I am grateful to Marianopolis College, which gave me my first opportunity to explore my interests in reproductive ethics, and to Queen's University, which in 1984 awarded me a Webster Fellowship in the Humanities to pursue my research. I want to thank all of my colleagues at Queen's in philosophy and in women's studies, particularly Michael Fox, Carlos Prado, and J. E. Bickenbach, who believed in me and my work, and Roberta Hamilton, Katherine McKenna, and Elizabeth Greene, who made me feel welcome in women's studies. I have also been fortunate to be able to discuss issues pertaining to reproduction with feminist scholars and practitioners at conferences and colloquia in medicine, law, theology, and philosophy; I am grateful to all of them. Many students have contributed to my thoughts on reproductive technology, particularly my students in Humanities 401 at Marianopolis College, and my students in Philosophy 495/895 at Queen's University. Patricia O'Reilly played a special role by sharing with me her interests and research in midwifery.

Harriet Simand's knowledge of reproductive health hazards, and her strength and personal integrity as a DES daughter, were an ongoing source of inspiration.

In the past two years I have come to regard three people as essential to may academic work: Linda Hall, Jackie Doherty, and Karen Hermer. They helped me master the intricacies of word processing and cheerfully contributed their knowledge and secretarial skills to the production of this manuscript.

I am grateful to John Michel and Lisa Freeman-Miller of Allen & Unwin, who were unfailingly encouraging and supportive, and to Barbara Katz Rothman for her detailed critique of my manuscript. Melissa Caplan spent an arduous summer assembling and checking the bibliography, and helped me to see many things that I would otherwise have missed. David Overall produced the index.

Most of all it has been the love and faith of my extended family that has freed me to write this book. I thank them all, but particularly my mother, Dorothy Overall, for being there; my brother, David Overall, for telling me to let it go; and my grandparents, Hazel and C. W. Bayes, for their courage and grace. My children, Devon and Narnia Worth, endured my absences, replenished my spirit, and always understood that "Mummy really wants to write." And my husband, Ted Worth, was in the beginning, is now, and ever shall be—in this life and in many to come.

1 *Introduction*

Is the use of prenatal diagnosis a unique form of insurance for parents that their offspring will be healthy? Or is it a covert but potentially dangerous manifestion of eugenics?

Is the practice of surrogate motherhood a valuable service for men whose wives are infertile? Or is it a type of reproductive prostitution of women?

Is fetal sex preselection a benign process that enables people to have the precious son or daughter for whom they long? Or is it a form of gynecide—that is, wholesale slaughter of females?

Is the recovery of eggs from surgically removed ovarian tissue a good source of experimental material for use in reproductive research? Or is it an insidious type of egg snatching and egg farming?

These questions are examples of just a few of the ethical issues now being raised about reproduction and reproductive technology. They are part of a rapidly growing philosophical subdiscipline—reproductive ethics—that is concerned with the wide range of moral questions arising in connection with human reproduction. Although some reproductive issues, such as those pertaining to contraception, abortion, and birth, have always been of deep significance throughout human existence, the past ten years have witnessed the development of new reproductive technologies, such as in vitro fertilization, embryo transfer, and sex preselection, which have almost as great a capacity for affecting human lives.

They will affect human lives—but, in particular, they will affect *women's* lives, and that potential does not always receive the emphasis it deserves. In the current debates about issues in reproductive ethics there is a striking contrast in approach between, on the one hand, those which highlight women's experience, needs, and behavior in connection with reproduction and those which minimize, ignore, or deny the central

relation between women and reproduction and instead pro-
fess concern for entities such as "society" or "the family." The
latter approach is antifeminist or nonfeminist in nature; the
former is feminist. This book develops a critique of antifeminist and nonfeminist approaches to reproductive ethics and
offers in their place a feminist analysis of issues in
reproduction.

Feminism: A Definition

Both historical and contemporary discussions show clearly
that the term "feminism" encompasses a variety of meanings,[1]
and not all of them are entirely consistent with one another.
Nevertheless it is possible to outline the minimal but essential
components of a feminist perspective.

First, a feminist perspective involves a commitment to
understanding women's experience, beliefs, ideas, relationships, behavior, creations, and history. It stresses women's
own perceptions; that is, how events, institutions, social
groups, and individuals are apprehended and interpreted by
women. It highlights those elements of women's personal and
social exerience which are common and shared as well as those
which are distinct and diverse. This focus is justified by the fact
that women's experience and history have for the most part
been suppressed, ignored, manipulated, and exploited, both
in the past and in the present. It is therefore necessary to
recover what has been lost, to give recognition to what has
been ignored, to revalue what has been depreciated in
women's experience. This recovery process involves a variety
of methods—from the informal and revelatory process of consciousness-raising to the more formal and scholarly research in
women's studies. What they have in common is a determination to avoid duplicating those methods used in the past
which, by treating women as, at most, objects to be studied,
have   misrepresented   and   misunderstood   women's
experience.

Second, a feminist perspective is founded upon and fully

informed by an awareness that women as women have been and are the victims of oppression under patriarchy, the system of male dominance.[2] Such a claim does not necessarily imply that "men are the enemy" or that all men rule all women. But it does imply that although women are oppressed as women, men are not usually oppressed as men.[3] This awareness includes a conception of what oppression—unjust limitations and barriers—is and of its physical, psychological, social, and legal manifestations. And it is not complete without attention to the ways in which women's oppression can vary depending upon other variables such as age, race, class, religion, nationality, and sexual orientation.

Third, a feminist perspective includes some sort of theory about the origins of the oppression of women. Such a theory entails not necessarily a belief in one general "cause" of sexual oppression but, rather, attention to the ways in which that oppression is maintained and perpetuated, as well as attention to the agents—both individual and institutional—of oppression. It is on this aspect of feminism perhaps more than any other that feminists have disagreed; disputes about the sources of women's oppression have led to the development, particularly within the last two decades, of feminist political theories ranging from liberal feminism to socialist and Marxist feminism to radical feminism.[4]

Fourth, a feminist perspective is guided by a determination to avoid perpetuating or acquiescing in the oppression of women and to contribute, whenever possible, to the further understanding and dissolution of sexual inequality. In this respect feminism moves beyond the awareness of women's victimization to a vision of women's present and potential empowerment. Such a vision includes a concept of what the end of oppression would mean and would be like and of what the goal of feminist revolutionary change should be. Feminists have favored a variety of means to end oppression, including gradual reform, the production of alternate institutions and systems, and separatism of various sorts.[5]

Finally, a feminist perspective is characterized by the deliberate and self-conscious (in a positive sense) nature of its worldview. In its most developed form it fosters the creation of new or alternate epistemic, ontological, ethical, and cultural systems.[6] This is the most original aspect of feminism, and also its least developed.

Antifeminist and Nonfeminist Perspectives

In the preceding definition of feminism the first and second characteristics are most crucial; the third, fourth, and fifth follow from them. Hence antifeminist and nonfeminist perspectives can most easily be understood in terms of their relationship to the first and second characteristics of feminism.

A type of conservatism, antifeminism rejects the feminist commitment to understanding women's experience and denies the claim that women have been and are the victims of oppression.[7] The antifeminist believes that women are not oppressed, for such a term implies unjust treatment of women. Instead he (or she) maintains that differential treatment of women is justified, often on the grounds of innate differences between the sexes that lead to distinct social functions for women and for men. The antifeminist also tends to support the enforcement and elaboration of alleged sex differences through state-controlled mechanisms. In short, antifeminism champions a type of socially sanctioned biological determinism in which sexual and reproductive differences between the sexes are fundamental to their different roles.[8]

In speaking of a nonfeminist approach, on the other hand, I am grouping a variety of different views. They are not necessarily overtly and actively misogynistic. However, a nonfeminist perspective is one that, deliberately or not, tends to ignore rather than deny women's experience and to suspend belief about the claim that women are oppressed. In this perspective what is most noticeable is not a deliberately antifeminist or antiwomen stance but, rather, one that is simply unaware of the hard-won insights of feminist writings. A nonfeminist approach, then, is androcentric[9]: that is, it overlooks women's experience, taking male perceptions and interpretations as the norm. It lacks the deliberately self-conscious character of feminist discourse, which is aware that there is more than one possible framework for the discussion of social and moral issues. Such an approach shows little or no awareness or understanding of the past and present oppression of women, and as a result it fails to question—and even helps to reinforce—patriarchal control over women.

Antifeminist and Nonfeminist Approaches to Reproductive Ethics

Human beings are embodied beings, and an understanding of reproduction is essential to understanding human relationships and what it is to be human within the context of patriarchy. Broadly construed, reproduction includes not only the immediate biological processes of procreation and the social uses to which they are put but also sexual interactions and relationships, and childrearing. In this book the focus is primarily upon issues pertaining directly to procreation, but it is impossible to discuss them independently of a concern for questions about sexuality and child care.

To examine reproduction requires not just an understanding of nature, of what is biologically given; it requires also an understanding of the social construction and organization of sexual, procreative, and child care relationships. In fact, such an understanding calls into question the assumption that it is legitimate or even meaningful to speak of what is biologically given outside the context of the human interpretations put on it. As Zillah Eisenstein says,

> Women can sexually reproduce and they lactate. These are biological facts. That women are defined as mothers is a political fact and reflects a political need of patriarchy, which is based partially in the biological truth that women bear children. The transformation of women from a biological being (childbearer) to a political being (childrearer) is part of the conflict expressed in the politics of patriarchy. Patriarchy seeks to maintain the myth that patriarchal motherhood is a

biological reality rather than a politically constructed necessity.[10]

Both antifeminists and nonfeminists, on the one hand, and feminists, on the other, have strived to understand human reproduction and to respond to the variety of issues raised by the social shaping of reproduction. The results of their investigations, however, have been very different.

Antifeminist and nonfeminist approaches to reproductive ethics are characterized by the tendency to concentrate on a few issues to the exclusion of others—which may in fact be equally or more important. *What* is overlooked, *that* it is overlooked, and *why* it is overlooked—all of this is as significant as what is actually discussed in reproductive ethics, but it is, of course, somewhat harder to recognize.

For example, contemporary philosophical discussions of reproduction have focused almost exclusively on the topic of abortion, and the literature on that subject is voluminous and complex. Moreover recent texts serving as general introductions to biomedical ethics or to contemporary social issues[11] almost always include a section on abortion but seldom on any other topics in reproductive ethics. This thanatological concentration is consistent with the general concern that philosophers have historically evinced for questions about death; it appears virtually to exclude any consideration of, for example, questions about birth.[12] It also entails lengthy and detailed discussions of the moral and metaphysical status of the embryo/fetus: for example, is it a person? If so, when does it become a person? If not, why is it not a person?[13] and so on. There is, however, relatively little discussion of the woman who is the co-creator and sole sustainer of the embryo/fetus, except insofar as she is treated as a container or "environment" for it. And on the rare occasions on which women are discussed within the context of abortion or birth, the fetus-woman relationship is most often seen as one of competition and antagonism rather than interaction and support.

Recent antifeminist and nonfeminist discussions of the uses of new reproductive technology have not done much to alter this myopic outlook. Once again, only a limited number of topics are considered to be worthy of discussion. In analyses of the implications of in vitro fertilization and surrogate motherhood, for example, we mainly find a concern for questions about so-called sexual ethics[14] (for example, is a surrogate mother committing adultery?[15]), about the security and sustenance of what is ambiguously referred to as "*the* family" (as if there were just one form of the family),[16] and about which woman is to be considered the "real mother" of the offspring produced through surrogacy.

Thus, in general an antifeminist or nonfeminist approach tends to avoid, overlook, or minimize what feminists would regard as crucial topics and issues in reproductive ethics and to concentrate on a rather small number of questions whose importance may, as a result, be exaggerated.

Second, antifeminist and nonfeminist approaches are characterized by a pervasive failure to examine or challenge certain underlying assumptions about reproduction that are widely held both by society in general and by the medical establishment in particular. The clearest example of this is found in discussions of infertility, its meaning, significance, and appropriate treatment. Infertility is an important topic because its growing incidence is usually offered as the main justification for the development of technologies of artificial reproduction. Antifeminist and nonfeminist experts from both medicine and the social sciences often assume that infertility is a legitimate problem only for women who are heterosexual and married[17]; that children are material commodities owned by their parents; that a family is incomplete, or not a family at all, if no children are present; and that a genetic link with one's children is psychologically and morally essential.[18]

These unexamined beliefs also have implications for what is assumed to be the appropriate and correct treatment of infertility. They suggest, for example, that people—especially men—have an inalienable right to be parents.[19] Yet it is also assumed that infertility should be treated only in women who are heterosexual and married[20]; that it should be treated so as to provide a child who is genetically related to the couple, and particularly to the father; and that therefore heroic measures, including in vitro fertilization, embryo transfer, and surrogate motherhood, may be preferable to adoption and to the less expensive, dangerous, and invasive procedure of artificial insemination by donor.[21] Finally, these beliefs are related to certain assumptions about women: that women are primarily dependent baby-making machines that, unfortunately, may threaten their offspring or fail to operate and therefore need a "technological fix."[22]

Are all of these beliefs true? The problem is not that antifeminist and nonfeminist writers *defend* them; in fact they usually offer virtually no justification whatsoever for holding them. The problem is that these ideas apparently are so self-evident to these writers that no one thinks to provide reasons for the ideas or that there could be any basis for questioning them.

Finally, antifeminist and nonfeminist approaches to reproductive ethics are characterized by a lack of insight into and concern for the implications of new reproductive technology for the well-being of women and children. One example is surrogate motherhood. Nonfeminist writers typically regard surrogate motherhood as, at best, a desirable, useful, and indeed necessary service that uncoerced women may offer for purchase by childless men. They believe that it is a relatively unproblematic social institution, requiring only careful legal regulation of its contractual aspects, as well as public scrutiny of its actual operation.[23] Little attention is paid in these discussions to the potential effects of the surrogate motherhood arrangement on children and on women, and there is no discussion of what the practice of buying reproductive services indicates about the social position of women.

Another example is fetal sex selection and preselection. Antifeminist and nonfeminist writers treat the use of these processes as inevitable and unproblematic. They seldom question the sexism implicit in a technology that would permit us to choose the human beings who will be our children on the basis of their sex alone. Such writers are remarkably undisturbed by the prospect of possible changes in the sex ratio that, given the almost universal parental preference for male offspring,[24] could be produced in some areas by widespread use of sex selection and preselection.[25] Instead most nonfeminist writers view fetal sex selection and preselection with great optimism as a potential cure for world population problems and a panacea for parents who would otherwise not get the kind of children they want.[26]

In general, then, as these examples show, antifeminist and nonfeminist discussions of reproductive ethics too often are almost oblivious to the possible consequences for children and women of the development and adoption of reproductive technology.

Feminist Approaches to Reproductive Ethics

Whereas much of patriarchal ideology defines women's "natural" function in terms of their capacities for sexual activity, procreation, and child-rearing, feminist analysis has recently begun to demonstrate that women's sexual, procreative, and child care abilities are manipulated, exploited, and appropriated to accommodate patriarchal interests.

This appropriation has been manifested historically through a variety of attitudes and behaviors.[27] In the arena of sexuality, for example, these include heterosexism and homophobia; pornography; contempt for women's bodies and women's sexuality; the institutions of incest, rape, sexual harassment, and prostitution; and sexual pressures and prohibitions of all types. In the arena of procreation the patriarchal appropriation of reproduction has produced compulsory motherhood—by means of contraception that is dangerous, unreliable, or often unavailable; abortion, which can be inaccessible or life-threatening; the prohibition of any life choices other than mothering, or the provision of work that mimics certain aspects of mothering; and the promotion of pronatalism and emphasis on fertility and fecundity, particularly in women. At the same time, not all women are judged suitable to be mothers. Some women have been the victims of involuntary sterilization; others have lost custody of and access to their children because of their sexual orientation. In the arena of child-rearing, patriarchal appropriation of reproduction takes the form of control over mothering, by means of an ideology of child-rearing that specifies what sort of mothers are desirable and what kind of children mothers should produce.[28] This is accompanied by a significant lack of support for mothering, evinced in the incompatibility of much productive labor and reproductive labor within patriarchy, and the absence of social mechanisms to support good child-rearing, such as paid maternity leave, adequate family allowances, and state-supported child care.

The most recent manifestation of the patriarchal appropriation of reproduction lies in the development and use of new reproductive technology. In contrast to the glorification of this technology by antifeminist and nonfeminist writers, feminists for the most part are not blinded by rosy visions of an approaching technological paradise, and generally adopt a more skeptical, sometimes even pessimistic stance toward issues in reproductive ethics. This is not, of course, uniformly true of all feminist theorists: Shulamith Firestone[29] is the exceptional example of a feminist who saw artificial reproduction as a liberating force for women. But more recent feminist writers who, unlike Firestone, have witnessed the implementation of the "technological fix" in reproduction have been less enthusiastic about the potential benefits of reproductive technology.[30]

In contrast to antifeminist and nonfeminist approaches, a specifically feminist approach to reproductive ethics fosters the recognition that there is a wide range of issues pertaining to human reproduction. For example, it helps us to see the significance of childbirth. The medicalization of the birth process, the usurpation of the role of midwives, and the place of birth (both in the sense of its physical location—in hospital, home, or clinic—and in the sense of its more general function in our society) are now recognized as genuine social and moral issues.[31] Feminist analyses have demonstrated that the way childbirth is handled reveals much about the status of women, as "patients" and as caregivers, and about the value we ascribe to infants and children.[32]

Furthermore, feminist discussions of reproduction have shown that there are other questions about abortion in addition to the undoubtedly important ones that center upon the fetus: questions having to do with reproductive freedom and choice, control of the body, and responsibility for one's actions.[33] Thus, in general a feminist approach transcends the often rather narrow range of issues recognized by antifeminist and nonfeminist writers and acknowledges the significance of women's experience in all areas of reproduction.

A feminist approach to reproductive ethics also challenges received opinions about reproduction. Feminist analysis has demonstrated that uncritical supporters of reproductive technology generally have narrow visions of what kind of family is "normal," what kind of chidren we should want, and especially what sort of responsibilities and roles women should have. Rejecting those visions, feminists examine critically the assumptions that underlie existing reproductive practices. For example, a feminist orientation to the problem of infertility asks: What are the pronatalist and pro-"family" pressures[34] that help to make infertility an almost unendurable burden, especially for women? In what ways is infertility a product of other interventions in the reproductive process? Why are women advised to endure the pain, uncertainty, and disappointments involved in in vitro fertilization, as a "treatment" for a low sperm court in their husbands, when artificial insemination by donor is easier, has a higher rate of success, and is pain-free?[35] How necessary is it, in fact, that one's child be one's own genetic product? Why is biological continuity especially important to men?[36] Feminism encourages the raising of questions about assumptions usually taken for granted in discussions of reproduction.

Finally, a feminist approach focuses attention upon what reproductive technology really is and upon its potential effects on children and women. For example, feminist writers have argued dramatically and effectively that surrogate motherhood is similar in some respects to prostitution,[37] that the surgical recovery of eggs and ovarian tissue from nonconsenting women is "egg-snatching,"[38] and that fetal sex selection may result in a sort of prenatal gynecide.[39] Thus the emphasis in feminist discussions is upon exploring in innovative ways all of the possible implications of the growing medical, legal, and social control of reproduction.

Feminism, Ethics, and Reproduction

It is clear that a feminist perspective contributes significantly to the reevaluation of issues in reproductive ethics and to the understanding of women and reproduction in patriarchy. So far, however, feminist discussions of reproduction and reproductive technology for the most part have been scattered and tentative. The aim of this book is to advance a cohesive feminist analysis of reproductive ethics.

For several reasons the analysis cannot claim to be complete. Not every possible issue is surveyed in detail; for example, contraception, reproductive hazards, and involuntary sterilization are discussed only briefly. And I do not discuss such related philosophical issues as population control and our obligations to future people. Moreover reproductive technology and the social structures of reproduction are subject to very rapid growth and change, which can overtake technical discussions of the subject. Finally, feminist theory itself is still at a stage of early development, and no contribution to the feminist discussion of reproduction can pretend to offer the final word on the subject.

Nevertheless, the book tries to extend and develop the feminist approach by incorporating the insights already achieved in feminist discussions of reproductive ethics and contrasting them with antifeminist and nonfeminist analyses. It examines some of the most important new technologies and their social uses and offers recommendations in regard to the formation of policy about reproduction. Most important, it attempts to highlight some significant ethical and social themes embedded within contemporary structures of reproduction: the manipulation of reproductive choices, the denigration of women's bodies, the overvaluing of fertility and a genetic link to one's offspring, and the commodification of reproduction.

To offer a feminist reassessment of reproductive ethics is, among other things, to make a claim for the inclusion—not the superiority—of women within moral decision making and policy. But the results of that inclusion are of such a magnitude that piecemeal alterations in morality and policy may no longer be adequate. According to Sandra Bartky, "feminists are not aware of different things than other people; they are aware of the same things differently."[40] This is partly right and partly wrong. For when feminists look at the "same things" differently, those things—issues, practices, values, behaviors, beliefs—cease to be the same.

Notes

An earlier version of part of this chapter, entitled "Reproductive Ethics: Feminist and Non-Feminist Approaches," appeared in *Canadian Journal of Women and the Law/revue juridique la femme et le droit* 1, no. 2 (1986): 271–278. The material is used here with the permission of the journal's editor.

1 See Alison M. Jaggar, *Feminist Politics and Human Nature* (Totowa, N.J.: Rowman & Allanheld, 1983); and Mary Midgley and Judith Hughes, *Women's Choices: Philosophical Problems Facing Feminism* (London: Weidenfeld and Nicholson, 1983), pp. 21–25.
2 For a discussion of the concept of patriarchy, see Zillah Eisenstein, *The Radical Future of Liberal Feminism* (New York: Longman, 1981), pp. 18–22.
3 Marilyn Frye, "Oppression," in *The Politics of Reality: Essays in Feminist Theory* (Trumansberg, N.Y.: Crossing Press, 1983), pp. 1–16.
4 These theories are ably discussed in Jaggar's book, and also in Catharine A. MacKinnon, "Feminism, Marxism, Method, and the State: An Agenda for Theory," in *Feminist Theory: A Critique of Ideology*, ed. Nannerl O. Keohane, Michelle Z. Rosaldo, and Barbara C. Gelpi (Chicago: University of Chicago Press, 1982), pp. 1–30.
5 See Sara Ann Ketchum and Christine Pierce, "Separatism and Sexual Relationships," in *Philosophy and Women*, ed. Sharon Bishop and Marjorie Weinzweig (Belmont, Calif.: Wadsworth, 1979), pp. 163–171.
6 Among many examples are the papers in *Discovering Reality: Feminist Perspectives on Epistemology, Metaphysics, Methodology, and the Philosophy of Science*, ed. Sandra Harding and Merrill B. Hintikka (Dordrecht, Holland: D. Reidel, 1983); and in *Beyond Domination: New Perspectives on Women and Philosophy*, ed. Carol C. Gould (Totowa, N.J.: Rowman & Allanheld, 1983).
7 My discussion of antifeminism owes much to Alison Jaggar's remarks

about the conservative view of women. See her "Political Philosophies of Women's Liberation," in *Philosophy and Women*, pp. 258–259.

8 See Janet Sayers's discussion of biological arguments against feminism in *Biological Politics: Feminist and Anti-Feminist Perspectives* (London: Tavistock, 1982), pp. 7–104.

9 Jackie Davies, "Commentary on J. E. Bickenbach's 'The Empty Garage?: Recent Feminist Critiques of Scientific Methodology'," delivered at the Department of Philosophy Colloquium, Queen's University, Kingston, Ontario, 29 November 1984.

10 Eisenstein, *Radical Future of Liberal Feminism*, p. 15.

11 For example, see Wesley Cragg, ed., *Contemporary Moral Issues* (Toronto: McGraw-Hill Ryerson, 1983); and Jan Narveson, ed., *Moral Issues* (Toronto: Oxford University Press, 1983).

12 Mary O'Brien, *The Politics of Reproduction* (Boston: Routledge & Kegan Paul, 1981), p. 20.

13 There are many instances of this approach. See, for example, John T. Noonan, Jr., "An Almost Absolute Value in History," Roger Wertheimer, "Understanding the Abortion Argument," and Michael Tooley, "A Defense of Abortion and Infanticide," in *The Problem of Abortion*, ed. Joel Feinberg (Belmont, Calif.: Wadsworth, 1973).

14 William J. Daniel, "Sexual Ethics in Relation to IVF and ET: The Fitting Use of Human Reproductive Power," in *Test-Tube Babies: A Guide to Moral Questions, Present Techniques and Future Possibilities*, ed. William Walters and Peter Singer (Melbourne: Oxford University Press, 1982), pp. 71–78.

15 Robert T. Francoeur, *Utopian Motherhood: New Trends in Human Reproduction* (Garden City, N.Y.: Doubleday, 1970), p. 104.

16 See John A. Henley, "IVF and the Human Family: Possible and Likely Consequences," in *Test-Tube Babies*, pp. 79–87; Herbert T. Krimmel, "The Case against Surrogate Parenting," *Hastings Center Report* 13 (October 1983): 35–39; and R. Snowden, G. D. Mitchell, and E. M. Snowden, *Artificial Reproduction: A Social Investigation* (London: George Allen & Unwin, 1983).

17 Leon R. Kass, "Babies by Means of In Vitro Fertilization: Unethical Experiments on the Unborn?" *New England Journal of Medicine* 285 (18 November 1971): 1176–1177, and Leon R. Kass, "Making Babies—The New Biology and the 'Old' Morality," *The Public Interest* 26 (Winter 1972): 20.

18 Robert Edwards and Patrick Steptoe, *A Matter of Life: The Story of a Medical Breakthrough* (London: Hutchinson, 1980), pp. 101–102; and Snowden et al., *Artificial Reproduction*, p. 43.

19 Edwards and Steptoe, *A Matter of Life*, pp. 101–102.

20 Snowden et al., *Artificial Reproduction*, p. 169.

21 R[obert] G. Edwards, "The Current Clinical and Ethical Situation of Human Conception In Vitro," in *Developments in Human Reproduction and Their Eugenic, Ethical Implications*, ed. C. O. Carter

(New York: Academic Press, 1983), p. 95; and John A. Robertson, "Surrogate Mothers: Not So Novel After All," *Hastings Center Report* 13 (October 1983): 28.

22 A phrase taken from Hilary Rose and Jalna Hanmer, "Women's Liberation, Reproduction, and the Technological Fix," in *Sexual Divisions and Society: Process and Change*, ed. Diana Leonard Barker and Sheila Allen (London: Tavistock, 1976), pp. 199–223.

23 See Robertson, "Surrogate Mothers," pp. 28–34; Michael D. Bayles, *Reproductive Ethics* (Englewood Cliffs, N.J.: Prentice-Hall, 1984), pp. 22–27; and Alan A. Rassaby, "Surrogate Motherhood: The Position and Problems of Substitutes," in *Test-Tube Babies*, pp. 97–109.

24 See Nancy E. Williamson, *Sons or Daughters: A Cross-Cultural Survey of Parental Preferences* (Newbury Park, Calif.: Sage Publications, 1976), and Nancy E. Williamson, "Sex Preferences, Sex Control, and the Status of Women," *Signs* 1 (1976): 847–862.

25 Amitai Etzioni, "Sex Control, Science, and Society," *Science* 161, no. 3846 (September 1968): 1109; John Postgate, "Bat's Chance in Hell," *New Scientist* 58, no. 840 (5 April 1973): 16.

26 Richard L. Meier, "Sex Determination and Other Innovations," in *Population in Perspective*, ed. Louise B. Young (New York: Oxford University Press, 1968), p. 410.

27 See MacKinnon, "Feminism, Marxism, Method and the State," pp. 15–19.

28 See, for example, Barbara Ehrenreich and Deirdre English, *For Her Own Good: 150 Years of the Experts' Advice to Women* (Garden City, N.Y.: Anchor Books, 1978); and Daniel Beekman, *The Mechanical Baby: A Popular History of the Theory and Practice of Child Raising* (Westport, Conn.: Lawrence Hill, 1977).

29 Shulamith Firestone, *The Dialectic of Sex* (New York: William Morrow, 1970, pp. 197–201.

30 See, for example, the papers in *Test-Tube Women: What Future for Motherhood?*, ed. Rita Arditti, Renate Duelli Klein, and Shelley Minden (London: Pandora Press, 1984); and *The Custom-Made Child? Women-Centered Perspectives*, ed. Helen B. Holmes, Betty B. Hoskins, and Michael Gross (Clifton, N.J.: Humana Press, 1981).

31 Adele E. Laslie, "Ethical Issues in Childbirth," *Journal of Medicine and Philosophy* 7 (1982): 179–195.

32 Barbara Katz Rothman, *Giving Birth: Alternatives in Childbirth* (Harmondsworth, England: Penguin, 1984); Ann Oakley, *Women Confined: Towards a Sociology of Childbirth* (New York: Schocken Books, 1980).

33 For example, Judith Jarvis Thomson, "A Defense of Abortion," *Philosophy and Public Affairs* 1 (Fall 1971): 47–66; Barbara Katz Rothman, "The Meanings of Choice in Reproductive Technology," in Arditti et al., *Test-Tube Women*, pp. 23–33; and Elizabeth W. Moen, "What Does 'Control over Our Bodies' Really Mean?" *International Journal of Women's Studies* 2 (March/April 1979): 129–143.

34 See Ellen Peck and Judith Senderowitz, eds., *Pronatalism: The Myth of Mom and Apple Pie* (New York: Thomas Y. Crowell, 1974); Martha E. Gimenez, "Feminism, Pronatalism, and Motherhood," in *Mothering: Essays in Feminist Theory*, ed. Joyce Trebilcot (Totowa, N.J.: Rowman & Allanheld, 1984), pp. 287–314; and Rebecca Albury, "Who Owns the Embryo?" in Arditti et al., *Test-Tube Women*, pp. 54–67.

35 Jalna Hanmer and Pat Allen, "Reproductive Engineering: The Final Solution?" in *Alice through the Microscope: The Power of Science over Women's Lives*, ed. The Brighton Women and Science Group (London: Virago, 1980), pp. 212–217; Jalna Hanmer, "Reproductive Technology: The Future for Women?" in *Machina Ex Dea: Feminist Perspectives on Technology*, ed. Joan Rothschild (New York: Pergamon Press, 1983), pp. 184–188.

36 O'Brien, *Politics of Reproduction*, pp. 29–64; Mary Kay Blakely, "Surrogate Mothers: For Whom Are They Working?" *Ms.* 11, no. 9 (March 1983): 20.

37 Andrea Dworkin, *Right-Wing Women* (New York: Perigee Books, 1983), pp. 174–188.

38 Genoveffa Corea, "Egg Snatchers," and Julie Murphy, "Egg Farming and Women's Future," both in Arditti et al., *Test-Tube Women*, pp. 37–51 and 68–75, respectively.

39 Betty B. Hoskins and Helen Bequaert Holmes, "Technology and Prenatal Femicide," in Arditti et al., *Test-Tube Women*, pp. 237–255.

40 Sandra Bartky, "Toward a Phenomenology of Feminist Consciousness," in Bishop and Weinzweig, *Philosophy and Women*, p. 254.

2 Sex Preselection

When we look at other women, we also see ourselves reflected in them; if we truly value ourselves, then we will value other women as well. The desire to reproduce ourselves, to give birth to other strong and independent women, is a healthy way of affirming our self-worth as women rather than denying women's worth. . . .[1]

But, if we think about reproducing ourselves on the basis of gender, we are morally no better than men who are hipped on the subject of sons.[2]

In this chapter I examine the possible justification for fetal sex preselection. Although widely discussed by scientists, mostly in nonfeminist or antifeminist terms, it has not yet received much attention from feminist philosophers. Hence one writer says that the topic is unfortunately characterized by "a lack of questioning about ethics and morality," and by the unchallenged assumption that fetal sex preselection is "an accepted and acceptable idea."[3]

There are three reasons for starting a feminist analysis of reproductive ethics with the topic of sex preselection. First, it presents the opportunity to look at some of the main moral questions that might be raised about conception—questions, for example, about what are considered to be the legitimate goals of procreation and the appropriate type of offspring to produce. Second, although the technology of sex preselection is still under development and not yet widely used, it promises to be of great significance to women and children. Third, the topic raises in a very immediate way some important issues for feminist theory.

"Fetal sex preselection" refers to the variety of techniques now under investigation which may enable prospective parents to predetermine, in the process of conception itself, what the sex of their child will be. The phrase should be clearly distinguished from "postconception fetal sex selection," which requires the discovery (usually through amniocentesis or chorionic biopsy) of the sex of the embryo or fetus at some point in its development, with subsequent abortion if it should turn out to be of the "wrong" sex.[4] A future method of post-conception fetal sex selection would involve the fertilization of eggs in vitro, determination of the sex of the resulting embryos, and implantation of an embryo of the desired sex.[5]

Unlike some other writers,[6] I distinguish between fetal sex preselection and postconception sex selection. Although the two procedures may produce some similar consequences, nevertheless some of the relevant issues are different, depending on whether or not an existing embryo or fetus and the possibility of abortion are involved. Subsequent chapters will discuss abortion and the status of the fetus; here I will concentrate upon the preconceptual issue of fetal sex preselection.

Several techniques for fetal sex preselection have been proposed.[7] At present these techniques are divided into those which can be undertaken by the prospective parents themselves and those which require some degree of technological intervention, culminating in artificial insemination of the woman. In the first category is included a variety of prescriptions regarding the prospective mother's diet, the timing of sexual intercourse in relation to the time of ovulation,[8] coital position, and douching in order to alter the acidity of the woman's vagina. The effectiveness of these techniques has not been established, and conflicting evidence has been presented as to precisely what changes in timing, diet, and so on will produce an embryo of the desired sex.

More promising, apparently, are the techniques in the second category. They involve different methods of separating the gynosperm—that is, sperm bearing the X chromosome, which produces daughters—from the androsperm—that is, sperm bearing the Y chromosome, which produces sons. Because of differences between X- and Y-bearing sperm in weight and motility, they can be separated through such processes as staining, filtering, and centrifugation. A woman could therefore be artificially inseminated with a sperm sample containing a high concentration of X- or Y-bearing sperm: her chances of conceiving a child of the desired sex are increased, although success is not guaranteed.

None of these processes are widely available; all are still in the developmental stage, and their effectiveness is not fully established in human beings. Moreover there is some indication that when sex preselection methods do work, they may be more effective in raising the probability of conceiving a son than of conceiving a daughter[9]—a fact that, it turns out, has a sinister significance in light of apparent parental preferences with regard to the sex of their offspring. However, with the rapid growth and development of other forms of reproductive technology such as in vitro fertilization and embryo transfer, it can be forecast that fetal sex preselection may soon be a real option for prospective parents.[10]

The primary ethical question is whether or not the use of sex preselection techniques of any sort can be morally justified. I shall discuss both the justification of individual choice about the use of sex preselection techniques,[11] a moral issue, and the justification of the promotion, availability, and use of sex preselection on a wide scale,[12] an issue of social policy.

Individual Choice about Sex Preselection

I shall start by considering some arguments against sex preselection put forward by philosopher Michael D. Bayles. His views on reproductive ethics display a striking combination of efforts to avoid sexist prejudice (that is, unfounded discrimination on the basis of sex alone) and an absence of any serious attention to women's experience in reproduction. Hence his views are nonfeminist rather than antifeminist in character. Bayles asks, "is it rational to desire a child of a particular sex?"[13] To answer the question, he cites two possible reasons for wanting a child of one sex rather than the other. The first is the preference for one sex over the other for its own sake; that is, the belief that one sex is intrinsically more valuable than the other. Bayles dismisses this reason very briefly by stating that it is a form of sexism, and "good reasons can be and have been given against this view by many authors, so such a desire is irrational"[14] and also wrong.[15]

The second reason Bayles calls "instrumental preference for a child of one sex or the other." This involves the belief that "the desire for a child of a particular sex is instrumental to fulfilling other desires."[16] Bayles regards this reason as also inadequate; it probably "mask[s] an irrational sexism."[17] He points out that reasons given in the past for instrumental preference of a child of a particular sex (almost always male)—reasons such as inheritance, need for workers, or carrying on the family name—are no longer relevant in the modern Western world. Moreover it is false to assume that "certain pleasures in child rearing"—leisure activities and shared work—can be achieved only with a child of one sex and not the other. Bayles says that although on the whole members of one sex may be better at some activities (such as ballet) than members of the other, nevertheless it is false that no members of the other sex can perform the same roles well, or that one set of roles is preferable to the other. "Were children allowed to develop freely their own interests and talents, children of the same sex would probably exhibit as much diversity as children of opposite sexes."[18]

Bayles concludes that sex preselection on the basis of instrumental sex preference is irrational and wrong. He admits only one exceptional case. In an instance in which the potential mother is a carrier of an X-linked genetic disease such as hemophilia, it would be rational to prefer girl children, who can at most be carriers of the disease, over boys, who are at risk of having the disease itself. "The preference here is not for a female child, but for a healthy child, and a female has a significantly better chance of being healthy."[19]

I shall accept without further comment Bayles's claim that sex preselection based on intrinsic sex preference is always irrational and wrong. But there are some problems with his second claim, that preselection based on instrumental sex preference, except to avoid offspring with sex-linked diseases, is also always irrational and wrong. This claim seems too restrictive, for there may be cases (perhaps few in actual number), unrelated to the risks of sex-linked diseases, in

which the preference for a child of one sex rather than the
other is not unjustified.

Yet is is not easy to delineate these cases. I cannot agree with
Mary Anne Warren, who argues that there are a number of
instances in which the decision to preselect the sex of one's
offspring is "motivated by an unselfish desire to ensure that
the child will have the best possible life." As an example, she
suggests that a couple might wish to have a son because a
deceased relative has willed his estate to go only to a son of
theirs, after their death, and they want the child to receive the
inheritance.[20] She also suggests that women in very oppressive societies might rationally prefer sons over daughters, since
although daughters would provide companionship and dom-
estic help, a female child would be abused and devalued.
Furthermore, she says, couples in places such as northern
India should not be blamed for choosing sons, who are
economic assets, over daughters, who are liabilities.[21] Even in
industrialized nations some people may justifiably wish to
have sons in order that the sons "may enjoy the freedoms
which women are still denied,"[22] or because the parents are
unwilling to bring daughters into a misogynistic world.[23] On
the other hand, a couple who opt for daughters "because they
do not want to raise potential [male] rapists or batterers" are
also making a rational choice.[24]. Or a couple may want a son
after having a run of daughters (or vice versa); they may want
at least one child of each sex; or they may believe that "because
of their own personal background or circumstances, they
would be better parents to a child of one sex than the other."[25]

Warren denies that these hypothetical choices are sexist and
therefore wrong. She briefly offers two main arguments. First,
of those cases in which sons are sought because they will
benefit (or benefit more than daughters) from living in a
patriarchy, she claims that it is not always wrong to profit from
an unjust situation: "If poor parents can benefit themselves
and their families by selecting sons, and if this does no direct
harm to anyone else, then it is not clear that what they do is in
any way unjust."[26] Second, of the case in which parents
choose a daughter on the grounds that females tend, on
average, to be less violent than males, she concedes that the
son they could have had instead might or might not have been

a violent person, but "since he does not exist he cannot have been treated unjustly."[27] (Presumably this latter claim also applies to cases in which the parents want one child of each sex or prefer a child of one sex because they feel they can raise it better.)

However, it is difficult to believe that deliberately producing male offspring in order that they will benefit from the oppression of women and girls need not produce any direct harm. Sex preselection cannot always be classified, as Warren implicitly does, as a victimless act.[28] These sons will probably benefit from and contribute to the exploitation of women; perhaps, given the motivation for which they were chosen, they will be educated and encouraged to do so. And Warren is extraordinarily insouciant about the prospects of a girl within a family that deliberately selects sons: the daughter's belief in her own equality may or may not be shaken, says Warren, but "she will, in any case, learn that her society values males more highly than females."[29]

But the chief problem in Warren's presentation of these reasons for sex selection lies in her failure to condemn their complicity with the patriarchal system. These cases must be evaluated on a broader base than that of the production of direct harm or injustice. Granted, it may in fact be kinder on an individual basis to avoid producing daughters who may run the risk of grievous injury through nutritional deprivation, genital mutilation, sexual abuse, exploitive labor, and dangerous procreation. But choosing sons for that reason is still a way of saying yes, however obscurely or reluctantly, to patriarchal power and the oppression of women. It is the expression of a failure to oppose the system.

What about Warren's second argument? It is of course trivially true that a person who never exists—such as a potential son who is unwanted because as a male he stands a greater chance of being violent than a daughter would, or a potential daughter who is unwanted because the parents feel they are better at raising sons—cannot be unjustly treated. This fact, however, fails in itself to justify the deliberate choice of a child of a specific sex. Although the unchosen child does not exist, the reason for the chosen child's existence nevertheless appears to be sexist. One is chosen and the other rejected because of generalizations about all members of their sex, generalizations that may well be false for the particular potential individuals whose existence, so to speak, hangs in the balance. It is not justified to refuse to hire a woman rather than a man because the woman might have characteristics often possessed by other women. It is not justified to evaluate any person based upon the probabilities that that person will possess the features of others of his or her sex. How, then, can it be justified to select one's offspring in order to avoid certain features often found in persons of one sex, or because one wants offspring of each sex?

A final suggestion made by Warren about the justification of the individual use of sex preselection is, however, more promising. She remarks that some women might choose daughters because they

> believe that under the present conditions they would have more in common with a child of their own sex and thus (they hope) a better relationship with her. A son might be able to share most of their particular interests and activities, but he could not share the basic experience of being female in a society which still values males more highly.[30]

This example suggests that in seeking good reasons for preferring children of one sex rather than the other we should focus more attention upon the *experience* of child rearing, an experience most salient historically for women but also significant, of course, to men. One cannot separate the desire for a child of a particular sex from the anticipated years-long process of rearing and caring for it. Although, as Bayles points out, one can of course go fishing with a daughter and bake cookies with a son, it just does not seem correct to suggest, as he does, that the sex of a close family member should make no difference to the already existing family members.

To see this, consider some analogies: instances in which the sex of a close family member is genuinely important and one might justifiably prefer a person of one sex rather than of the other. These cases are one's relationships with one's mate and one's relationship with one's parents.

First, one can potentially have a loving sexual relationship with members of either sex. Yet when seeking a mate it is surely not wrong to prefer a member of one sex rather than the other. Is it sexist for a homosexual to exclude members of the other sex?

Adrienne Rich has suggested that for women heterosexuality is "compulsory": it "may not be a 'preference' at all but something that has had to be imposed, managed, organized, propagandized, and maintained by force."[31] The institution of compulsory heterosexuality, she believes, dominates and in most cases ultimately destroys the "lesbian continuum"—the range of woman-identified experience. Heterosexuality is not innate but learned and enforced by means of strong social mechanisms. Moreover it is evident that many individuals are heterosexist: they evince an unjustified bias in favor of heterosexual relationships and behavior.

Nevertheless these ideas about heterosexuality do not necessarily imply that the preference on the part of a heterosexual for a sexual partner of the other sex is unreasoned prejudice, any more than is the preference of a lesbian for a sexual partner of her own sex. For it seems likely that in terms of the lived *experience* of women (and men also), one's sexual orientation, whether toward the same or the other sex, is often felt to be deep-seated, natural, and central to one's personality. Regardless of how an individual's sexual orientation has been produced and is maintained, and even if that individual does not discriminate on the basis of sexual orientation, she or he is unlikely to be able to choose to want a sexual partner of either sex. For example, even very strong political convictions would be insufficient to induce a committed heterosexual feminist to seek a mate from among members of her own sex. In light of the experience of sexual orientation, then, I suggest (providing one is not guilty of heterosexist bias) that when seeking a mate it is not wrong to prefer members of one sex rather than of the other.

Second, consider relationships with one's parents. Surely persons of either sex can be excellent parents. But is it sexist for offspring—of any age—to prefer one parent over the other, perhaps temporarily or at different stages in their development? Would it be irrational for, let's say, a motherless child whose father is a wonderful parent to long for a mother (rather than another father)? I believe that it would not.

There is an underlying reason why the sex of the person with whom one has a close relationship is important and relevant to that relationship. One need not make any sexist generalizations about the capacities, talents, or roles of females and males to believe that the sex of an individual is a core part of that person's identity. I am not adopting here what has been called the "essentialist" view—that there are definite universal masculine and feminine characteristics independent of cultural differences.[32] It is undeniable that through complex socialization processes each of us learns our gender role, the complex set of traits and behaviors stereotypically expected of members of each sex within a particular culture.[33] Gender roles are acquired, not innate. However, even if males and females were somehow exposed to identical or at least very similar socialization processes, some important differences between female and male persons would persist. These differences arise from the experiences and capacities associated with being biologically female or biologically male, and they make one's sex central to one's identity.

At the moment cultural conditioning makes the differences between the experiences of females and the experiences of males diverse and deep. As feminist consciousness-raising techniques have taught, there is a tremendous value for women in sharing experiences that are the product of such social conditions. If and when the forms of discrimination found in patriarchal society are reduced, these differences would also diminish. But they would not disappear. There is an irreducible minimum of difference between male and female experience which results from the biological differences between the sexes.

What that minimum is cannot yet be specified, in the absence of any totally nonsexist culture to provide empirical evidence.[34] At the least it would probably rest, for females, for example, in the experience of the capacity to ovulate, menstruate, gestate, and lactate, as well as the sexual experiences, pleasures, and vulnerabilities associated with being female. Even if a woman remains celibate or childless, she is affected by her awareness of her capacity to engage in sexual activity or to procreate. No woman is a woman, a female, only when pregnant or engaged in sexual activity: the fact of being female permeates her sense of self and her ways of relating to the world. (The fact of being male likewise permeates a man's sense of self. But it may be harder for him to recognize that fact, since in a patriarchal culture to be a person is, preeminently, to be male. Hence men may tend to take their awareness of themselves as male to be simply an awareness of themselves as persons.) Like the feminist philosopher Caroline Whitbeck, I believe that these experiences "do not readily fall into either the nature category or the nurture category."[35] They are shaped but not entirely constituted by our nurture as members of one sex or the other, and they are founded upon but not reducible to our biological nature. These fundamental differences between the experiences of the sexes are not just the result of socialization, but they are not just biological either, since they are constituted by our *awareness* of the capacities unique to our sex.

If one's sex is central to one's own identity, then it should not be surprising that the sex of other persons will be significant in some relationships. Not, I hasten to add, in all relationships: I doubt that the sex of the other person is, or at least should be, central when interacting with salespersons, government officials, elevator operators, repair persons, or even students, teachers, or coworkers. But in relationships involving strong friendship, love and/or sexual intimacy, the sex of the other is highly important.

In relationships such as those I discussed earlier—with one's mate or one's parents—the sex of the person chosen or preferred is significant for reasons of either sexual similarity or sexual complementarity. That is, one deliberately seeks a person whose experiences and capacities as a member of one sex rather than the other are similar or complementary to one's own.

The idea of sexual similarity is, I think, straightforward. What I am suggesting is that when we say an adolescent girl needs her mother, for example, we mean she needs not merely her parent but her female parent. And when a lesbian seeks a partner, she wants a sexual and love relationship with a woman because she (the partner) is a woman.[36] What is sought is a likeness, an affinity, of experience and capacities—the groundedness of being with one's own kind. The notion of sexual complementarity, on the other hand, involves both a difference from and an adding to. It is not merely a matter of dissimilarity, although the attraction of the different, the foreign, the unknown, may be there. But the desire for sexual complementarity, whether in a parent or in a mate or friend, is the desire for the new, for what will change and enlarge one's own experience by opening it to another kind of experience.

Of course, in suggesting this I am not claiming that one never experiences differences with members of the same sex as oneself or affinities with members of the other sex. I am suggesting only that one's sexual identity provides a reason, in some relationships, for preferring either persons with the same sexual (not gender) identity or persons with a different sexual (not gender) identity.

These ideas of sexual similarity and complementarity are also applicable in other close relationships, such as one's relationship with one's children. They could therefore be involved in some parents' sex preferences for their children. I do not by any means suggest that they are always involved, or that they are the only factors involved. I claim only that it is possible that in some cases the preference of a potential mother for a daughter, for example, may be founded upon the desire for sexual similarity in her offspring, whereas the preference for a son may be founded upon the desire for sexual complementarity. Here it is not stereotyped gender roles that form the basis for the preference but, rather, the sexual identity of the infant. Thus in these cases (if they occur) to want, let us say, a baby girl rather than a boy is rather like wanting a husband (rather than a wife) or a mother (rather than a father). One would be seeking a child of a specific sex because of the anticipated rewards and pleasures to be gained through a parenting relationship with a younger human being who is either like oneself or different from oneself in the central and fundamental respect of sexual identity.

So, attention to the lived experience of close human relationships suggests that in these circumstances (as well as those in which there is a serious risk of sex-linked disease) there may be a good reason for preferring children of one sex rather than the other. Such a preference need not be sexist; that is, it need not entail the unreasoning desire for children of one sex and rejection of children of the other.

But what remains questionable is whether the reason I have described is also *sufficient* to justify the practice of sex preselection. In other words, is the reason not only good but good enough as grounds for deliberately choosing the sex of one's offspring?

Moral choices are not and cannot be made independently of their social context. In a culture free of misogyny, sex preselection, if it occurred at all, would not be a moral issue; in a society oppressive to women, preselection for any reason remains problematic. For it is essential to consider the meaning of the decision to preselect one's offspring (even for very good reasons) as it would be understood within societies essentially patriarchal in their social structure. Such a decision would almost inevitably be interpreted as resting on sexist grounds, and if it involved the choice of male offspring, it might, as I suggested earlier, serve to reinforce biases against females. Hence it cannot be concluded that the good reason I have cited to prefer children of one sex rather than the other is sufficient to justify the use of preselection techniques. What counts against acting on these reasons is the patriarchal and misogynist context in which such choices would be made.

Social Policy for Sex Preselection

While examining some grounds for individual choice about sex preselection, I have postponed any consideration of the possible general adoption of fetal sex preselection. Such a consideration raises social policy questions about the promotion and availability of these techniques. To this topic I now turn.

The existing literature discussing sex preselection of offspring is concerned mainly with attempting to delineate the probably social consequences if the techniques are widely used and successful.[37] All such predictions are founded primarily upon existing knowledge regarding sex preferences. Further data can also be gained from the study of different societies that now have varying sex ratios.[38]

Unfortunately, under present circumstances, when people's offspring sex preferences are presumably determined by factors other than a desire for sexual similarity or complementarity, no balanced sex ratio among children resulting from the general adoption of sex preselection can be predicted. Study after study confirms that, in fact, both men and women prefer sons. Surveys of the accumulated evidence indicate that in almost all societies around the world, (1) in general, male children are preferred over girls—to a greater extent by men than by women;[39] (2) a boy is strongly preferred as the first child; (3) if there is to be only one child, a boy is preferred; (4) if an odd number of children is desired, most would rather have more boys than girls; and (5) parents may be more likely to stop bearing children after obtaining a son than after obtaining a daughter—that is, families with only girls are more likely to continue to reproduce to obtain a boy than are families with only sons likely to try for girls.[40]

In light of this very pronounced preference, the predicted consequences of the general adoption of fetal sex preselection techniques fall into two groups: those that are generally beneficial and those that are generally harmful to society at large.[41] The latter group is dominated by particularly dangerous consequences for women. I shall briefly summarize both sets of consequences in order finally to evaluate the justification of the use of sex preselection on a wide scale.

The foreseen beneficial consequences include a reduction in the incidence of sex-linked diseases;[42] "greater rationality in family formation";[43] happy parents and happy children (the parents exercise choice and get the kinds of children they want; the children are spared suffering because of being the "wrong" sex[44] and are treated better by the parents); "a better balance of male/female companionship among the elderly";[45] and reduction of the birth rate. The latter, it is claimed, would occur because parents would no longer need to have "just one more" in order to obtain a child of the desired sex. More radically, writers such as John Postgate[46] have proposed that the use of sex preselection techniques, inevitably resulting in the birth of far more boys than girls, would reduce the population because there would be so many fewer women to bear children.

On the other hand, the predicted harmful consequences of general adoption of sex preselection seem to both outnumber and outweigh the beneficial ones, and they call into question the underlying assumptions of those who are optimistic about the general use of the techniques. First, sex preference has been shown to be related to desired birth order, in that people usually prefer a son first and then a daughter.[47] But some studies have found certain important differences between first- and second-born children, regardless of their sex. In terms of ability and academic and professional success, first-borns are overrepresented.[48] Second-born children, however, are more likely to be socially adept and popular.[49] More recently some other research has called into question the reliability of these generalizations.[50] What can be said, however, is that *if* birth order makes a significant difference in the characteristics of children, then the use of sex preselection techniques could confirm existing stereotypes about the sexes and relegate women to a 'second class' status because they would be denied the advantages of being the first-born.[51] It has further been suggested that there is little advantage in being wanted if one is wanted only as a second child.

"And, what about the mistakes? Suppose a daughter is born after 'failure' of a technique."[52] Such a child might suffer even more serious psychological problems than children now born of the "wrong" sex. (It is not altogether clear, either, what the effect would be of being born of a predetermined "right" sex.[53])

Independent of the effects of the birth order factor, other writers have foreseen that general use of sex preselection techniques would incur an increase in gender stereotyping[54] and a slowdown or even reversal in any material progress toward sexual equality. "Parents who are willing to invest heavily—both financially and emotionally—in experimental sex selection techniques to fulfill their reproductive needs, might be less willing to accept deviations from their idealized visions of femininity or masculinity than would parents who are not so motivated."[55] One writer also foresees greater bias against homosexuals and lesbians.[56]

A society with a surplus of men is predicted to be a dangerous and unjust place—especially for women. Says sociologist Amitai Etzioni, "A significant and cumulative male surplus will . . . produce a society with some of the rougher features of a frontier town."[57] He predicts more criminals, fewer "agents of moral education" (that is, women), more interracial and interclass tensions,[58] more prostitution, more homosexuality, and a pattern of delay in marriage, or no marriage partners at all, for many men. Postgate's predictions of the effects of a "man child pill" are even more chilling:

> All sorts of taboos would be expected and it is probable that a form of *purdah* would become necessary. Women's right to work, even to travel alone freely, would probably be forgotten transiently. Polyandry might well become accepted in some societies; some might treat their women as queen ants, others as rewards for the most outstanding (or most determined) males.[59]

The world would come to resemble either "a giant boy's public school or a huge male prison." (Astonishingly, after this horrifying recital, he describes these consequences as mere "matters of taste rather than serious concern!"[60]) To this, another writer adds that women will be "run off their feet" dealing with the rise in ill health and the results of male violence and war.[61]

In view of the worldwide evidence in regard to offspring sex preferences and to the seriousness of the potential consequences of general adoption of fetal sex preselection techniques, their use on a wide scale is virtually impossible to justify. From a feminist perspective, the single most important consideration is the probability that the societal position of women and girls could be considerably worsened. The technology of sex preselection enables people, particularly men, to act upon their biases against women; it is not an exaggeration to regard the potential results as a form of gynecide—that is, a wrongful form of sexual discrimination that reduces the relative number of females. (The magnitude of the consequences would, of course, depend upon the degree to which technologies of sex preselection are used, and this might well vary from one country to another, since sex preferences themselves also vary from place to place. But there is very little evidence that the techniques would work to women's benefit.)

True, some commentators have claimed that an "invisible hand"[62] would eventually right any sex ratio imbalance,[63] but there are no data to support this contention. Some writers argue that "once these unbalanced cohorts enter the marriage market, the benefits to couples of having daughters may increase, changing the entire preference structure."[64] But even if this is correct, such an effect would require a generation to take place. It seems unlikely, however, that parents would choose not to have sons because of boys' poor prospects in the marriage market. Since marriage is not typically regarded as central in the life of men, it is probably that sons would continue to be preferred because of their other salient roles—for example, as breadwinners. Moreover it is implausible to suppose that parents would make choices about the sex of their children based on an awareness of general probabilities; it is always open to a parent to hope that his son will be successful in finding a spouse in a crowded marriage market, even if other sons are not. In addition, the fact that much of the existing sex preselection technology may not increase the chances of conceiving a daughter suggests that it may not even be possible to offset a preponderance of boys once it occurs.

Yet another writer has gone so far as to claim that sex preselection could be "a major force for sex equality."[65] The claim is that when the preference for males is implemented and females are fewer in number, women will be considered more valuable. They will be more desirable in marriage and more easily able to leave an abusive husband to seek a new one. Furthermore, the small number of women available for sex-typed occupations will produce an increase in wages in those occupations.

But this scenario is also implausible. First, it assumes what is certainly open to challenge: that marriage is, or ought to be, of prime importance in all or most women's lives. Second, Nancy Williamson's studies of five small preindustrial "daughter-preferring" societies found that even when daughters are valued, women do not enjoy a position of equality with men. "The work done by men is considered more honorific and men hold relatively more power in religious and political activities."[66] In these groups daughters are valued as a medium of exchange and for their reproductive capacity—neither of which turns out to be conducive to acquisition of equality or power. Becoming more valuable as marriage partners or within sex-typed occupations is not a route to liberation for women.

Nevertheless, even those commentators seriously concerned about the potential harmful consequences of the general adoption of fetal sex preselection have felt that little can be done to limit its use[67] because of the sheer practical difficulties inherent in such regulation.[68] Of course, if regulation is justified, some sex preselection techniques would be easier to control than others. At this stage it seems likely that the most effective techniques will involve separating gynosperm and androsperm by means of filtering or centrifugation. Such a procedure would presumably have to be carried out in a laboratory. If this occurs, then there is some prospect of controlling the use of the techniques by regulating—and perhaps severely limiting—both the funding for research into sex preselection and the number of clinics at which the procedure is offered. Unfortunately, such a policy would probably also have the effect of ensuring that only the well-off have the opportunity to use sex preselection, since only they will be able to travel to the clinics and to afford its cost. In response to this problem, it has been suggested that the use of sex preselection could perhaps be discouraged through measures such as taxation,[69] or by offering it only to couples who already have one child.[70] In addition, some of its worst effects could be reduced by means of positive incentives to bear the less preferred sex,[71] if technology permits.

Some writers nevertheless believe that little *should* be done to govern the use of sex preselection because such regulation would serve to undermine the limited degree of reproductive freedom that women have already achieved.[72] The inequities that result from the social restriction of procreative freedom in regard to abortion are well known. The curtailment of the use of fetal sex preselection, beyond what might be necessary for requirements of health and safety of the technique, therefore seems difficult to justify.[73]

But the nature of reproductive choice and its regulation through public policy are complex subjects: it is not merely a matter of conflict between social control and individual liberty.

It is significant that in the context of fetal sex preselection, "reproductive choice" seems to mean the opportunity for prospective parents—particularly men—to specify the kinds of offspring they want and to set certain standards for what will be considered acceptable children. As I shall show in later chapters, this interpretation of reproductive choice is also embedded in the social uses of other types of reproductive technology, and its legitimacy is open to moral challenge.

Since the dangers of widescale use of sex preselection arise from the strong preference for males expressed in almost all cultures, and since such sex preference is, clearly, learned,[74] the only way ultimately to prevent or avoid these dangers lies in the radical reeducation of people's beliefs about and attitudes towards women. Such a change must be an important component of long-term feminist goals. For the present, however, it is essential to avoid contributing to any growth of androcentric interest in the use of the techniques. Mere "moral exhortation"[75] not to use them, which has been advocated by some feminists desperately worried about their probable effects, is not enough, because it fails to get at the root of those effects. Nor is the suggestion made by one writer of "turning loose" the sex preselection technologies among women who would opt for daughters[76] a satisfactory solution. And one can only label naive John C. Fletcher's suggestion that "[w]omen now hold the upper hand in the restraint of technological sex selection. All they have to do is to say 'no' and not give ground."[77] As subsequent chapters will show, such a view drastically underestimates the growing male control of reproduction.

I arrive, then, at a position with regard to the justification of sex preselection that, though consistent, is scarcely comfortable. On the one hand, I would want to insist that because of its likely consequences, widespread use of sex preselection is not justified; these technologies should not be extensively researched[78] or promoted, and certainly not encouraged or imposed. Yet its use should not be prohibited or severely limited either. Moreover there are some individual cases— perhaps, in practice, rare—in which there are good (although perhaps not sufficient) reasons for the use of sex preselection techniques: that is, those in which the prospective parents seek to avoid the risk for their offspring of sex-linked diseases and those in which they choose the sex of the child on the basis of a desire for what I have called sexual similarity or complementarity. Hence the use of technologies for fetal sex preselection is not necessarily sexist—although it may very well be, and given present sex preferences, the dangers of their use are considerable.

Notes

1 Comment by Laura Punnett, in Emily Erwin Culpepper, moderator, "Sex Preselection Discussion," in *The Custom-Made Child? Women-Centred Perspectives*, ed. Helen B. Holmes, Betty B. Hoskins, and Michael Gross (Clifton, N.J.: Humana Press, 1981, p. 215.

2 Comment by Tabitha [M.] Powledge in ibid.

3 Jalna Hanmer, 'Reproductive Technology: The Future for Women?" in *Machina ex Dea: Feminist Perspectives on Technology*, ed. Joan Rothschild (New York: Pergamon Press, 1983), p. 191.

4 See Viola Roggencamp, "Abortion of a Special Kind: Male Sex Selection in India," in *Test-Tube Women: What Future for Motherhood?* ed. Rita Arditti, Renate Duelli Klein, and Shelley Minden (London: Pandora Press, 1984), pp. 266–277, for discussion of a specific case.

5 V. Jeffery Evans, "Legal Aspects of Prenatal Sex Selection," in *Sex Selection of Children*, ed. Neil G. Bennett (New York: Academic Press, 1983), pp. 149–150.

6 For example, see Roberta Steinbacher, "Futuristic Implications of Sex Preselection," in *The Custom-Made Child?*, p. 188; Tabitha M. Powledge, "Toward a Moral Policy for Sex Choice," in *Sex Selection of Children*, p. 210; and Mary Anne Warren, *Gendercide: The Implications of Sex Selection* (Totowa, N.J.: Rowman & Allanheld, 1985), p. 104.

7 Jalna Hanmer, "Sex Predetermination, Artificial Insemination and the Maintenance of Male-Dominated Culture," in *Women, Health and Reproduction*, ed. Helen Roberts (London: Routledge & Kegan Paul, 1981), p. 175; M. Ruth Nentwig, "Technical Aspects of Sex Preselection," in Holmes at al., *The Custom-Made Child?* pp. 181–186; Betty B. Hoskins and Helen Bequaert Holmes, "Technology and Prenatal Femicide," in Arditti et al., *Test-Tube Women*, pp. 238–241; Gale Largey, "Reproductive Technologies: Sex Selection," in *Encyclopedia of Bioethics*, ed. Warren T. Reich

(New York: Free Press, 1978), 4:1439–1441; Robert H. Glass and Ronald J. Ericsson, *Getting Pregnant in the 1980s: New Advances in Infertility Treatment and Sex Preselection* (Berkeley, Calif.: University of California Press, 1982), pp. 113–129.

 8 See William H. James, "Timing of Fertilization and the Sex Ratio of Offspring," in Bennett, *Sex Selection of Children*, pp. 73–99.

 9 Glass and Ericsson, *Getting Pregnant in the 1980s*, pp. 123–124; Neil G. Bennett and Andrew Mason, "Decision Making and Sex Selection with Biased Technologies," in Bennett, *Sex Selection of Children*, pp. 101–102.

10 Nancy E. Williamson, "Parental Sex Preferences and Sex Selection," in Bennett, *Sex Selection of Children*, pp. 135–138.

11 Tabitha M. Powledge, "Unnatural Selection: On Choosing Children's Sex," in Holmes et al., *The Custom-Made Child?* pp. 193–199; Michael D. Bayles, *Reproductive Ethics* (Englewood Cliffs, N.J.: Prentice-Hall, 1984), pp. 33–36.

12 Amitai Etzioni, "Sex Control, Science, and Society," *Science* 161, no. 3846 (September 1968): 1107–1112; Marc Lappé and Peter Steinfels, "Choosing the Sex of Our Children," *Hastings Center Report* 4 (February 1974): 1–4; John Postgate, "Bat's Chance in Hell," *New Scientist* 58, no. 540 (5 April 1973): 12–16; Charles F. Westoff and Ronald R. Rindfuss, "Sex Preselection in the United States: Some Implications," *Science* 184 (10 May 1974): 633–636.

13 Bayles, *Reproductive Ethics*, p. 34.

14 Ibid.

15 Compare Powledge, "Unnatural Selection," p. 196; Robyn Rowland, "Reproductive Technologies: The Final Solution to the Woman Question?" in Arditti et al., *Test-Tube Women*, p. 361; Hoskins and Holmes, "Technology and Prenatal Femicide," p. 248; Clyda S. Rent and George S. Rent, "More on Offspring-Sex Preference: A Comment on Nancy E. Williamson's 'Sex Preferences, Sex Control, and the Status of Women,'" *Signs* 3 (1977): 512.

16 Bayles, *Reproductive Ethics*, p. 35.

17 Cf. Powledge, "Toward a Moral Policy for Sex Choice," p. 203.

18 Bayles, *Reproductive Ethics*, p. 35.

19 Ibid.

20 Mary Anne Warren, *Gendercide*.

21 Ibid., p. 85.

22 Ibid., p. 87.

23 Ibid., p. 176.

24 Ibid., p. 128.

25 Ibid., p. 84.

26 Ibid., p. 86.

27 Ibid., p. 87.

28 Ibid., p. 186.

29 Ibid., p. 143.

30 Ibid., p. 87.
31 Adrienne Rich, "Compulsory Heterosexuality and Lesbian Existence," in *Women: Sex and Sexuality*, ed. Catharine R. Stimpson and Ethel Spector Person (Chicago: University of Chicago Press, 1980), p. 79.
32 Anne Dickason, "The Feminine as a Universal," in *"Femininity," "Masculinity," and "Androgyny,"* ed. Mary Vetterling-Braggin (Totowa, N.J.: Littlefield, Adams, 1982), p. 11.
33 Elizabeth Rice Allgeier and Naomi B. McCormick, "Introduction: The Intimate Relationship between Gender Roles and Sexuality," in *Changing Boundaries: Gender Roles and Sexual Behavior*, ed. Elizabeth Rice Allgeier and Naomi B. McCormick (Palo Alto, Calif.: Mayfield, 1983), p. 5.
34 For a discussion of the difficulties involved in discerning that minimum, see Patrick Grim, "Sex and Social Roles: How to Deal with the Data," in Vetterling-Braggin, *"Femininity," "Masculinity," and "Androgyny,"* pp. 128–147.
35 Caroline Whitbeck, "The Maternal Instinct," in *Mothering: Essays in Feminist Theory*, ed. Joyce Trebilcot (Totowa, N.J.: Rowman & Allanheld, 1984), p. 186.
36 Letitia Anne Peplau and Steven L. Gordon, "The Intimate Relationships of Lesbians and Gay Men," in Allgeier and McCormick, *Changing Boundaries*, p. 231.
37 Some writers have expressed reservations about the degree of willingness and ability of the general population to adopt sex preselection techniques. See, for example, Pebley and Westoff, "Women's Sex Preferences," pp. 180–181; Westoff and Rindfuss, "Sex Preselection," pp. 635–636; Williamson, "Sex Preferences, Sex Control, and the Status of Women," pp. 855–857; Williamson, "Parental Sex Preferences and Sex Selection," pp. 138–140; Glass and Ericsson, *Getting Pregnant in The 1980s*, p. xv. They suggest that some techniques— for example, those which do not require artificial insemination—might be more acceptable than others and that the degree of acceptance, while low at first, might gradually increase.
38 Marcia Guttentag and Paul F. Secord, *Too Many Women? The Sex Ratio Question* (Newbury Park, Cal.: Sage Publications, 1983).
39 But this preference is less pronounced in the United States, where women are more likely to say that they want a balance in the sex of their offspring. See Anne R. Pebley and Charles F. Westoff, "Women's Sex Preferences in the United States: 1970 to 1975," *Demography* 19 (May 1982): 178.
40 See Nancy E. Williamson, *Sons or Daughters: A Cross-Cultural Survey of Parental Preferences*, (Newbury Park, Calif.: Sage Publications, 1976); Nancy E. Williamson, "Sex Preferences, Sex Control, and the Status of Women," *Signs* 1 (1976): 847–862; Pebley and Westoff, "Women's Sex Preferences," pp. 177–189.
41 See Powledge, "Toward a Moral Policy for Sex Choice,"

pp. 202–206. Warren provides a provocative discussion of both groups. See Warren, *Gendercide*, pp. 108–178.

42 Largey, "Reproductive Technologies," p. 1439.

43 Richard L. Meier, "Sex Determination and Other Innovations," in *Population in Perspective*, ed. Louise B. Young (New York: Oxford University Press, 1968), p. 410.

44 Powledge, "Toward a Moral Policy for Sex Choice," p. 202.

45 Bayles, *Reproductive Ethics*, p. 36.

46 Postgate, "Bat's Chance in Hell," p. 14.

47 Westoff and Rindfuss, "Sex Preselection in the United States," p. 635.

48 Williamson, "Sex Preferences, Sex Control, and the Status of Women," p. 859.

49 Lucille Forer with Henry Still, *The Birth Order Factor* (New York: Pocket Books, 1977), passim.

50 Warren, *Gendercide*, pp. 140–142.

51 Williamson, "Sex & Preferences," p. 860; Rowland, "Reproductive Technologies," pp. 361–362.

52 Hoskins and Holmes, "Technology and Prenatal Femicide," p. 248.

53 Lappé and Steinfels, "Choosing the Sex of Our Children," p. 2; John C. Fletcher, "Is Sex Selection Ethical?" in *Research Ethics*, ed. Kare Berg and Knut Eric Tranoy (New York: Alan R. Liss, 1983), p. 343.

54 Cf. Barbara Katz Rothman, *The Tentative Pregnancy: Prenatal Diagnosis and the Future of Motherhood* (New York: Viking/Penguin, 1986), pp. 138–139, on the possible effects of gender stereotyping as a result of the use of sex selection.

55 Lappé and Steinfels, "Choosing the Sex of Our Children," p. 2.

56 Ibid.

57 Etzioni, "Sex Control, Science, and Society," p. 1109.

58 Cf. Rowland, "Reproductive Technologies," p. 362.

59 Postgate, "Bat's Chance in Hell," p. 16.

60 Ibid.

61 Rowland, "Reproductive Technologies," p. 362.

62 Williamson, "Sex Preferences, Sex Control, and the Status of Women," p. 861; also Williamson, "Parental Sex Preferences and Sex Selection," p. 130.

63 Westoff and Rindfuss, "Sex Preselection in the U.S.," p. 636; Meier, "Sex Determination," p. 410; Nathan Keyfitz, "Foreword," in *Sex Selection of Children*, p. xii.

64 Pebley and Westoff, "Women's Sex Preferences," p. 187.

65 Keyfitz, "Foreword," p. xii; cf. Williamson, "Parental Sex Preferences and Sex Selection," p. 142.

66 Williamson, *Sons or Daughters*, p. 111.

67 Lappé and Steinfels, "Choosing the Sex of Our Children," p. 4; Bayles, *Reproductive Ethics*, pp. 36–37; Powledge, "Unnatural Selection," p. 197; Powledge, "Toward a Moral Policy for Sex Choice," p. 207.

68 For a discussion of the legal aspects of sex preselection, see Evans, "Legal Aspects of Prenatal Sex Selection," pp. 147–20.

69 Powledge, "Toward a Moral Policy for Sex Choice," p. 211.

70 Melissa Caplan, "Sex Preselection Techniques: A Desirable, and Morally Justifiable Innovation," unpublished paper (Montreal, Quebec, 1983), p. 6.

71 Bayles, *Reproductive Ethics*, p. 37.

72 Largey, "Reproductive Technologies," p. 1439; John C. Fletcher, "Ethics and Public Policy: Should Sex Choice Be Discouraged?" in *Sex Selection of Children*, p. 248.

73 See Warren, *Gendercide*, pp. 179–191.

74 Janice G. Raymond, "Sex Preselection: A Response," in *The Custom-Made Child?* pp. 209–210.

75 Powledge, "Unnatural Selection: On Choosing Children's Sex," p. 198.

76 Remark by Janice G. Raymond, "Sex Preselection," p. 221.

77 Fletcher, "Is Sex Selection Ethical?" p. 345.

78 See Powledge, "Toward a Moral Policy for Sex Choice," pp. 208–209.

3 The Embryo/Fetus

In a paper on abortion published fourteen years ago, philosopher Roger Wertheimer proposed the following thought experiment:

> Close your eyes for a moment and imagine that, due to advances in medical technology or mutation caused by a nuclear war, the relevant cutaneous and membranous shields became transparent from conception to parturition, so that when a mother put aside her modesty and her clothing the developing fetus would be in full public view. Or suppose instead, or in addition, that anyone could at any time pluck a fetus from its womb, air it, observe it, fondle it, and then stick it back in after a few minutes. . . . What then would we think of aborting a fetus? . . . And what does that say about what you *now* think?[1]

Wertheimer was only slightly ahead of his time. Current technology permits the fetus to be placed "in full public view" and permits doctors, at least, to "pluck a fetus from its womb." What is philosophically significant are the ways in which these new capacities affect and reflect moral attitudes toward the embryo/fetus and, less directly, toward women.

This chapter discusses ethical questions about prenatal human life, the whole range of human growth from the fertilized ovum, through the blastocyst/morula/zygote stages and the embryonic and fetal phases, to birth. I refer to the living entity that undergoes these stages as the "embryo/fetus," a shorthand phrase to encompass all of its development. Although it is a somewhat awkward term, neither "embryo" nor "fetus" by itself is an adequate label to cover the full scope of prenatal evolution.

Despite this concern with the embryo/fetus, I shall not

discuss some questions about it which are usually raised by philosophers and theologians. For example, nothing is said about the supposed ensoulment of the embryo/fetus, or about its personhood (or lack of personhood).[2] It is assumed only that one need not adopt an all-or-nothing view. For even if the embryo/fetus is not regarded as a person, it is not nothing,[3] and important questions will still remain as to what sort of being it is and how it ought to be treated.

The primary concern here is not the ontological status of the embryo/fetus but rather its moral status: that is, the nature of our moral views about it. Questions about abortion are examined here only briefly, since they will be discussed extensively in chapter 4. Instead I shall examine our current attitudes as they are revealed within a broad range of treatments now being done to and for the embryo/fetus. Then, from a feminist perspective I shall raise some questions about the legitimacy of those attitudes. Finally, I shall suggest the outline of an alternative moral approach to treatment of the embryo/fetus.

Benefits and Harms

The current scientific, medical, and social treatment of the embryo/fetus is roughly of two types: benefits and harms. (The word "treatment" is used in this context very generally to refer to any sort of behavior toward the embryo/fetus, not just recognized medical treatment.) Some treatments apparently help the embryo/fetus in a variety of ways. I say "apparently" because even some of the intended benefits turn out to be harmful. Other treatments, whether intentionally or not, straightforwardly harm it in one way or another.[4] What these two different types of treatments suggest is a conflict within current attitudes toward the embryo/fetus. To paraphrase Wertheimer, we cannot decide whether we want to take it out or do it in.[5]

Consider first the current treatments of the embryo/fetus that apparently benefit it. The most contentious and noticeable of these is, of course, the antiabortion (or, to use its own

preferred name, "pro-life") movement. This varied group
defends the alleged right to life of the embryo/fetus on the basis
of its supposed personhood. In Canada, for example, one
activist, former politician Joe Borowski, sought unsuccessfully
to change the Canadian Criminal Code provisions that govern
abortion by having the fetus declared a legal person.[6] The
argument rested on Section 7 of the Canadian Charter of
Rights and Freedoms, which guarantees "everyone" rights to
"life, liberty and security of the person," and on the claim that
"everyone" includes the fetus.[7] Pro-life activists see what
they call the unborn child as "the most defenceless of all
human beings",[8] whose existence and well-being must be
championed against those who threaten it. Every embryo/
fetus has a right to life, they say, including those that are
deformed: "If all mentally normal fetuses have a full human
right to life then it follows that *all fetuses*, whether physically or
mentally handicapped, *must have these same rights. We must be
consistent.*"[9]

Next among those who promote apparent benefits for the
embryo/fetus is a growing group of physicians, scientists,
lawyers, and ethicists who are concerned with what they call
"prenatal abuse." Prenatal abuse is unjustified mistreatment
of the embryo/fetus; it is a form of child abuse that begins
before birth. These individuals defend the alleged rights of the
embryo/fetus to be free of unnecessary pain, to be free of the
debilitating effects of drug and alcohol use by the mother, to
avoid deformity as a result of environmental hazards, and to
receive adequate nutrition and health care. As a result, they
promote a variety of measures to safeguard the entitlement of
the embryo/fetus to these "rights"—measures ranging from
provision of food supplements for the mother to legal regulation of maternal behavior.

For example, one writer advises that "prudent physicians"
would prescribe folic acid supplements to *all* high-risk patients
during the last two weeks of *each* menstrual cycle, apparently
regardless of whether a pregnancy is contemplated or
anticipated.[10] Concern for prenatal abuse has produced the
suggestion that pregnant women have obligations to undergo
prenatal screening and to avoid work, recreation, and medical
care choices that are hazardous to the embryo/fetus.[11] It is

claimed that health care professionals ought to be required to report both actual and potential fetal abuse.[12] According to these writers, laws prohibiting pregnant women from obtaining or using alcohol, tobacco, or drugs likely to damage the embryo/fetus would be justified, even if such laws applied only to pregnant women.[13] They raise the question whether the fetus might be considered a possible victim of criminal offenses such as assault,[14] and suggest that legal mechanisms may be necessary to enforce the embryo/fetus' "right" to care and protection from abuse. One lawyer goes so far as to suggest that defense of the embryo/fetus may require what he calls "forcible bodily intrusions"; that is, assault on the pregnant woman.[15] Another holds that parents should "be held accountable to their children if they knowingly and willfully choose to transmit deleterious genes or if the mother waives her right to an abortion if, after prenatal testing, a fetus is discovered to be seriously deformed or mentally defective."[16] And it is interesting to note that the concept of what constitutes prenatal abuse is gradually being expanded, so that in some cases even a planned birth at home has been described as an instance of prenatal abuse.[17]

A third type of apparent benefit for the embryo/fetus sought by some advocates is fetal surgery. Thanks to new medical techniques, it is now possible to treat the fetus as a patient.[18] Some undesirable medical conditions in the fetus can be dealt with by means of prenatal surgery to correct the condition. There are treatments for fluid build-up in the brain, chest, or abdomen; blocked bladders; fetal hernia; and fetal growth retardation.[19] Moreover at the University of Colorado Health Sciences Center, where fetal surgery is performed, a theologian and a neonatologist have been appointed as advocates for fetuses who are candidates for intrauterine therapy.[20] By these means some doctors come to develop an apparent relationship with the fetus; they regard the fetus as having a right to diagnosis or themselves as having a right to diagnose "their patient," the fetus.[21]

A fourth type of apparent benefit for the embryo/fetus throughout and at the very end of its prenatal existence is the use of fairly major technological interventions to monitor its development and birth. Techniques such as chorionic villi sampling, amniocentesis, ultrasound, and fetoscopy open an apparently benevolent window on the womb. Such processes seem to benefit the fetus by providing early information about any medical problems it may have. Birth technology includes fetal monitoring, induction of labor, artificial rupture of the amniotic membranes, and episiotomy.

Perhaps the most notorious of interventions at birth is the use of cesarean section, an operation whose incidence has increased tremendously within the last decade. These cesareans are undertaken for the supposed benefit of fetuses that, for one reason or another, are judged to be unsuited to ordinary vaginal birth. One writer says, "where the need to preserve the unborn child's life or health conflicts with the mother's wish for vaginal delivery, the child's interests should take priority. If the mother's insistence on vaginal delivery causes death or injury of the child, the mother could be subject to civil liability or criminal prosecution".[22] This writer further advises that in a case in which a mother persists in refusing a cesarean, the physician's duty is to seek emergency judicial approval for the operation.[23] And indeed, this is precisely what has happened in some cases: cesareans have been undertaken against the will of the mother and enforced through court orders.[24]

What possible reasons could there be for claiming that at least some of the apparent benefits just described may actually harm the embryo/fetus? General reasons for misgivings will be suggested later. At this point only some specific concerns about these treatments will be mentioned. First, although they appear to provide benefits, they are not without risks to the embryo/fetus. For example, although the use of ultrasound has been regarded as entirely safe and has become routine in many pregnancies, laboratory research has "demonstrated fetal abnormalities, fetal and maternal deaths in animal studies, and chromosomal and other abnormalities in human cell studies".[25] Thus ultrasound tests may subject the fetus to long-term health risks. Fetal surgery is another obvious example.[26] In one case the fetus' head "was punctured six times between the twenty-fifth and thirty-second weeks of pregnancy to withdraw fluid. Yet despite this treatment, the baby was born with severe brain damage and other disabilities".[27]

Second, and perhaps more radically, it might be questioned whether the benefits for the embryo/fetus of the treatments just described necessarily always outweigh the harms they produce. For example, insofar as the pro-life movement is successful in preventing an abortion from taking place, is the fetus thereby benefited more than it is harmed? Some evidence suggests that the offspring of women who sought abortions and were denied them fared significantly less well than wanted children in regard to mental health, social adjustments, and school performance.[28] Without unduly blaming the mothers of these children, who are compelled by unjust laws to make the best of a very difficult situation, it could be argued that it is not always and necessarily in the best interests of a fetus to be born to a woman who does not want it.[29] It appears that preventing an abortion could even contribute to rather than reduce the infliction of harm on the fetus, or on the person the fetus will become.

In response to this argument, however, one defender of the right to prenatal care questions whether "not being wanted is always so great a deficiency that it would be better to terminate such pregnancies".[30] The claim is that the hazards of being unwanted are not sufficient to make life not worth living for the embryo/fetus. Admittedly, it would be both implausible and insensitive to argue that all unwanted children should never have existed. But this concession is not inconsistent with the more general claim that for some fetuses, the harms of not being aborted may outweigh the benefits, and that denying an abortion to a woman may not be in the best interests of her embryo/fetus.

In assessing abortions, therefore, it is essential to consider very carefully the underlying ethical question whether any life whatsoever is better than no life at all. Two ethicists comment:

> Fetal surgery may salvage a fetus whose prospects prove to be dismal. Rather than death in the womb or shortly after birth, it will survive only to face a series of painful operations, institutional existence, or perpetual childish dependence on parents or others. To the extent that life-preservation is a worthy pursuit, such results may be

counted successes; but this success must be balanced against the cost in lives of low quality.[31]

The general assumption on which the provision of various forms of apparent good for the embryo/fetus is premised is that any human life form is always benefited through treatment that prolongs its life. Existence, even in a seriously damaged condition, is always preferable to nonexistence. But this assumption is at least open to question, for a life lived in pain, unawareness, or severe disability may not be worth living.[32]

The harmful treatments inflicted on the embryo/fetus are almost a mirror image of the apparent benefits. They include, first, abortion, the reported incidence of which has increased massively during the years in which it has been legally permitted in North America under certain carefully regulated conditions. Like some other feminists,[33] I believe that although women are entitled to legal access to abortion, we must not lose sight of the fact that abortion involves the termination of fetal life. Not all prenatal life is necessarily worth preserving, and some abortions may be justified by reference to the embryo/fetus's own best interests.[34] But clearly in many cases abortion is a serious harm to the embryo/fetus. Aside from the pain that the abortion procedure may occasion in developed fetuses, abortion is a harm to the embryo/fetus not so much because of what it is but because of the loss of what it could otherwise have become.

The second type of harmful treatment of the embryo/fetus includes reproductive hazards of various kinds, both what could be called maternal hazards—that is, those directly occasioned by the mother—and environmental hazards—those produced by the behavior of other individuals and institutions.[35] A woman who smokes, drinks heavily, or makes use of drugs—prescription or nonprescription, legal or illegal—may be putting her embryo/fetus at risk. And similarly, such environmental conditions as second-hand cigarette smoke, severe air or water pollution, and contaminants in the workplace constitute a possible threat to the developing embryo/fetus.[36]

Even more obviously harmful to the embryo/fetus is experimentation on it.[37] Once again, the harm inflicted here includes possible pain, mutilation, and loss of potential for future life. In the United States at least until federally supported experimentation was brought to an end,[38] this research included studies of the effects of certain processes and substances both on fetuses scheduled to be aborted and on those already aborted.[39] Moreover, some writers foresee that there may be a movement in the future to a situation in which embryos are "farmed": that is, created and sustained as a source of spare tissue and organs for more mature human beings.[40] These treatments, although they may seem to be justified by reference to the claim that future fetuses will benefit,[41] ordinarily do not benefit the embryos or fetuses themselves on which they are performed.[42]

Finally, a fourth type of harm to the embryo/fetus derives from the vast range of new reproductive technology now under development and study. This includes sex preselection, discussed in chapter 2, as well as in vitro fertilization (IVF), embryo transfer, and the freezing of embryos, techniques for artificially producing, harvesting, and preserving embryos. In the process of in vitro fertilization, ova (the female gametes, also called eggs) are surgically removed under general anesthesia from a woman's ovaries. (Ordinarily the woman is administered hormones in order to stimulate her ovaries to produce several eggs simultaneously.) The eggs are then fertilized in a glass dish ("in vitro") with sperm obtained by masturbation from a man who is usually the woman's husband or partner. The resulting embryos are transferred to the woman's uterus by means of a thin catheter inserted through her cervix, in the hope that at least one of them will implant in the uterine wall and a normal pregnancy will result.[43] So-called spare embryos can be frozen for future use by the same woman or by another to whom the embryos are donated.

This technology will be discussed at greater length in later chapters. Its classification here as harmful to the embryo/fetus may be controversial.[44] For it is often argued that such technology is a benefit to the embryo/fetus that is thereby produced, since without such effort it would not have existed at all. One writer states,

a higher incidence of birth defects in . . . offspring [produced through artificial reproduction] would not justify banning the technique[s] in order to protect the offspring, because without these techniques these children would not have been born at all. Unless their lives are so full of suffering as to be worse than no life at all, a very unlikely supposition, the defective children of such a union have not been harmed if they could not have been born healthy.[45]

This is another version of the undefended assumption noted earlier, that almost any existence is better than none. Thus life as a four-celled embryo, produced through in vitro fertilization and frozen in an embryo bank, or implanted at great risk in a surrogate mother, is assumed to be preferable to never having existed. But it is worth remarking that even ardent defenders of the social uses of reproductive technology admit that techniques such as in vitro fertilization are intended to operate in the best interests of infertile couples, not (like adoption, for example) in the best interests of the fetuses and children thereby produced.[46] For example, the Ontario Law Reform Commission defends embryo donation because for a small group of people it offers the only chance to have a child, and "this group should not be denied the advantages offered to those whose desire for a child can be accommodated" by gamete donation.[47] Furthermore, the use of new reproductive technology, like fetal surgery and birth technology, entails risks to the embryo/fetus, risks threatening both its future well-being and its present existence.[48] For these reasons I classify the use of new reproductive technology as a harm rather than a benefit to the embryo/fetus. More perhaps than any of the other types of treatment, this technology should raise questions about who or what is actually benefited by its use.

The Commodification of Reproduction

The conflict between treatments that apparently benefit the embryo/fetus and those that harm it thus turns out to be less profound than it first appears. For at least some apparently beneficent treatments are similar to harmful treatments insofar as they involve risk with little or no benefit to the embryo/fetus, and they are founded on the assumption that any life is better than no life at all. This observation invites further consideration of what is really involved in the current treatments of the embryo/fetus and what they suggest about moral attitudes towards it.

I suggest that all of the various forms of treatment of the embryo/fetus are evidence of the gradual commodification of reproduction. "Commodification of reproduction" refers to the processes by which economic relationships of various kinds are introduced into the social patterns of human reproduction. In particular the embryo/fetus is becoming a type of consumer good that can be made to order and purchased on the open market. Parents thus become the consumers of special reproductive services designed to enhance the quality of the fetus-product.

The various ways in which the embryo/fetus is treated show that it is regarded as a product, a human creation in a new sense. For now the embryo/fetus has become an entity that human beings can set out consciously to plan, schedule, and improve upon. To a high degree citizens in the Western world at least appear to have the freedom to choose whether to reproduce, when to reproduce, what to reproduce, and the number of offspring to reproduce—a godlike responsibility. So it is not surprising that two researchers on in vitro fertilization describe their work as "assisting in creation by using God's materials: the sperm of the husband, the egg of the wife and the brains of the scientist."[49] And one ethicist claims,

It seems to me that laboratory reproduction is radically human compared to conception by ordinary heterosexual intercourse. It is willed, chosen, purposed and controlled and surely these are the traits that distinguish *Homo Sapiens* from others in the animal genus, from primates down. Coital reproduction is therefore less human than laboratory reproduction—more fun, to be sure, but with our separation of baby making from love making, both become more human because they are matters of choice and not of chance.[50]

Thus the embryo/fetus is in some ways like a work of art and in other respects like an ongoing scientific experiment, never to be considered entirely finished. Technology now enables human beings to repair and improve on the characteristics of the embryo/fetus. As a result, one legal expert claims that what he calls "procreative autonomy" includes the "right to take positive steps to enhance the possibility that offspring will have desired characteristics." This right would include the entitlement to abort fetuses or to refuse to implant embryos with undesired gender or genetic traits. People, he says, should have the freedom to pick egg, sperm, or gestational donors to maximize desirable physical features.[51] Technology also enables us to store embryos and to select those that will be implanted in a uterus, experimented upon, or disposed of.[52] Medical and bioethical discussions of in vitro fertilization routinely refer to the extra embryos that are produced as "spare" embryos,[53] as if they were commercial products of which the organized householder would do well to keep extras on hand. One ethicist describes these tendencies as "treat[ing] the embryo too much like unclaimed luggage"—yet even he casually recommends destroying an embryo if both of the gamete donors who contributed to its creation should happen to die.[54]

As a new consumer product, the embryo/fetus has an exchange value at several points in its growth; it is a luxury item that one might or might not want or need. The actual cost of an embryo can be seen quite clearly in the prices charged throughout North America for in vitro fertilization and embryo transfer. The cost of a more developed fetus, free of foreseeable defects, is manifested in the prices charged in the United States for prenatal screening and fetal surgery.

The embryo/fetus has become a new type of property; it is now the sort of thing one can own.[55] If an individual does not have one of her (or, very often, his) own, she or he can obtain one from others who do not want theirs. A recent book about artificial reproduction takes this premise to its logical limit when it proposes a solution to the situation in which a couple, the "joint owners" of an embryo, disagree as to what is to be done with it. According to the book,

King Solomon's remedy of equal division might well be the best [solution]. At this early state, each surgically separated half would be able to develop normally—thus each partner would have one of a pair of identical twin embryos.[56]

Now I do not believe that buying and selling are inherently evil, or that there is something morally objectionable about every commercial transaction. It is specifically the introduction of economic considerations into reproduction about which I have reservations. But what is wrong with this gradual process of commodification of reproduction may not be immediately evident, and in fact it has been vigorously defended. One lawyer justifies it by pointing out that "substantial sums" are spent for the investigation and treatment of infertility, for childbirth, and for neonatal care,[57] and this is not objectionable. Similarly, the sale of gametes and embryos has been defended partly by the argument that "many means of achieving natural reproduction—the surgical treatment of reproductive impairments, for example—depend upon the existence of paid services, where profit is involved."[58] And these practices, the argument suggests, do not seem to be morally unacceptable.

Perhaps, however, the moral innocuousness of paying for these latter sorts of medical care stems from the fact that they do not involve the buying and selling of reproductive products and services themselves—that is, eggs, sperm, embryos, and the use of a uterus. It is this type of commercial exchange that is morally troubling.

The commodification of reproduction creates the potential for manipulation, corruption, exploitation, and misuse of power. Special reproductive services—the buying of a high-quality embryo produced through in vitro fertilization, for example—are now available only to the wealthy. From here it is but a short distance to the point where women will have the "opportunity" to sell their embryos. Indeed, the process of uterine lavage already enables one woman to give her embryo to another; and there seems little reason to doubt that on the present model of sperm vendors and surrogate mothers, it will soon be possible for such women—or their representatives or middlemen—to sell them. And it will be poorer women who

will be the suppliers of this commodity. The business of providing embryos creates a new opportunity for using the bodies
of women and exerting control over their reproductive
capacities.[59] Businesses will have the chance to profit from the
transactions between buyers and sellers of reproductive products and services. Deceit and possibly medical danger will be
introduced, since people will be tempted to lie in order to
complete a sale: much as a similar problem enters into the sale
of blood and blood products in the United States today.[60]

It is striking, then, that the buying and selling of gametes
and embryos has been defended by reference to legal statutes
that legitimize the purchase and sale of blood or blood consti-
tuents, on the supposed ground that "it is in the public interest
to stockpile supplies of blood and to encourage people to
contribute to them".[61] Presumably, then, the implication is
that it is likewise in the public interest to "stockpile" gametes
and embryos. Such an assumption is founded upon a charac-
teristically nonfeminist inattention to the effects of reproductive technology on women.

At this point it is important to return to the question suggested earlier: Who really benefits from the ways in which the
embryo/fetus is treated? Though much of the behavior toward
it is apparently intended to promote its well-being, a closer
examination suggests that it is the inventors, producers, and
promoters of fetal treatments who more often gain from them.
Scientists and physicians make the decisions about which
women will have abortions, which women will be eligible for
in vitro fertilization and will donate eggs and embryos, and
which embryos will be transferred. And they—the scientists
and physicians—profit from the subsequent execution of
those decisions. Reproductive and birth technology provide a
lucrative income and often the rewards of media adulation to
those who make it available.

In addition to these consequentialist considerations pertaining to the commodification of reproduction, there is also a
further area of concern, less easy to delineate but important
nevertheless. A person is not the kind of thing that may be
bought or sold. The immorality of such exchanges extends, I
submit, both to what was once a person and to what may
become a person. Thus the buying or selling of a human corpse

would be prima facie wrong, not so much because of what it is but because of what it was. Possibly, in some cases, compelling reasons could be given to override the wrongness of such transactions, but the burden of proof would rest on those who wished to engage in them. In the case of the embryo/fetus, one need not make any judgment either that it is or that it is not a person. If it is not a person, clearly it may, given the right combination of circumstances, become one, and for that reason it should not be bargained with. Thus the buying or selling of a human embryo/fetus would be prima facie wrong, not so much because of what it is but because of what it will be. Once again, the burden of proof would rest upon those who wished to engage in such transactions. As a result, the commodification of reproduction—at least in regard to the embryo/fetus—seems to be *inherently* as well as instrumentally wrong because of its violation of the prima facie obligation not to buy or sell what is, was, or will be a person.

Some Connections

I now want to posit some connections between the treatment of the embryo/fetus and attitudes toward other, more developed human beings, particularly children and women. These connections reveal the nonfeminist and even antifeminist elements inherent in much of that treatment.

First, the current treatment of the embryo/fetus is an extension to the prenatal period of some of the less praiseworthy attitudes toward children of middle-class North Americans. A recent study of private adoption in Canada cites "the importance of the 'law of supply and demand' in the development of processes to 'distribute' children within our society," and argues that "when children are in scarce supply they are viewed as particularly valuable[;] . . . today healthy, Caucasion infants are in very short supply".[62] Another writer suggests, "The child in North America has become a luxury item, a pet, a sign of conspicuous consumption for the well-off, and a financial burden for the poor."[63]

According to current assumptions, the child is an expression of its parents, especially the mother, and reflects their abilities and talents as well as their weaknesses and errors in judgment. Parents have a duty to make their offspring as good as possible, according to very definite standards of intelligence and accomplishment, by providing their children with every opportunity and means to improve on their strengths and overcome their faults.[64]

Reproductive technology such as prenatal diagnosis, fetal surgery, sex preselection, and selective abortion (of defective fetuses or those of the "wrong" sex) is an extension of this approach to child-rearing for it permits, at the prenatal stage, more and more detailed specifications of the type of child that is wanted. One feminist points out that claims have been made on behalf of in vitro fertilization that the offspring produced are more intelligent and socially adept than other children and that people are sometimes requesting the procedure with donated gametes because they find their partner's characteristics undesirable.[65] So not only have the standards for what are considered acceptable offspring been raised in recent times, but the application of those standards has extended back in time to the period before birth. What is the place of children who are thus artificially created and improved upon? One writer desribes the child who is produced via artificial insemination by donor as having "a 'prosthetic' role to play in the family."[66] This appears to suggest that the created child is a synthetic but much enhanced substitute for the real thing. There is a connection, then, between the treatment of children and the treatment of the embryo/fetus. As one writer puts it, "too much emphasis has been placed upon the ownership of . . . embryos, reflecting the obsession our society has with the ownership of, as opposed to the caring for, children."[67]

How is the treatment of the embryo/fetus connected with social attitudes toward women? I suggest that the various ways in which the embryo/fetus is experimented upon, repaired, and improved are connected with some general feelings about women's bodies. Women's bodies have traditionally been regarded as dark and dangerous places, threatening to the men who use them sexually and even to the babies who emerge, not always intact, from them.[68] Now, however, the female body is seen as dangerous even to the embryo/fetus because the pregnant woman cannot be trusted not to abuse it, pass on defective genes to it, or even kill it, let alone to protect it from environmental harm and give birth to it safely. One ethicist who has done much to promote awareness of prenatal abuse clearly regards the mother as one of the greatest dangers to the embryo/fetus, and suggests that mothers are the likeliest class of defendant in future legal actions for prenatal injury.[69] Similarly, another lawyer apparently regards the dangers of prenatal abuse by mothers as serious and wide-ranging; he proposes that

> states could amend or interpret child abuse, feticide, or abortion laws to include a wide range of behavior by pregnant women that is likely to cause harm to their unborn children. Under such statutes, it would be possible to punish a woman who refused to take a necessary medication (as, for example, a diabetic mother who failed to take insulin) or who knowingly exposed herself to teratogenic substances or environments.[70]

This argument mislocates the responsibility for reproductive hazards: it is the pregnant woman herself who is seen as the primary danger to her embryo/fetus, since it is she who exposes it to reproductive dangers in the workplace and elsewhere.[71] Such an approach fails to acknowledge that one's exposure to teratogenic environments may not be within one's power; it is difficult to control the purity of the air we breathe and the water we drink. And employees have little or no power over reproductive hazards in the workplace. Moreover, even those activities (such as smoking and consuming alcohol) that appear to be directly the responsibility of the pregnant woman are encouraged and supported by corporations and indirectly by the state itself. Thus what is omitted is a concern for the social context of pregnancy and birthing and for public responsibilities to pregnant women, and the result is to blame the pregnant woman who is herself the victim of reproductive hazards.[72]

A feminist critic of new reproductive technology argues that those engaged in research on this technology regard women as "ineffective, wasteful, storers of eggs" and embryos.[73] This observation is borne out by the words of two researchers on in vitro fertilization, who classify the procedure among those that afford "man" [*sic*] "the objective of trying to improve on nature's errors or mistakes."[74] Moreover, another scientist states,

> One of the highest responsibilities of any society must surely involve the conception of its children with the greatest possible skill and devotion, to assure them of the best life possible. The introduction of conception in vitro, and the breadth of its related studies, helped to transform such responsibility from theory into fact, and deserves the widest financial and ethical support.[75]

If, as this quotation implies, conception in vitro is thought to assure children of the best life possible, one wonders whether it will not soon be advocated for all conceptions. Indeed, the scientist just quoted seems convinced of the inefficient and downright dangerous nature of ordinary conception: "For me, a glance at some of the unfortunate products of natural conception—triploid and trisomic children, others suffering from genetic lesions, some ending as disordered growths in the mother's body, is sufficient to demand that some sort of intervention is *essential* in conception to ensure that children are born as normal as we can possibly ensure."[76]

It is fortunate, then, from this point of view that men have stepped in to improve upon the deficiencies of the female reproductive system.[77] The scientist continues, "Man [*sic*] should contribute to the ongoing task of creating man [*sic*] because God [has] shared his creative powers with us."[78] And in a similar vein, a theologian sees experimentation on embryos as a manifestation of "our need to get a control of ourselves." He says, "we take our biology from being that which we *live*, to be that which we *observe*, and so to be that which we *conquer*."[79] There is a connection, then, between the current treatment of the embryo/fetus and social attitudes toward women: intervention in and on behalf of the embryo/fetus is thought to be necessitated by the danger and inefficiency of the female body.

An Alternative

I now want to propose an alternative approach to the current treatment of the embryo/fetus. What follows is intended to give aid and comfort neither to antiabortionists nor to defendants of fetal experimentation. Individuals on both of the sides delineated here seem fundamentally mistaken, and it is therefore not surprising that despite apparent differences the two should have much in common. They share a nonfeminist (or even antifeminist) androcentric approach and a lack of concern for the implications of the treatment of the embryo/fetus for women and children. They are influenced by those tendencies in patriarchal thought toward dichotomization and moral absolutism which have been criticized by feminists. To avoid those extremes the alternative approach proposed here adopts a sort of *via negativa*. That is, it says more about what should *not* be done than about what should be done in the treatment of the embryo/fetus.

I suggest, first, that there should be stringent restrictions on all programs, institutions, research projects, and contracts that serve to promote the commodification of reproduction. Just as economic considerations should not rule sexual relationships, so also they should not goven reproductive relationships. On a legal and political level this would mean the prohibition of any commercial arrangements by which sperm, ova, embryos, or embryo parts are bought or sold. And it would mean that all contracts for babies by surrogate motherhood would be rendered invalid.

On this issue some of the recommendations of *The Warnock Report on Human Fertilisation and Embryology* are far preferable to, for example, those of the Ontario Law Reform Commission's *Report of Artificial Reproduction and Related Matters*. The Law Reform Commission in effect endorses the commodification of reproduction in its recommendation that "gamete banks, that is, banks that buy and sell sperm, ova, and embryos, should be permitted to operate on a commercial basis," subject only to the modest limitations that such banks operate under licence and be regulated in respect to "payment by users to defray reasonable costs and, perhaps, to provide a reasonable profit."[80] The Commission provides for "reasonable payment" for sperm and ovum donors[81] and suggests a panoply of legal regulations to govern but not outlaw surrogate motherhood. By contrast, *The Warnock Report* recommends legislation "to render criminal the creation or the operation in the United Kingdom of agencies whose purposes include the recruitment of women for surrogate pregnancy or making arrangements for individuals or couples who wish to utilize the services of a carrying mother" and also to render unenforceable in the courts all surrogacy agreements.[82] These recommendations will be discussed further in chapter 6; for now I wish only to suggest that the Warnock Committee seems correct in its assumption that payments for and profit-making from these services are difficult to limit and likely to lead to serious exploitation.

On a much deeper level, the level of our thinking about the status of the embryo/fetus and our moral obligations to it, the exclusion of economic considerations from reproductive relationships would mean ceasing to think of the embryo/fetus as an ongoing work of art or scientific experiment, ceasing to think of it as a product to be improved upon through human ingenuity, ceasing to think of it as a bit of property or piece of consumer goods with a dollar value. And it is not clear how so profound a revolution in our thinking could be brought about. For in making these recommendations it is not suggested that all of our practices of prenatal screening, prenatal care, or abortion are always unjustified. On the contrary, they could be of very real value both to women and to future children. But in their present uses they are founded upon the wrong assumptions about the embryo/fetus, and they tend toward morally dubious goals.

Second, I propose that less emphasis should be placed on providing apparent benefits for the embryo/fetus, and instead the Hippocratic injunction, "primum non nocere," should be stressed. At least within ethical discussions, the seemingly old-fashioned moral obligation of nonmaleficence appears to be virtually ignored.[83] Yet it is surely essential to morality. While promoting the good is of course morally important, the principle of nonmaleficence is significant in a more fundamental way: It implies that the burden of justification must always be on those who wish to cause harm rather than on those who wish to avoid it. To refrain from hurting or injuring living beings and the environment in which they live and move and have their being is both the minimum and also the sine qua non of responsible moral behavior. "The duty of nonmaleficence does not merely prohibit intentional harm—except in special circumstances—and require the justification of risks by probable benefits. It also requires that agents be thoughtful and act carefully."[84]

The principle of nonmaleficence has special relevance to the embryo/fetus. As biologists point out, growth processes in the embryo/fetus are largely interrelated and as yet poorly understood. Interfering in one process may unintentionally disrupt another.

Furthermore, physicians are as yet ignorant about what differences are to be expected in the "normal" rates of development among different "normal" fetuses. Different children grow at different rates; no reason to think that fetuses don't. But that means that chemical and physical indices that seem "abnormal" may turn out to be within the "normal" range once that range gets mapped out. As physicians devise new tests and procedures, they are very likely to repair "errors" that would correct themselves. Some "errors" may be harmless and may not need to be "corrected."[85]

Sometimes, of course, literal nonmaleficence is impossible: doing harm is unavoidable. But in that case, surely, our responsibility is to do the least harm possible. An example of this responsibility is described by Margaret Somerville and will be discussed at greater length in chapter 4. She proposes that physicians who perform abortions have a moral obligation to use "the least mutilating means of abortion which are reasonably available" and to take "all reasonable measures to preserve the life of the foetus in so far as these are consistent with carrying out the abortion."[86]

The final step along my via negativa involves a reassessment of the ontological assumptions apparently taken for granted when the embryo/fetus is discussed in a way that divorces it from the woman within which it flourishes. It is because of the development of efficient forms of abortion as well as in vitro fertilization, uterine lavage, embryo transfer, prenatal diagnosis, and fetal surgery that we have become accustomed to thinking of the embryo/fetus as a separate and independent being. As one feminist philosopher has argued, there is, at least in the context of disputes about abortion, a conceptualization of the embryo/fetus "based on the categories that are familiar to men's experience, so that being pregnant is represented on the one hand as similar to having a tumor, or on the other as being hooked up to an adult stranger who is dependent on that hookup for survival, or more remote yet, as occupying a house with another person whose presence constitutes more or less of a threat to one's life."[87] From the point of view of the medical profession, "pregnancy has become a disease with *two* potential patients—the pregnant woman and the fetus—and of those, the fetus is medically and technically by far the more interesting one."[88]

Thus the embryo/fetus and the woman are seen as adversaries who are in competition with each other.[89] As one writer describes it, in sporting terms, "the unborn is *in* the race and has something to compete with other than just a right which 'crystallizes at birth'."[90] The embryo/fetus is seen as "a completely autonomous human being"[91] whose needs may be in conflict with those of its mother. The mother becomes "the route to the fetus,"[92] an incubator,[93] or, more sinister still, a nine-month jail cell.[94]

As an alternative to this approach, some feminists suggest that we reconsider the embryo/fetus in terms of its relationship to the woman who gestates it. "The interests of fetus and woman are so intimately bound that one cannot speak of their distinct, let alone conflicting, interests without simplifying distortion."[95] At the same time, it is worth remembering that despite the complex interaction of the two, the mother was a separate and independent individual before her pregnancy began and will be again when it ends. She has various physiological and perhaps also emotional bonds with her embryo/fetus but is not dependent upon it for her continued existence. The embryo/fetus, by contrast, although it will be independent of its mother to a degree at the end of its gestation, was obviously not independent prior to conception and is totally dependent for its existence on the woman who gestates it. It is not yet a child, though it may become one. Thus "although the pregnant woman and the fetus are interdependent, the relationship is not symmetrical."[96] And a feminist theologian adds that fetal development should be described as "an *interaction* between a fetal life form and a woman's body, which far from a 'mere' passive host, is *the* life system that enables continuous fetal development from its simple to its complex form."[97]

Fourteen years ago Roger Wertheimer predicted that if the developing embryo/fetus could be viewed and manipulated, attitudes toward it would change. About this he was quite correct; but what he did not foresee was that those changes might be morally undesirable. As the capacity to manipulate the embryo/fetus grows, the increasing tendency to commodify it and to view it as a work of art or an ongoing experiment should be resisted. Instead of treating the embryo/fetus as a distinct, separate, independent entity, it should be seen in a more holistic fashion as connected with its mother, who is not a danger to it but the source of its ongoing sustenance. Certainly it is now possible, in Wertheimer's words, to "pluck a fetus from its womb," but that capacity should not obscure the significance of its relationship with the woman who gestates it.

Notes

An earlier version of this chapter, entitled "'Pluck a Fetus from Its Womb': A Critique of Current Attitudes toward the Embryo/Fetus," appeared in *The University of Western Ontario Law Review* 24 (1986): 1–14. The material is used here with the permission of the journal's editor.

I wish to thank Sanda Rodgers-Magnet, Abby Lippman, Margaret Somerville, and Peter Singer for their very helpful comments on this chapter.

1 Roger Wertheimer, "Understanding the Abortion Argument," in

Moral Problems, ed. James Rachels (New York: Harper & Row, 1975), p. 86, Wertheimer's emphasis.

2 Unlike some writers, I do not think that debates about personhood are hopelessly confused; nor do I believe that the assignment of the label "person" reflects a necessarily arbitrary decision. This is the view taken by H. W. Jones, Jr., in "The Ethics of In-Vitro Fertilization—1981," in *Human Conception In Vitro,* ed. R. G. Edwards and Jean M. Purdy (London: Academic Press, 1982), pp. 353–354, and by Lori B. Andrews, "Ethical Considerations in In Vitro Fertilization and Embryo Transfer," in *Human In Vitro Fertilization and Embryo Transfer,* ed. Don P. Wolf and Martin M. Quigley (New York: Plenum Press, 1984), p. 406. Nevertheless the prospect of making philosophical progress in the personhood debates about the fetus seems dim, and for that reason the issue is set aside here.

3 Here I disagree with Joseph Fletcher, for example, who comes close to regarding the fetus as nothing when he states that a fetus that is inviable or to be terminated cannot be harmed or injured, and compares it to a corpse. See Joseph Fletcher, *Humanhood: Essays in Biomedical Ethics* (Buffalo: Prometheus Books, 1979), p. 99.

4 It has been pointed out that in some cases "whether a treatment is a harm or a benefit may depend on the context of the situation and not necessarily be an inherent component of the treatment itself" (Abby Lippman, 17 December 1985, private communication).

5 Wertheimer, "Understanding the Abortion Argument," p. 85.

6 See Anne Collins, *The Big Evasion: Abortion, the Issue that Won't Go Away* (Toronto: Lester & Orpen Dennys, 1985).

7 Ibid. pp. 46–47.

8 Bishop Lacey, quoted in Collins, p. 90.

9 Ellen Tabisz, quoted in Collins, pp. 206–207, Tabisz's emphasis.

10 Margery W. Shaw, "Conditional Prospective Rights of the Fetus," *Journal of Legal Medicine* 5, no. 1 (1984): 84. See also Edward W. Keyserlingk, "The Unborn Child's Right to Prenatal Care," Part I and Part II, *Health Law In Canada* 3, nos. 1 and 2 (1982): 10–21, 31–41.

11 John A. Robertson, "Procreative Liberty and the Control of Conception, Pregnancy, and Childbirth," *Virginia Law Review* 69, no. 3 (April 1983): 450.

12 Shaw, "Conditional Prospective Rights," p. 100.

13 Robertson, "Procreative Liberty," p. 442; compare Shaw, "Conditional Prospective Rights," p. 74.

14 Margaret A. Somerville, "Reflections on Canadian Abortion Law: Evacuation and Destruction—Two Separate Issues," *University of Toronto Law Journal* 31, no. 1 (1981): 11–12.

15 Robertson, "Procreative Liberty," p. 437.

16 Shaw, "Conditional Prospective Rights," p. 111.

17 Janet Gallagher, "The Fetus and the Law—Whose Life Is It

Anyway?" *Ms.* (September 1984): 134. For a critique of the view that state mechanisms should "impose medical treatment or life-style prohibitions upon the mother in the interests of perceived superior claims of the foetus," see Sanda Rodgers-Magnet, "Foetal Rights and Maternal Rights: Is There Conflict?" (Paper delivered at the Sixth National Biennial Conference of the National Association of Women and the Law, Ottawa, Ontario, 22 February 1985).

18 See E. Peter Volpe, *Patient in the Womb* (Macon, Ga.: Mercer University Press, 1984).

19 Collins, *The Big Evasion*, p. 223.

20 William Ruddick and William Wilcox, "Operating on the Fetus," *Hastings Center Report* 12, no. 5 (October 1982): 10.

21 Barbara Katz Rothman, *The Tentative Pregnancy: Prenatal Diagnosis and the Future of Motherhood* (New York: Viking/Penguin, 1986), p. 28.

22 Robertson, "Procreative Liberty," p. 455.

23 Ibid., p. 456.

24 See Gallagher, "The Fetus and the Law," and Ruth Hubbard, "The Fetus as Patient," *Ms.* (October 1982): 28, 32.

25 Dianne Patychuk, "Ultrasound: The First Wave," *Healthsharing* 6, no. 4 (Fall 1985): 26.

26 Collins, *The Big Evasion*, p. 224.

27 Hubbard, "The Fetus as Patient," p. 32.

28 W[endell] W. Watters, M. Cohen, D. Carr, and J. Askwith, "Response to Edward W. Keyserlingk's Article: The Unborn Child's Right to Prenatal Care," *Health Law in Canada* 4, no. 2 (1983): 33; and Wendell W. Watters, *Compulsory Parenthood: The Truth about Abortion* (Toronto: McClelland and Stewart, 1976), pp. 201–216.

29 Ruddick and Wilcox, "Operating on the Fetus," p. 13.

30 Edward W. Keyserlingk, "Clarifying the Right to Prenatal Care: Reply to a Response," *Health Law in Canada* 4, no. 2 (1983): 38.

31 Ruddick and Wilcox, "Operating on the Fetus," p. 11.

32 Thus Margery Shaw goes so far as to suggest that severely defective fetuses might have a "right to die" (Shaw, "Conditional Prospective Rights," pp. 96–97).

33 E.g., Kathleen McDonnell, *Not an Easy Choice: A Feminist Re-Examines Abortion* (Toronto: The Women's Press, 1984).

34 For a discussion of the idea of abortion for the sake of the fetus, see Paul F. Camenisch, "Abortion: For the Fetus's Own Sake?" in *Medical Ethics and Human Life*, ed. John E. Thomas (Toronto: Samuel Stevens, 1983), pp. 135–143.

35 For a detailed description of both kinds of hazards, see Shaw, "Conditional Prospective Rights," pp. 66–75.

36 See Nancy Miller Chenier, *Reproductive Hazards at Work: Men, Women and the Fertility Gamble* (Ottawa: Canadian Advisory Council on the Status of Women, 1982).

37 See R. G. Edwards, "The Case for Studying Human Embryos and Their Constituent Tissues In Vitro," in *Human Conception In Vitro*, pp. 371–388; and R. G. Edwards, "The Current Clinical and Ethical Situation of Human Conception In Vitro," in *Developments in Human Reproduction and Their Eugenic, Ethical Implications*, ed. C. O. Carter (London: Academic Press, 1983), pp. 97–109, for a discussion of the many long-term benefits to be gained from experimentation on the embryo. For a defense of fetal experimentation, see Joseph Fletcher, *Humanhood: Essays in Biomedical Ethics* (Buffalo: Prometheus Books, 1979), pp. 93–105; and Robert S. Morison and Sumner B. Twiss, Jr., "The Human Fetus as Useful Research Material," *Hastings Center Report* 3 (1973): 8–10. See John A. Robertson, "Embryo Research," *The University of Western Ontario Law Review* 24, no. 1 (1986): 15–37, for an overview of ethical issues pertaining to research on embryos.

38 See Susan Abramowitz, "A Stalemate on Test-Tube Baby Research," *Hastings Center Report* 14, no. 1 (February 1984): 5–9.

39 See John C. Fletcher and Joseph D. Schulman, "Fetal Research: The State of the Question," *Hastings Center Report* 15, no. 2 (April 1985): 6–12.

40 Peter Singer and Deane Wells, *The Reproduction Revolution: New Ways of Making Babies* (Oxford: Oxford University Press, 1984), pp. 138–141.

41 Charles C. Baron, "Fetal Research: The Question in the States," *Hastings Center Report* 15, no. 2 (April 1985): 13.

42 Edwards, "The Current Clinical and Ethical Situation of Human Conception In Vitro," p. 102.

43 Linda S. Williams, "But What Will They Mean for Women? Feminist Concerns about the New Reproductive Technologies," (Ottawa: CRIAW/ICREF Feminist Perspectives Feministes, 1986), pp. 12–13; *Fertility and Sterility* 46, Supplement 1 (September 1986): 32S. I am grateful to Robert Reid for bringing the latter to my attention.

44 I do not share many of the reservations about reproductive technology that have been put forward by members of the Right to Life movement. See "For and Against: The Essence of the Arguments," in *Test-Tube Babies: A Guide to Moral Questions, Present Techniques and Future Possibilities*, ed. William A. Walters and Peter Singer (Melbourne: Oxford University Press, 1982), pp. 36–48.

45 Robertson, "Procreative Liberty," p. 434.

46 Singer and Wells, *The Reproduction Revolution*, p. 79.

47 Ontario Law Reform Commission, *Report on Artificial Reproduction and Related Matters*, II (Toronto: Ministry of the Attorney General, 1985), p. 148.

48 For an overview of discussions of risk-taking for the embryo/fetus, in the context of research pertaining to in vitro fertilization, see LeRoy Walters, "Human In Vitro Fertilization: A Review of the

Ethical Literature," *Hastings Center Report* 9, no. 4 (August 1979): 27–28.

49 Carl Wood and John Kerin, "Ethics," in *Clinical In Vitro Fertilization*, ed. Carl Wood and Alan Trounson (Berlin: Springer-Verlag, 1984), p. 184. Compare Carl Wood and Ann Westmore, *Test-Tube Conception* (Englewood Cliffs, N.J.: Prentice-Hall 1984), p. 103; and R. G. Edwards, "Fertilization of Human Eggs In Vitro: Morals, Ethics and the Law," *Quarterly Review of Biology* 50th Anniversary Special Issue 49 (1976): 379.

50 Joseph Fletcher, *Humanhood: Essays in Biomedical Ethics*, p. 88.

51 Robertson, "Procreative Liberty," pp. 430–431. The main limitation on this right is that its exercise must not make the resulting children worse off than they would otherwise be (ibid., p. 432).

52 See Genoveffa Corea, "Egg Snatchers," in *Test-Tube Women: What Future for Motherhood?* ed. Rita Arditti, Renate Duelli Klein, and Shelley Minden (London: Pandora Press, 1984), pp. 44–45, for a brief description of the extent of existing commercial uses of reproductive products.

53 Council for Science and Society, *Human Procreation: Ethical Aspects of New Techniques* (Oxford: Oxford University Press, 1984), p. 81. See also "Discussion on the Ethics of Fertilization In Vitro," in *Human Conception In Vitro*, ed. Edwards and Purdy, pp. 360–362.

54 George J. Annas, "Redefining Parenthood and Protecting Embryos: Why We Need New Laws," *Hastings Center Report* 14, no. 5 (October 1984): p. 51.

55 In vitro fertilization researchers Carl Wood and John Kerin say, in regard to the embryos produced by their programmes, "The embryos belong to the patients" (Wood and Kerin, "Ethics," p. 181). A. O. Trounson says much the same thing in "Discussion on the Ethics of Fertilization In Vitro," in *Human Conception In Vitro*, p. 366.

56 Singer and Wells, *The Reproduction Revolution*, p. 104.

57 Andrews, "Ethical Considerations in In Vitro Fertilization," p. 413.

58 Ontario Law Reform Commission Reports, p. 171.

59 Some ethicists argue that such women will "benefit by receiving the market price for their services" (Peter Singer, 13 January 1986, private communication). This argument is dealt with in chapter 5.

60 Cf. Singer and Wells, *The Reproduction Revolution*, pp. 81–82. In my view the provision of blood products differs from the provision of reproductive products insofar as the "need" for reproductive products may in part be socially created. The infertile undergo very real suffering, but it is not the same as that undergone by an individual who is in dire need of a blood transfusion. Of course, as Peter Singer points out (13 January 1986, private communication), some blood is used in optional operations. This suggests that in some instances the need for blood is indirectly socially created.

61 Ontario Law Reform Commission Report, p. 171.

62 Evelyn E. Ferguson, "'The Real Cabbage Patch Kids': An Examination of the Canadian Private Adoption System," Occasional Papers in Social Policy Analysis (Toronto: Ontario Institute for Studies in Education, 1984), pp. 1, 12.

63 Collins, *The Big Evasion*, p. 185.

64 For a history of the development of perfectionist attitudes toward children, see Daniel Beekman, *The Mechanical Baby: A Popular History of the Theory and Practice of Child Raising* (Westport, Conn.: Lawrence Hill, 1977).

65 Robyn Rowland, "Social Implications of Reproductive Technology," *International Review of Natural Family Planning* 8, no. 3 (1984): 191.

66 Sue Teper and E. Malcolm Symonds, "Artificial Insemination by Donor: Problems and Perspectives," in Carter, *Developments in Human Reproduction and Their Eugenic, Ethical Implications*, p. 44.

67 Rowland, "Social Implications of Reproductive Technology," p. 196.

68 See Barbara Ehrenreich and Deirdre English, "Complaints and Disorders: The Sexual Politics of Sickness," in *Seizing Our Bodies: The Politics of Women's Health*, ed. Claudia Dreifus (New York: Vintage Books, 1977), pp. 43–56; and Barbara Ehrenreich and Deirdre English, *For Her Own Good: 150 Years of the Experts' Advice to Women* (Garden City, N.Y.: Anchor Books, 1978), pp. 33–39.

69 Keyserlingk, "The Unborn Child's Right to Prenatal Care," p. 12.

70 Robertson, "Procreative Liberty," p. 443. Cf. Shaw, "Conditional Prospective Rights," p. 70.

71 Gallagher, "The Fetus and The Law," p. 134.

72 Lippman, 17 December 1985, private communication; Watters et al., "Response to Edward W. Keyserlingk's Article," p. 34.

73 Julie Murphy, "Egg Farming and Women's Future," in Arditti et al., *Test-Tube Women*, pp. 71–72.

74 Wood and Kerin, "Ethics," p. 180.

75 R. G. Edwards, "Human Conception In Vitro: New Opportunities in Medicine and Research," in *In Vitro Fertilization and Embryo Transfer*, ed. Alan Trounson and Carl Wood (Edinburgh: Churchill Livingstone, 1984), p. 244.

76 Edwards, "The Current Clinical and Ethical Situation of Human Conception In Vitro," pp. 92–93, my emphasis.

77 Peter Singer has pointed out that female scientists and doctors are also involved in work on in vitro fertilization (13 January 1986, private communication). Nevertheless the main public defenders of the technique are male.

78 Paraphrase of Robert Francoeur by R. G. Edwards in "The Current Clinical and Ethical Situation of Human Conception In Vitro," p. 91.

79 Oliver O'Donovan, *Begotten or Made?* (Oxford: Clarendon Press, 1984), p. 62, O'Donovan's emphasis.

80 Ontario Law Reform Commission Report, p. 172.

81 Ibid., p. 276.

82 The Committee of Inquiry into Human Fertilisation and Embryo-logy, *A Question of Life: The Warnock Report on Human Fertilisation and Embryology*, introduction and conclusion by Mary Warnock (Oxford: Basil Blackwell, 1985), p. 47.

83 There is a certain irony in the fact that this maxim is cited by R. G. Edwards in his discussion of his own work on in vitro fertilization ("The Current Clinical and Ethical Situation of Human Concep-tion In Vitro," p. 91).

84 Tom L. Beauchamp and James F. Childress, *Principles of Biomedical Ethics* (New York: Oxford University Press, 1979), pp. 99–100.

85 Hubbard, "The Fetus as Patient," p. 32.

86 Somerville, "Birth Technology," p. 25.

87 Caroline Whitbeck, "The Moral Implications of Regarding Women as People: New Perspectives on Pregnancy and Personhood," in *Abortion and the Status of the Fetus*, ed. William B. Bondeson, H. Tristram Engelhardt, Jr., Stuart F. Spicker, and Daniel H. Winship (Dordrecht, Holland: D. Reidel, 1984), p. 254.

88 Hubbard, "The Fetus as Patient," p. 32. Ruddick and Wilcox, "Operating on the Fetus," refer to the "pediatric" contract under-taken with some obstetricians whereby the woman agrees to subordinate her interests to those of the fetus (p. 12).

89 Collins, *The Big Evasion*, p. 214.

90 Keyserlingk, "The Unborn Child's Right to Prenatal Care," p. 36, Keyserlingk's emphasis.

91 Sir William Liley, quoted in Collins, *The Big Evasion*, p. 217.

92 Ontario Medical Association, "Discussion Paper on Directions in Health Care Issues Relating to Childbirth" (1984): 12.

93 Watters et al., "Response to Edward W. Keyserlingk's Article," p. 32.

94 Collins, *The Big Evasion*, p. xiii.

95 Ruddick and Wilcox, "Operating on the Fetus," p. 13.

96 Janet Farrell Smith, "Rights-Conflict, Pregnancy, and Abortion," in *Beyond Domination: New Perspectives on Women and Philosophy*, ed. Carol C. Gould (Totowa, N.J.: Rowman & Allanheld, 1983), p. 268. Smith provides an excellent discussion of the ways in which this asymmetrical relationship affects the moral rights, duties, obligations, and responsibilities of the pregnant woman and the fetus.

97 Beverly Wildung Harrison, *Our Right to Choose: Toward a New Ethic of Abortion* (Boston: Beacon Press, 1983), p. 212, Harrison's emphasis.

4 *Abortion*

In the previous chapter some general problems in the treatment of the embryo/fetus were examined. I shall now discuss at greater length the issue of abortion—a topic that, in light of its philosophical history, commands a chapter to itself. Here the approach taken in chapter 3 will be extended to show that a plausible view of the morality of abortion requires both a concern for the well-being of the embryo/fetus and a respect for women's autonomy.

Until recently it seems fair—and obvious—to say, the main objection to abortion by those who find it morally wrong has depended primarily upon the indubitable empirical fact that abortion results in the death of the embryo/fetus.[1] (Some objections to abortion may also be founded upon overt or covert misogyny: a desire to punish women for "illicit" sexual behavior or to control women through the denial of reproductive choice.[2] In later chapters I shall examine both the patriarchally enforced connections and disconnections between sexuality and reproduction, and the use of reproductive technology to control women. For now, however, I shall assume that the central and arguably most defensible objection to abortion is that it kills the embryo/fetus.)

But with the arrival of new developments in reproductive technology and neonatal care, what was once an indubitable empirical fact is changing. It is becoming clear that abortion really consists of two potentially distinct aspects: (1) the (premature) emptying of the uterus (that is, the expulsion of the embryo/fetus), and (2) causing the death of the embryo/fetus.[3] In the past (1) has virtually always resulted in (2); the embryo/fetus dies either during or immediately after the process of prematurely removing it from the uterus. So closely linked have these two events been that some philosophers have even defined abortion as consisting essentially of (2).[4]

However, that (1) and (2) are distinct, though causally related, has been recognized at least implicitly by other philosophers—for example, within the context of discussion of the Roman Catholic doctrine of double effect.[5]

It is because abortion consists of these two events that two alleged rights are commonly discussed in connection with the abortion issue. These are (a) the alleged right of the pregnant woman to control her own body, and (b) the alleged right of the embryo/fetus to life. The two are in conflict, and this is because until now the exercise of one alleged right has precluded the exercise of the other. If the woman exercises her alleged right to control her body by having her uterus emptied, the embryo/fetus dies; if the embryo/fetus exercises, or better, is permitted to exercise, its alleged right to life, this severely reduces (if not eliminates) the woman's control over her body.

Furthermore, the fact that abortion consists of these two events and that therefore the two alleged rights are in apparent conflict has led to the generation of two staunchly opposed positions about the morality of abortion, commonly called the "liberal" position and the "conservative" position. The liberal position, putting its emphasis on event (1) of the abortion process and alleged right (a), avows that abortion is not (at least in most cases) morally wrong. The conservative position, putting its emphasis on event (2) of the abortion process and alleged right (b), avows that abortion is (at least in most cases) morally wrong.[6] The liberal position has ordinarily been associated with feminism, whereas the conservative position appears to be nonfeminist or antifeminist in character.

However, the very nature of abortion and of the related moral issues is changing and will change further because of recent developments in reproductive technology. These developments will mean that the two hitherto causally linked events, (1) the emptying of the uterus and (2) the death of the embryo/fetus, can be severed. The expulsion of the embryo/fetus will no longer mean its death.

This possibility is suggested by the production of embryos through in vitro fertilization.[7] Ordinarily, if fertilization and embryo development proceed normally, the embryo is either implanted in its donor mother or a surrogate or is stored in a frozen state for possible future use. So far embryos are usually developed in vitro only to the sixteen-cell stage before being implanted. However, the development of frozen embryo banks suggests that the actual length of time of the embryo's independence of the uterus can be considerably extended beyond a few days.[8] Moreover, perhaps even more important, a type of "embryo adoption" can be effected by removing an embryo through uterine lavage from the uterus of one woman and implanting it directly in that of another.[9]

What these processes suggest is that there is a time, near the beginning of its development, albeit so far a very limited time, when the embryo/fetus need not be dependent for its existence upon the occupancy of a uterus, or at least, of any particular uterus—for example, that of its biological mother. And of course at the other end of prenatal existence the age of viability—the point at which a relatively developed fetus is able to survive ex utero with the help of sophisticated support systems—is gradually declining. Therefore although it remains true that the embryo/fetus in utero is fully dependent upon the woman who sustains it, in such a way that its well-being is not usually separable from hers, it can be anticipated that in the future, expulsion from the uterus will ordinarily not result in the death of the embryo/fetus. This potential development provides the opportunity for a reexamination of the issue of the morality of abortion. It permits us to keep quite separate the two alleged rights mentioned earlier, of the woman to control her body and of the embryo/fetus to its life.

In this chapter I shall recast the issues surrounding abortion in a way that may satisfy both the liberal and the conservative. It preserves the woman-oriented insights of the liberal position without being forced to sacrifice all of the conservative's concern for the embryo/fetus. This new approach emerges by focusing upon what seems to be rather wide consensus about some aspects of abortion. The consensus may not have been very apparent until now because of the fact that the emptying of the uterus resulted in the death of the embryo/fetus. But if, instead, we examine our responses—our "intuitions," as some have called them—about each of these events separately, a surprising degree of agreement appears. This agreement may help to reduce the confusion discussed in chapter 3 in attitudes toward and treatment of the embryo/fetus.

(However, it does not by any means solve all the problems associated with abortion. Rather, it would be fair to say that it displaces them.)

Abortion and the Embryo/Fetus

Like many others, I propose to discuss abortion in terms of rights. To say that a person has a right to have or to do something is to imply that it would be wrong to interfere with her having it or doing it.[10] I do not assume that any rights are necessarily absolute—that is, that they hold whatever else may be the case. However, rights must be regarded as special claims or entitlements that can be set aside or interfered with, if at all, only on the basis of other compelling moral grounds.

R. M. Hare points out that rights are "the stamping ground of intuitionists",[11] and as I have indicated, I shall argue on the basis of our responses to, or "intuitions" about, some specific moral situations. However, the intuitions advanced here are not in support of claims about the possession of rights. Instead, they are used to support claims about the *absence* of rights.

Let us begin with the heart of the conservative position: claim (b), that the embryo/fetus has a right to life. Does it indeed have such a right? If so, when is the right acquired—at the time of conception, motility, viability? If not, why not? What distinguishes it from beings that do in fact possess this right? These questions are apparently endlessly debatable. In this discussion I assume no views about the embryo/fetus' alleged right to life; I am agnostic as to the answers to the questions listed above.

Instead I offer a different statement about rights and the embryo/fetus—or rather, about the absence of rights: (c) The pregnant woman (or anyone else, e.g., a physician) has no right to kill the embryo/fetus.

The claim is not without precedents, and indeed seems to match the intuitions of many who have written about abortion. Judith Jarvis Thomson, for example, who espouses a liberal view about the morality of abortion, has this to say:

I am not arguing for the right to secure the death of the unborn child. It is easy to confuse these two things in that up to a certain point in the life of the fetus it is not able to survive outside the mother's body; hence removing it from her body guarantees its death. But they are importantly different. . . . A woman may be utterly devastated by the thought of a child, a bit of herself, put out for adoption and never seen or heard of again. She may therefore want not merely that the child be detached from her, but more, that it die. . . . [But] the desire for the child's death is not one which anybody may gratify, should it turn out to be possible to detach the child alive.[12]

Other philosophers have expressed agreement with this view[13]; for example, Mary Anne Warren remarks, "if abortion could be performed without killing the fetus, she [the mother] would never possess the *right* to have the fetus destroyed, for the same reasons that she has no right to have an infant destroyed."[14] Margaret A. Somerville argues that it is both unethical and illegal (within the context of Canadian law) for a physician intentionally and unnecessarily to kill the fetus, because even when an abortion is legally performed neither the mother nor the physician has the moral or legal right to kill it unnecessarily.[15]

What exactly does (c) mean? In general, if X has a right to life, then Y has no right to kill X. Conversely, if Y has a right to kill X, then X has no (or a very minimal) right to life. However, even if X (in this case, the embryo/fetus) has itself no right to life (i.e., no right not to be killed) or even if we do not know whether it has a right to life, this does not imply that another being, Y, has the right to kill X. Nor does this imply that it is morally right to kill X. There is no prima facie obligation on any other being, Z, to permit Y to kill X; and indeed, under some circumstances Z may even have an obligation to prevent Y from killing X. That is, even if X has no right to life, it may nevertheless be wrong to kill X;[16] therefore Y does not have a right to kill X.

Claim (c) may appear to threaten the heart of the liberal position and to be inconsistent with a feminist approach to abortion. But notice that in both Thomson's and Warren's formulation of (c), explicit reference is made to the important distinction between events (1) expelling the embryo/fetus from the uterus, and (2) causing the death of the embryo/fetus. It is this distinction that helps to make the claim plausible. Reflection upon several actual and possible cases will illustrate and lend support to (c).

Consider first the fact that occasionally, after a late abortion involving the injection of a saline solution into the woman's uterus, the fetus is born alive. An attempt is ordinarily made to resuscitate the baby, damaged though it may be by the abortion process. No one would suppose that the mother of such a baby has a right to strangle it, slit its throat, suffocate it, or otherwise kill it. Nor has anyone else, including the physician who performed the abortion and subsequent delivery, any such right on behalf of the mother.

Similarly, imagine that a baby is born very prematurely to a woman who had wanted an abortion but failed to obtain one (whether because of legal barriers, lack of access to abortion facilities, or whatever). Babies born as early as twenty-six weeks' gestational age, and sometimes less, may survive.[17] Suppose, then, that this unwanted baby is delivered spontaneously at twenty-six weeks. Once again, no one would be inclined to say that the mother or anyone else (whether acting independently or on the mother's behalf) has a right to kill it.

Third (and this is the most difficult example), consider the case of a typical "test-tube baby": that is, a one- to sixteen-cell embryo existing outside its biological mother's uterus in a culture medium. Tiny and undeveloped as it is, its parents (and anyone else) do not have a *right* to destroy it or have it destroyed. Here I disagree with arguments put forward by Helga Kuhse and Peter Singer. The former states, "there is no moral difference between discarding surplus human embryos and deliberately not creating them in the first place."[18] In another paper, Kuhse and Singer together appear to maintain that a couple who have donated sperm and eggs for in vitro fertilization have a right to refuse to permit excess embryos resulting therefrom either to be implanted (in the woman herself or in a surrogate) or to be frozen; in other words, they have a right to have the embryos "tipped down the sink" and thus destroyed.[19]

This, however, is mistaken. The parents do not have this right, mainly because they do not own the embryo. An individual does, in a limited sense at least, own his or her genetic material: a woman can be said to be the owner of her ova; a man of his sperm.[20] Women may soon donate or sell their eggs to egg banks, just as men now sell or donate their sperm to sperm banks. While objections deserve to be raised about the selling of genetic materials—in other words, about *what* can be done with them and the *ways* in which they are disposed of—there can be no doubt that one's gametes are one's own to dispose of, at least in the sense that they do not belong to anyone else. The individual from whom they are obtained has the clearest entitlement to determine their disposal, including their destruction—although there may be good consequentialist reasons to limit that entitlement (for example, to limit the person's ability to determine which individuals may be the recipients of the gametes). To the extent that an individual may be said to be the owner of her or his body parts, that individual also owns her or his own gametes and has some rights as to their preservation and destruction. There are, of course, problems in regarding parts of the body as one's property,[21] and there are important limitations on what one can do with parts of one's body. But there is at least an important sense in which my arm *is* mine (and no one else's), and in that sense my gametes are also mine.[22] Thus the couple in Kuhse and Singer's example does have the right to have these materials "tipped down the sink" (destroyed)—if, for example, one of them should change his or her mind about participation in the in vitro fertilization process.

By contrast, the sense of "mine" that pertains to one's body parts or one's gametes does not extend to embryos, even to embryos produced by means of one's own gametes. No one owns the embryo or fetus: for as an entity that may become a person, it is not something that can be owned. Joel Feinberg shows this very clearly by means of two arguments:[23] First,

> if fetuses were property, we would find nothing odd in the notion that they can be bought and sold, rented out, leased, used as collateral on loans, and so on. But no one has ever seriously entertained such suggestions.

Of course, as human reproduction becomes increasingly commodified, these suggestions may be entertained more seriously, but their conceptual and moral inappropriateness remains. According to Feinberg's second argument,

> one would think that the father would have equal or near-equal rights of disposal if the fetus were "property." It is not in his body, to be sure, but he contributed as much genetically to its existence as did the mother and might therefore make just as strong (or just as weak) a claim to ownership over it. But neither claim would make very good conceptual sense.

Once again, the claim fails to make sense because the embryo/fetus is not the sort of thing that can be owned. Unlike an individual egg or sperm cell, an embryo may become a person, and it is therefore different from mere body parts.

Some might be tempted to argue that an individual ovum or sperm may become a person also. For example, Peter Singer and Deane Wells state that since it is not wrong to destroy one's gametes, it is also not wrong to destroy an embryo, an embryo being simply a fortuitous coming together of egg and sperm.[24] But that that claim is misleading at best is shown by the fact that it is an embryo, not an egg or sperm cell, which is transferred to a woman's uterus after external fertilization. The embryo, but not the ovum or sperm alone, may become a person.

Thus because no one—not even its parents—owns the embryo/fetus, no one has the *right* to destroy it, even at a very early developmental stage, and the couple in Kuhse and Singer's example are not entitled to tip the embryo down the sink. This is not to deny that the genetic parents are ordinarily authorized to make some decisions about the fate of the embryo/fetus.[25] The point here is simply that to destroy an embryo is not an automatic entitlement held by anyone, including its genetic parents.

If the three cases cited so far are persuasive with regard to the claim that the mother (and everyone else) has no right to kill the embryo/fetus, it might be thought that this absence of a right is due to the location of the embryo/fetus. In the first two examples the fetus is born; it is now a baby outside the mother's body. In the third case the embryo exists independently in a petri dish.

However, it is not because of some change in location, or because of development in a location independent of the mother's body, that there exists no right to kill it. To suppose that merely location determines this absence of right is to confuse claim (c) with some aspect of another claim, to be called (d), which will be discussed later. From the perspective of a woman experiencing pregnancy, the location of the embryo/fetus is naturally of the utmost importance, and that fact must be taken account of. But the point being made here is just that the location itself of the embryo/fetus can neither endow a right upon it nor deny a right to it.

At this point it should be noted that althouth the mother (and everyone else) has no right to kill the embryo/fetus, it may nevertheless in some cases not be wrong for her—or, more likely, a physician deputized by her—to kill the embryo/fetus or to permit it to die. For to say that a person has no right to do something does not preclude her doing it, on occasion, and being morally right in doing so. An obvious example in this context is a case in which the embryo is threatening the mother's health—for example, when growing in the fallopian tube. Other possible examples include cases of severe fetal deformity or illness. Thus the general possibility must be recognized that at times it might be right for someone in some circumstances to kill the embryo/fetus or to allow it to die, and this might be so regardless of its location—whether in its mother's uterus or growing in a petri dish, and regardless of the fact that she (and everyone else) has no general right to kill it.

Abortion and the Pregnant Woman

Now consider the heart of the liberal position: claim (a), that the mother has the right to control her own body. Like (b), about fetal rights, (a) has been endlessly debated. Thomson states, "if a human being has any just, prior claim to anything at all, he [*sic*] has a just, prior claim to his own body," and she suggests that "everyone would grant that."[26] But as she indicates, much of the dispute has concerned the possible limitations on that alleged right and the degree to which it can be overcome by other rights, such as alleged rights of the embryo/fetus. In this discussion although I assume that the parts of a woman's body are hers and no one else's, I make no general assumptions about women's alleged right to control their bodies; I am agnostic as to the solutions to the problems just cited.

Instead, I offer a different statement about rights and women, or rather, once again, about the absence of rights: (d) The embryo/fetus has no right to occupancy of its mother's (or anyone else's) uterus.[27]

This claim is a specific instance of the more general principle that no one has the right to the use of anyone else's body: that is, presumably, part of what makes rape and slavery wrong. Maintaining our bodily integrity and autonomy is essential to our identity and sense of ourselves as persons; this is true no less in the case of pregnancy than in other cases. As I shall argue in chapter 6, the relationship of a pregnant woman to her reproductive organs and capacities cannot be likened to the relationship of landlord to rental property. It is precisely because her body in no way resembles a building awaiting occupancy that it is impossible for anything—including the embryo/fetus—to have a right to the use of it.

Claim (d) is very clearly illustrated by Thomson's famous violinist example. Suppose that a famous violinist is ill and will survive only by being hooked up to some specific individual's kidneys. "[N]obody has any right to use your kidneys unless you give him such a right; and nobody has the right against you that you shall give him this right—if you do allow him to go on using your kidneys, this is a kindness on your part, and not something he can claim against you."[28]

Claim (d) appears to undermine the conservative position on abortion. But once again, the distinction between emptying the uterus and causing the death of the embryo/fetus must be maintained, and a brief consideration of some possible cases will lend support to (d).

Imagine, first, that an egg is withdrawn from a woman and is fertilized in vitro with her partner's sperm. However, during the time in which the embryo is growing to a multicellular stage, the woman unfortunately is killed in a car accident. No one could plausibly say that another woman must be made the host(ess?) of the "orphan" embryo. For the embryo has no right to the occupancy of another woman's body. The fact that it is dependent—first on the culture medium in which it divides and then upon a uterus, should one be available—does not give it the right to inhabit a woman's body.

Now suppose that in the same type of case, several eggs are withdrawn and fertilized. One is reimplanted, develops, and becomes a healthy baby successfully delivered nine months later. The other embryos are frozen for possible later use. But then several years go by and the woman enters her forties: she feels too old to have another baby. Or imagine that in the meantime she develops diabetes, a condition that may make pregnancy perilous for her and the embryo/fetus. The frozen embryos then have no right—against the interests of her health and her life situation—to be implanted. For they too have no right to the occupancy of their biological mother's uterus. Those who may be inclined to say that these embryos do have such a right are confusing that claim either with the more usual but unproved conservative claim that the embryo/fetus has a right to life, or with claim (c), that no one has the right to kill the embryo/fetus.

However, it should also be noted that claim (d), that the embryo/fetus has no right to occupancy of any woman's uterus, does not imply that it will never be wrong for a woman to terminate its occupancy—that is, to abort it. Circumstances may be such that it would be wrong for her to end the pregnancy, in that she has incurred some degree of responsibility for the embryo/fetus. For example, it might be wrong for a mother to abort her embryo/fetus when its conception was planned, it is well advanced in development, and her only reason is that she is tired of her pregnancy;[29] the abortion might also be wrong when its only justification is that the embryo/fetus has been discovered to be of the "wrong" sex. Thus the general possibility should be recognized that it might sometimes be wrong for a woman in some circumstances to end the embryo/fetus' occupancy of her uterus, and this might be so regardless of the fact that it has no general right to such occupancy.

Some Implications

If it were not for developing reproductive technology, the two claims, (c) and (d), put forward here would continue to generate an insoluble conflict, in practice if not in theory. To say that no one has a right to kill the embryo/fetus seems to say that abortion is wrong; but to say that the embryo/fetus has no right to occupancy of its mother's (or anyone else's) uterus seems to say that abortion is not wrong.

If, however, it is becoming more and more possible for an embryo/fetus to survive outside its mother's body, or to be transferred successfully to the uterus of another woman who wants a child, abortion need no longer entail so much moral conflict. It could then be said that a woman may have an abortion, in the sense of expelling the embryo/fetus from her body, and the embryo/fetus may live. The solution could satisfy both the liberal, whose desire is to provide abortions for women who want them, and the conservative, whose aim is the preservation of fetal life. The feminist concern for women's reproductive control is not necessarily incompatible with a concern for the embryo/fetus.

Thus the position on abortion outlined here has both theoretical and practical advantages over the old battle lines. That is, it both helps to make sense of moral beliefs about the topic and it suggests actual positive consequences for behavior. I turn now to a consideration of these potential advantages.

When a spontaneous miscarriage occurs, people mourn—and perhaps not only for the woman whose pregnancy has ended but for the loss of a being they regard as valuable. In fact, as chapter 3 showed, great efforts have been and are being made to preserve and enhance the life of the embryo/fetus in utero. While some treatments (such as fetal surgery) have the potential to oppress both the pregnant woman and her fetus, other forms of care (such as a nutritious diet and adequate prenatal care) are usually beneficial to both and willingly assumed by pregnant women.

Yet these practices are rather difficult to reconcile with the usual liberal view on abortion, which tends to see the embryo/ fetus as merely a disposable part of the mother's body. From an extreme liberal point of view, care for the embryo/fetus can be understood only by reference to the woman's care for herself, or by her desire to have a healthy child at the end of the pregnancy, or perhaps by the need to avoid unnecessary medical costs of providing for disabled children. And the liberal view is not improved by arguing that no body part is a *mere* part; or that a part takes its meaning from the whole, and that a person may value or despise parts of her body. For a woman may freely and legitimately choose to undergo cosmetic surgery, to donate a kidney, or to have her uterus removed: while such choices may be foolish or wise, hasty or well thought out, informed or ignorant, no one would argue that she should consider her moral responsibilities to her face, her kidney, or her uterus.

But the view defended here—that there is no general right to kill the embryo/fetus—raises the possibility that individuals also have responsibilities to the embryo/fetus itself. They lead us to suspect that perhaps no one has a *right* to injure, mutilate, or cause pain to it—that is, that there is at least a prima facie responsibility of nonmaleficence to it. The embryo/fetus therefore appears to have a different moral status than that which is possessed by a body part.

In saying this I wish to emphasize not just the responsibility of the pregnant woman, as do most advocates of prenatal care, but the social responsibility toward the embryo/fetus on the part of entities such as the state, corporations, and the medical care system. Furthermore, these responsibilities should not be permitted to override the consideration of the pregnant woman's health; that is, performance of the least mutilating type of abortion procedure for the fetus should not impose serious health risks upon the woman.

If abortion is justified, then it should be performed in a way that gives the child a chance of survival, if there is any chance at all. The effort to save the aborted child and to find ways of saving all who are justifiably aborted would be a token of sincerity that the death of the child really was not in the scope of the intention.[30]

What exactly is the intention of a woman seeking an abortion is, surely, an empirical question. Often she may not have thought beyond the immediate goal of no longer being pregnant. In addition, she may feel that she does not want and/or is not able to care for an infant, or the child that it will become. Most people do not regard a desperate woman who attempts to abort herself as a potential killer. It is recognized, implicitly, that what she is trying to do is to end her pregnancy, to remove the embryo/fetus from her body. Moreover, most people probably feel particularly sympathetic to women who seek abortions when pregnancy results from rape or incest, or when it seriously threatens their life or health. Once again, the woman seems to be saying that she does not want, and will not permit, the embryo/fetus to occupy her uterus. Her goal is clearly to end her pregnancy, but not necessarily to kill the embryo/fetus. And to say that the former may not be wrong, although the latter may be, is preferable to the more peculiar view of those who seem inclined to believe that an embryo/fetus has a right to life—except when it is the product of rape.

Is it the case that some women seeking abortions specifically desire the death of the embryo/fetus? Steven L. Ross argues that, indeed, some women "cannot be satisfied *unless* the fetus is killed; nothing else will do."[31] This desire, he says, is derived from the unique relationship of the parent to the embryo/fetus: that it is genetically related to her, and that she (as well as the father) has the most legitimate claim to raise the child. Thus for some, the feeling that "she and not any one else ought to raise whatever children she brings into the world" is a "deeply felt personal preference";[32] failure to raise one's own child can be avoided only by killing the embryo/fetus.

This kind of feeling, however, if and when it occurs (and the existence of surrogate mothers proves that it is not universal), does not justify killing the embryo/fetus. Although the relationship to the embryo/fetus is unique (and Ross does not fully understand it, for he says, "We cannot . . . love the fetus even if we wanted to, as we cannot be said to love anything we have not interacted with"[33]—there are certainly some women who would claim that they have both interacted with and loved their fetus), the mother does not own it and therefore is not entitled to have it killed. (Moreover, as I will argue in chapter 7, it is important not to overestimate the moral significance of the link with one's genetically related offspring.)

Hence writers like H. Tristram Engelhardt, Jr., are mistaken when they claim that the use of abortifacient devices that guarantee the death of the embryo/fetus is justified by "a woman's interests in not being a mother," and that "one would wish as well to forbid attempts, against the will of the mother, to sustain the life of an abortus prior to the established [legal] upper limit for abortions."[34] The policy at many North American hospitals that perform abortions is to attempt to resuscitate aborted fetuses that show signs of life. And surely, if abortion is seen primarily as the emptying of the uterus and no one has the right to kill the embryo/fetus, then some of the irony attendant upon "requiring a lifesaving medical team to be prepared to rush into the operating clinic in the event that the abortion team fails to achieve the fetus's death"[35] is reduced. There is, perhaps, an important moral distinction between killing and letting die. But once the mother's personal autonomy is respected by honoring her request to end her pregnancy (because the embryo/fetus has no right to occupy her uterus), there seems to be little reason for assuming that there is never anything morally wrong with letting the aborted fetus die. There may be cases in which this would be right—for example, if the embryo/fetus is irretrievably deformed or damaged by the abortion process—but this will not be true in all cases, and, as I suggested earlier, the abortion procedure itself should ideally be designed to minimize damage to the embryo/fetus. That is, the mother (and everyone else) is entitled to demand neither that the embryo/fetus be killed after abortion nor that it not be resuscitated.

This position permits the reexamination of some morally peculiar views about viability. Many have been inclined to agree with American abortion policy, which treats viability as the cutoff point for most permissible abortions. This view suggests that it is all right to expel the embryo/fetus from the uterus until the point in its development when it is able to survive outside the uterus—at which time it becomes impermissible to expel it. The anomaly is made even worse by the fact that while the age of fetal viability is declining, the age at which abortions can be performed safely (for the woman) is moving up. But neither sheer length of gestation nor capacity for survival outside the uterus confers on the embryo/fetus a right to occupancy of the uterus. Engelhardt points out that if reproductive technology develops to the point that an embryo/fetus could be brought to term in vitro, then "all conceptuses would be viable in the sense of being at a stage at which there are known survivors."[36] He then asks whether this should result in the prohibition of all abortions. But if we agree that the embryo/fetus has no right to occupancy of the uterus, we can see that such a general prohibition would not be justified in these circumstances. Achievement of viability does not confer rights on the embryo/fetus.

Having detailed some advantages of this approach to the abortion issue, it must be conceded that it also raises a good many problems. If fetal survival outside the uterus becomes more and more frequent, and the two claims, (c) and (d), are accepted, then the moral quandaries will merely shift from the actual process of abortion to the events that follow the abortion. These problems include, but are not confined to, the following.

First, if fetal survival becomes commonplace, would there be an obligation to preserve all aborted fetuses? As Somerville points out, "arguing that the lives of viable to-be-aborted fetuses should be preserved even though they may be aborted is artificially to create a group of new-borns at much higher risk of being defective than babies born at term." These babies "are at a high risk of being mentally or physically handicapped by their premature expulsion into the world and . . . therefore require specialized and expensive treatment."[37]

Second, what limitations, if any, should be placed on the availability of abortion, understood as the emptying of the uterus? Those who advocate "embryo adoption"—the transfer of an embryo from an unwilling woman to a willing adoptive mother—argue that a woman "should be free to surrender her fetus for adoption at any time during pregnancy."[38] Since the embryo/fetus has no right to occupancy of its mother's uterus, this appears justifiable. But "embryo adoption" at all points during pregnancy is not yet technically possible, and in any case it raises its own moral problems: Should all aborted embryo/fetuses be candidates for adoption? What about those with defects? What women should be able to become their adoptive mothers? How should the decision be made?

Finally, the present reality is that there is still a period, perhaps about twenty-three weeks in length, in which an embryo/fetus is totally dependent upon the body of a woman for its continued existence. So it is necessary to consider the general policy implications of the position adumbrated here for this period of time in prenatal life. I suggest that claim (d) is most relevant to the early months of embryonic development. The fact that the embryo/fetus has no right to occupancy of its mother's (or any other woman's) uterus would sanction very early abortions on request, despite the fact that the embryos aborted will not now survive. Claim (c), on the other hand, is most relevant to later months of fetal development. The fact that the mother (or anyone else) has no right to kill the embryo/fetus requires the performance of abortions in a way that, without compromising the pregnant woman's medical care, causes least mutilation and maximizes the fetus' chances of survival.[39]

It should now be clear that the development of new reproductive technologies both permits and requires the reevaluation of existing views about abortion. When fetal survival becomes routinely possible, it will be necessary to confront some very difficult practical questions about the treatment of the embryo/fetus. But these developments also enable us to make the crucial distinction between emptying the uterus and killing the embryo/fetus, and to see that while the embryo/fetus has no right to occupancy of its mother's (or anyone's) uterus, she (along with everyone else) has no right to kill the embryo/fetus.

Notes

An earlier version of part of this chapter, entitled "New Reproductive

Technology: Some Implications for the Abortion Issue," appeared in
The Journal of Value Inquiry 19 (1985): 279–292. The material is used
here with the permission of the journal's editor.

1 Once again, "embryo/fetus" will be used here generally to refer to
  the developing zygote/embryo/fetus throughout its nine-month
  gestation, except when referring specifically to very early stages of
  gestation, when the term "embryo" will be used.
2 Cf. Janet Radcliffe Richards, *The Sceptical Feminist: A Philosophical
  Inquiry* (Harmondsworth, England: Penguin Books, 1980),
  pp. 263–290.
3 Mary B. Mahowald makes a similar distinction between different
  concepts of abortion. Abortion, she says, is either the "premature
  termination of pregnancy" or the "termination of fetal life." See
  "Concepts of Abortion and Their Relevance to the Abortion
  Debate," *Southern Journal of Philosophy* 20 (Summer 1982): 195.
  Compare Sissela Bok, Bernard N. Nathanson, and LeRoy Walters,
  "Commentary: The Unwanted Child: Caring for the Fetus Born
  Alive after an Abortion," *Cases in Bioethics*, rev. ed. ed. Carol
  Levine and Robert M. Veatch (Hastings-on-Hudson: The Hastings
  Center, 1984), pp. 3, 5.
4 For example, see Joel Feinberg, "Abortion," in *Matters of Life and
  Death: New Introductory Essays in Moral Philosophy*, ed. Tom Regan
  (New York: Random House, 1981), p. 183.
5 See Susan T. Nicholson, "The Roman Catholic Doctrine of
  Therapeutic Abortion," in *Feminism and Philosophy*, ed. Mary
  Vetterling-Braggin, Frederick A. Elliston, and Jane English
  (Totowa, N.J.: Littlefield, Adams, 1978), p. 392. The distinction is
  also employed by John Morreall in "Of Marsupials and Men: A
  Thought Experiment on Abortion," *Dialogos* 37 (1981): 16; by
  Steven L. Ross in "Abortion and the Death of the Fetus," *Phil-
  osophy and Public Affairs* 11 (1982): 232; by Daniel I. Wikler in
  "Ought We to Save Aborted Fetuses?" *Ethics* 90 (1978): 64; and by
  Raymond M. Herbenick in "Remarks on Abortion, Aban-
  donment, and Adoption Opportunities," in *Philosophy and Publics
  Affairs* 5 (1975): 98.
6 A "moderate" position on abortion, not discussed here, has also
  been defended. See L. W. Sumner, "Toward a Credible View of
  Abortion," *Canadian Journal of Philosophy* 4 (1974): 163–181.
7 An informative discussion of in vitro fertilization is given by John
  F. Leeton, Alan O. Trounson, and Carl Wood, in "IVF and ET:
  What It Is and How It Works," in *Test-Tube Babies: A Guide to Moral
  Questions, Present Techniques and Future Possibilities*, ed. William
  A. W. Walters and Peter Singer (Melbourne, Australia: Oxford
  University Press, 1982), pp. 2–10.
8 Ectogenesis, the growth of the fetus outside the human uterus, is
  discussed by William A. W. Walters in "Cloning, Ectogenesis,
  and Hybrids: Things to Come?" in *Test-Tube Babies*, pp. 115–117.

9 See Robert A. Freitas, Jr., "Fetal Adoption: A Technological Solution to the Problem of Abortion Ethics," *The Humanist* (May/June 1980): 22–23.

10 Cf. Ronald Dworkin, *Taking Rights Seriously* (Cambridge, Mass.: Harvard University Press, 1977), p. 188.

11 R. M. Hare, "Abortion and the Golden Rule," in *Philosophy and Sex*, ed. Robert Baker and Frederick Elliston (Buffalo: Prometheus Books, 1975), p. 357.

12 Judith Jarvis Thomson, "A Defense of Abortion," in *Moral Problems*, 2d ed., ed. James Rachels (New York: Harper & Row, 1975), p. 106.

13 Jane English, "Abortion: Introduction," in Vetterling-Braggin et al., *Feminism and Philosophy*, p. 422; Frances Myrna, "The Right to Abortion," in *Ethics for Modern Life*, ed. Raziel Abelson and Marie-Louise Friquegnon (New York: St. Martin's Press, 1982), pp. 114–115; David S. Levin, "Abortion, Personhood and Vagueness," *Journal of Value Inquiry* 19 (1985): 202–203.

14 Mary Anne Warren, "On the Moral and Legal Status of Abortion," in *Today's Moral Problems*, ed. Richard Wasserstrom (New York: Macmillan, 1975), p. 136, my emphasis.

15 Margaret A. Somerville, "Reflections on Canadian Abortion Law: Evacuation and Destruction—Two Separate Issues," *University of Toronto Law Journal* 31, no. 1 (1981), p. 12.

16 Cf. Charles B. Daniels, "Abortion and Potential," *Dialogue* 18 (1979): 223, 1 n.

17 Ernle W. D. Young, "Caring for Disabled Infants," *Hastings Center Report* 13 (August 1983): 16.

18 Helga Kuhse, "An Ethical Approach to IVF and ET: What Ethics Is All About," in Walters and Singer, *Test-Tube Babies*, p. 34.

19 Helga Kuhse and Peter Singer, "The Moral Status of the Embryo," in Walters and Singer, *Test-Tube Babies*, pp. 57 ff.

20 See Robert P. S. Jansen, "Sperm and Ova as Property," *Journal of Medical Ethics* 11 (September 1985): 123–126.

21 See, for example, Warren, "On the Moral and Legal Status of Abortion," p. 121; Feinberg, "Abortion," p. 204; Sara Ann Ketchum, "The Moral Status of the Bodies of Persons," *Social Theory and Practice* 10 (Spring 1984): 25–27; and Leon R. Kass, "Thinking about the Body," *Hastings Center Report* 15 (February 1985): 23.

22 See Lori B. Andrews, "My Body, My Property," *Hastings Center Report* 16 (October 1986): 28–38. However, Andrews regards embryos as well as gametes as personal property and enthusiastically endorses financial compensation for body parts. For a dissenting view, that gametes "are, strictly speaking, not our private property, in the sense of individual interest, control and possession," see Joseph Fletcher, *Humanhood: Essays in Biomedical Ethics* (Buffalo: Promethus Books, 1979), p. 118.

23 Feinberg, "Abortion," p. 204.

24 Peter Singer and Deane Wells, *The Reproduction Revolution: New Ways of Making Babies* (Oxford: Oxford University Press, 1984), pp. 87–89. For criticisms of this view, see B. F. Scarlett, "The Moral Status of Embryos," *Journal of Medical Ethics* 2 (1984): 79–81. See also the response to Scarlett's arguments by Peter Singer and Helga Kuhse, *Journal of Medical Ethics* 2 (1984): 80–81.
25 The position advanced here is very like that taken in *A Question of Life: The Warnock Report on Human Fertilisation and Embryology*, by Mary Warnock (Oxford: Basil Blackwell, 1985), p. 56.
26 Thomson, "A Defense of Abortion," pp. 95, 90.
27 Cf. Ellen Frankel Paul and Jeffrey Paul, "Self-Ownership, Abortion and Infanticide," *Journal of Medical Ethics* 5 (1979): 134.
28 Thomson, "A Defense of Abortion," p. 96.
29 Thomson gives a similar example, p. 105. Cf. Morreall, "Of Marsupials and Men," p. 11.
30 Germain Grisez, "Abortion: Ethical Arguments," in Wasserstrom, *Today's Moral Problems*, p. 102.
31 Ross, "Abortion and the Death of the Fetus," p. 238, his emphasis.
32 Ibid., p. 240.
33 Ibid., p. 243.
34 H. Tristram Engelhardt, Jr., "Viability and the Use of the Fetus," in *Ethics and Public Policy*, ed. Tom L. Beauchamp and Terry P. Pinkard (Englewood Cliffs, N.J.: Prentice-Hall, 1980), pp. 307–308.
35 Wikler, "Ought we to Save Aborted Fetuses?" p. 60. Cf. Paul and Paul, "Self-Ownership," p. 133; and Thomas P. Carney, *Instant Evolution: We'd Better Get Good at It* (Notre Dame, Ind.: University of Notre Dame Press, 1980), p. 16.
36 Engelhardt, "Viability and the Use of the Fetus," p. 307.
37 Somerville, "Birth Technology," pp. 23, 22.
38 Freitas, "Fetal Adoption," p. 23.
39 Cf. Sissela Bok, Bernard N. Nathanson, and LeRoy Walters, "Commentary: The Unwanted Child," pp. 2, 3, and 6.

5 Childbirth

Woman: I would like to have a natural birth.
Doctor: Of course, if you think you can, I'll go along with it.
Remember, though, that the most important thing is the
baby and not your own wishes or comfort.[1]

Unlike some of the reproductive processes and events
discussed so far, childbirth is ubiquitous. Although professional philosophers have had very little to say about it,
childbirth has been discussed rather extensively, both by
feminist and by nonfeminist and antifeminist writers.
Feminist theorists have provided telling critiques of current
childbirth practices in the Western world[2] and have offered
insightful reevaluations of the history of childbirth.[3] What
emerges from these studies is a picture of conflict: conflict
between the goals of women in childbirth and the goals of their
attending physicians,[4] whose obstetric practices frequently
manifest an antifeminist and misogynistic orientation.

Building upon the foundations laid by feminist theorists, I
shall not, for the most part, discuss this more familiar material
or attempt to deal with all of the moral questions concerning
childbirth.[5] Instead I shall present a critique of some crucial
underlying assumptions—both moral and ontological—made
by nonfeminists and antifeminists about the nature of
childbearing itself and the relationship of the parturient
woman to her fetus. These theorists see birth mostly through
the eyes of male physicians and overlook women's experience
in childbearing. Ignoring the very real conflict between maternal and medical perspectives on childbirth, they instead describe (a better word would be "invent") other conflicts:
between the pregnant woman and her fetus, and between the
requirements of safety and other human needs and desires. As
the discussion will show, a belief in the existence of these

conflicts, and obstetric practices founded upon that belief, are entirely consonant with the themes of nonfeminists and anti-feminists in their analysis of the reproductive issues already discussed.

Conflict between Pregnant Woman and Fetus

Chapter 3 described the concern of some nonfeminist and antifeminist writers for what has been called prenatal abuse. There it was suggested that this concern seems to be connected to certain attitudes toward women, according to which the female body is a threat to the embryo/fetus: the pregnant woman cannot be trusted not to abuse it, pass on defective genes to it, or even kill it, let alone to protect it from environmental harm and give birth to it safely. What is assumed by those who adopt this attitude is that there is a serious potential for conflict between the pregnant woman and the embryo/ fetus.

Such an assumption also underlies nonfeminist and antifeminist views of childbirth, which is seen as a crisis point at which the maternal/fetal conflict is most strongly dramatized. According to "the medical belief in an adversary relationship between the mother and the baby,"

the baby must be stopped from ripping its mother apart, and the surgical scissors [performing an episiotomy, that is, a cut in the mother's perineum] are considered to be more gentle than the baby's head. At the same time, the mother must be stopped from crushing her baby, and the obstetrical forceps are seen as being more gentle than the mother's vagina.[6]

Thus in a 1984 discussion paper of the Ontario Medical Association (OMA) entitled "Issues Relating to Childbirth,"[7] the pregnant woman and her fetus (and, later, the baby) are seen as adversaries competing to get their needs filled. The pregnant woman is primarily a container or environment for the fetus; her interests are often different from—even in conflict with—those of her fetus. The paper states,

> We are . . . beginning to see claims for dual medical-legal rights and new responsibilities, one set for the mother and an increasingly well-defined set for the fetus. There is a growing need to discuss how we are going to resolve social conflicts between the rights of the mother and the rights of the fetus and newborn. Quite separately, appropriate and useful medical care for the fetus will require the mother to assume some risks without any benefit to herself since for some procedures she is the only route to the fetus.[8]

There are a number of problems with this type of approach to the pregnant woman/fetus relationship. First, seeing the pregnant woman as the "route to the fetus" has the effect of literally depersonalizing her, reducing her to a mere environment in which the fetus grows. It obscures the fact that she is, or ought to be, an independent and autonomous adult, with full decision-making powers and legal rights to determine what occurs to and within her own body. The discussion paper's approach appears to demote the pregnant woman to a derivative ontological and moral status, making questions of her safety and well-being secondary to questions about the safety and well-being of the fetus.

Moreover, the excerpt just quoted suggests an understanding of the maternal/fetal relationship which is couched in terms of the (potentially conflicting) rights of each. Yet, as the discussion in the previous chapter suggested, the use of the concept of rights is neither a morally appropriate nor a pragmatically fruitful approach to this relationship. In chapter 4 two claims were made about rights in connection with the fetus and pregnant woman: First, that the pregnant woman (or anyone else, e.g., a physician) has no right to kill the embryo/fetus; second, that the embryo/fetus has no right to occupancy of its mother's (or anyone else's) uterus. Comparable claims remain true up to and throughout the birth of the baby: during childbirth the woman is not entitled, by right, to harm the fetus, but equally important, the fetus itself is not entitled, by right, to the use of its mother's body. To acknowledge that a fetus has no right to the occupancy of its mother's uterus is to recognize that the pregnant woman is not a sort of incubator or house belonging temporarily to the fetus.[9]

Within the context of childbirth, however, while something like the first claim about rights is usually stressed, the second is often entirely denied: it is assumed that at and around the time of birth the fetus is entitled to a variety of uses of and services from its mother. Thus John A. Robertson says, in regard to compulsory cesarean sections, "To impose on the mother a duty to undergo surgical delivery where it is necessary to save the child's life or to prevent it from being injured is not unreasonable when she has chosen to lend her body to bring the child into the world."[10]

It could be said, in the words of Judith Jarvis Thomson, that a position such as this requires women "to be not merely Minimally Decent Samaritans, but Good Samaritans to unborn persons inside them."[11] Thomson, whose reservations about killing the fetus were mentioned in chapter 4, is writing in this quotation about abortion, but the distinction applies as well to birthing. Her point is that women are often compelled, by moral pressure and, in the case of abortion, by legal sanction, to sacrifice themselves for the embryo/fetus. What is required of them is supererogation, or at least what would be supererogation in regard to more developed human beings—that is, the performance of acts far beyond minimum moral requirements. Thus the antifeminist perspective on childbirth sees the alleged conflict between pregnant woman and fetus as an unequal struggle: the pregnant woman is the potential oppressor of her fetus. During birth she must therefore voluntarily abdicate her power over it, and if she will not, the resolution of this unequal conflict requires the oppression of the pregnant woman by medical and legal authorities.

What sorts of sacrifice are expected of pregnant women in the process of birth? First, parturient women are ordinarily expected to abandon any preference they may have for birthing at home. In most of the Western world, and particularly in North America, women are supposed to give birth in a hospital. Moreover, they are not permitted much choice in their attendants at birth; in particular, they are often prevented (and again, this is a special problem in North America) from having the services of midwives, and even close friends and relatives (other than her husband, if she has one) are not allowed to be present.

Giving birth in the hospital requires further sacrifices of the parturient women. She must often accept extensive technological intervention in her labor, sometimes at the expense of lack of personal attention from birth "attendants." For example, she may be left *unattended* except for the presence of a fetal heart monitor, which gives the misleading impression that she is being watched. External monitors require straps around the woman's abdomen and impose limitations on her movements during labor. Internal monitors require electrodes that are passed through the woman's vagina and are clipped or screwed into the fetus's scalp.[12]

Additional medical interventions in the course of a hospital birth include the following:[13]

Shaving of the perineal area

Enemas

Intravenous feeding

Artificial induction of labor, which may, in some cases, be done for the sake of the physician's convenience[14]

Withholding of food and liquids during labor

Stimulation of labor by means of oxytocin

Analgesia and anesthesia

Artificial rupture of membranes (amniotomy)

Use of the lithotomy (horizontal supine) position and stirrups for delivery

Episiotomy, which does not seem to reduce the incidence of tears,[15] and may even be associated with a greater incidence of lacerations

Use of forceps

Cesareans

Postnatal separation of mother and infant.

For the laboring woman a hospital birth can be an extraordinarily alienating experience:

Her clothes are sent away and she wears a standard gown. Her name is appended a hospital number. She is cleansed (shaved, washed and given an anema). Communication with her family and friends is monitored by the staff and severely curtailed. Instruments are attached to her to monitor the child's heart beat. Drugs are given to partially anesthetize her. She is physically inspected mainly in the area of her genitals. She is expected to remain lying down and, at inspections, near delivery and afterwards, her legs are in straps which retain them in a raised and apart position.[16]

Thus the sacrifices inherent in many hospital births also include such psychological costs as loss of autonomy and self-esteem.[17]

Although these sacrifices are presented as being mainly for the sake of the fetus's welfare, in fact it is not entirely clear that the infant always, or even usually, benefits from them. Fetal heart monitors, to take just one example, are inaccurate; they can create the impression of fetal distress, resulting in unnecessary procedures such as cesarean sections. The necessary immobilization may be uncomfortable for the woman and even detrimental to her and the fetus.[18] In general, it seems likely that the twentieth-century drop in infant mortality rates owes little to the procedures of hospital births and much to improved maternal diet, clean water, and adequate sanitation, housing, and working conditions.[19] There is no evidence of a causal relationship (in addition to a mere correlation) between the gradual drop in neonatal mortality rates in the last century and the rise in rates of hospital births.

Hence there is nothing self-evident about the value orientation exemplified in standard hospital birth practices. If some physicians regard the pregnant woman as a "route to the fetus" who during childbirth must sacrifice her interests to those of the fetus, they ought to *defend* that approach and not merely assume that it is legitimate. And so even if it is assumed, for the sake of argument, that on some occasions and in some circumstances (though certainly not all) the pregnant woman's interests and those of her fetus are not compatible, then the predominant question must be: To what degree, if at all, should the pregnant woman sacrifice her interests or permit them to be sacrificed? It is certainly not obvious that decisions about care for pregnant woman and fetus should necessarily subordinate the woman's freedom, interests, and well-being to those of her fetus.

Barbara Katz Rothman points out that in situations in which, for example, a cesarean section for the benefit of the baby is being contemplated, "the decision is seen as a *medical* decision rather than a moral or ethical one."[20] Yet in other situations outside the context of reproduction, when a decision must be made whether to risk one person's health in order to benefit another, the choice would be recognized, correctly, as constituting a moral problem. In childbirth apparently, decisions that essentially involve the weighing of varying values are falsely interpreted by medical personnel as being nothing more than medical choices. John A. Robertson makes this interpretation explicit when he states,

> Decisions whether or not to reproduce and decisions about rearing can be distinguished as more significant to the individual or as more rooted in a tradition of autonomy, than decisions affecting how one conducts parturition. Indeed, *childbirth decisions involve questions of medical practice*, in which regulation has traditionally been the norm.[21]

Within this interpretation of the nature of childbearing moral choices are being made, but they are not even recognized as such, and they are not given the appropriate and necessary justification that a moral choice requires. It is simply assumed, without question, that the well-being of the fetus takes priority.[22]

It may be that those who favor maternal sacrifice for the sake of the fetus implicitly justify their views by reference to two aspects of the birthing situation: first, the fact that in most births the fetus is, compared to earlier stages in pregnancy, highly developed (if it is not already a person, then it will very soon become one); and second, the fact that in all births the fetus is, until its emergence, entirely dependent for its survival on the pregnant woman (it is a highly needy and vulnerable being).

Nevertheless, regardless of the status and needs of the fetus at birth, it—like any other human being—cannot have a right to the use of another person's body. As Sara Ann Ketchum argues, in her examination of the moral status of the bodies of persons,

> Vital need cannot yield a right to other persons. The fundamental moral distinction—the one we must make in order for there to be any ethics at all—is that between persons and objects. Persons have rights and obligations; we owe them obligations and we have rights that we hold against them. We have rights *to* objects, and to consideration on the part of other persons, but we can never have a right to use another person as an object. To claim that A has a right to B's body—and in particular that A's need *confers* a right to B's body—is to claim that morally speaking A has a right that B be an object in A's world. But that would contradict the fundamental assumption of ethics; I cannot have a right that the distinction between persons and objects be blurred to suit my needs.[23]

Beyond its unquestioning emphasis upon the priority of fetal rights, a further problem with the assumption that there is a conflict between maternal and fetal rights and needs is that it is not at all obvious that fetus and pregnant women *should* in fact always be viewed as adversaries, competing to get their needs filled. As was argued in chapter 3, ordinarily during the course of pregnancy activities and resources—for example, mild exercise, nourishing food, and unpolluted air—that are beneficial for the mother are also beneficial for the fetus. Conversely, activities and environments—such as smoking, dangerous work environments, and exposure to disease—that are harmful for the fetus are also harmful for the pregnant woman. This relationship of shared benefit and vulnerability does not cease during the activity of childbirth.

Furthermore, it is unlikely that a pregnant woman sees herself as being in competition with her fetus; on the contrary, women ordinarily want the best for their future baby and are willing to go to considerable lengths to secure it.[24] Although it is undoubtedly true that some women may be unhappy during pregnancy, or may fear (perhaps with very good reason) the process of giving birth, those women who are involved in preparing and planning for the circumstances of their child's birth certainly perceive themselves as acting on behalf of, and in the best interests of, their fetus.

Could that perception be delusory? Some physicians apparently believe that it is, and accordingly, in keeping with the growing tendency to see the fetus as a patient, they have suggested that the fetus needs an advocate, particularly in the context of childbirth. For example, the OMA Discussion Paper states, "Whichever way we expand or change perinatal care, the change should not be in any way at the expense of the fetus or the newborn (healthy or handicapped), who are in no position to advocate for themselves."[25]

A number of assumptions are built into this deceptively simple statement. The first is that the fetus is in need of an advocate. Against whom does it need an advocate? In light of the belief discussed earlier, that the fetus and the pregnant woman are adversaries, it might seem true that the fetus is in need of an advocate to defend it against the misjudgment and/or incompatible wants and needs of the mother. On the other hand, if it is not correct always to assume that the fetus and pregnant woman are adversaries, then there seems to be much less reason to assume that the fetus is in need of an advocate.

Now perhaps the point about fetal advocates is just that the fetus cannot speak for itself during childbirth and cannot defend its own interests; it therefore needs someone who will speak on its behalf and look out for its well-being. The silence of the fetus is indisputable, but what is disputable is who should be the person who speaks on its behalf. The OMA Discussion Paper appears to assume that it is the physician's responsibility to protect the fetus from potentially unwise and self-oriented choices that may be made by the pregnant woman. In other words, the assumption is that the advocate for the fetus/newborn is, or should be, the doctor, not the pregnant woman/new mother.

However, insofar as there is ever a necessity to override the pregnant woman's decisions—whether because of her lack of knowledge or lack of competence—this necessity would have to be demonstrated, and not simply assumed to hold in all cases. Surely in no other human relationship does an unrelated person believe he has grounds unilaterally to appoint himself another's advocate without prior invitation. Certainly such a belief runs counter to the general practice in most other aspects of parent/child relationships.

This general practice is ably described by Paul Thompson, in a discussion of the *"prima facie* prerogative [of parents] to choose on behalf of their children."[26] Thompson points out that there is a great range of activities in which it is justifiably assumed that parents have a legitimate right to determine their children's participation.[27] There is no general reason to suppose that childbirth is different; there are no compelling grounds (such as the expectation of great harm) to justify overriding the parent's prerogative. Hence insofar as the fetus needs an advocate, there is no reason to regard the physician rather than the pregnant woman as the appropriate advocate.

Conflict between Safety and Other Values

In his discussion of childbirth, Michael Bayles also criticizes the belief that the physician should be the advocate of the fetus. He describes it as follows:

> Many physicians claim that they best represent the interests of the fetus. They do not deny that almost all women are interested in the well-being of their baby, but the woman's interests can conflict with those of the baby. For example, the woman's interests in the psychological and social aspects of birth are probably greater than those of the child, and women might sacrifice the physical safety of the fetus for their own psychological fulfillment. Even if maternal-infant bonding is beneficial for the baby, it is not as important as its physical well-being. Moreover, it is precisely in the area of physical safety that physicians have expertise. Consequently, it is claimed, they should make the decisions about childbirth.[28]

Interestingly, although Bayles rejects the notion that the physician is the appropriate advocate for the fetus, he nevertheless accepts, along with many antifeminist theorists, the assumption that there may be a conflict between the psychological needs of the pregnant woman and the requirements of safety for her and the fetus.

Much of the historical and contemporary discussion of childbirth states or assumes that the requirements of safety in birthing may not be compatible with other values or goals sought by the pregnant woman. For example, the OMA Discussion Paper assumes that in medical care generally and in birthing in particular there is a conflict between considerations of safety and "psycho-social needs." The paper worries about whether there is a "mechanism" to ensure that changes in medical practice "keep the safety of mother and fetus in balance with the psycho-social needs of the pregnant patient."[29] Similarly, it suggests that the concern of some women is to make "the episode of pregnancy . . . an opportunity in life to personally grow and experience to the fullest a basic aspect of their femininity"; these women want to have this experience within "acceptable limits of safety." The paper says that the "challenge to the health care system" is to try to provide this kind of experience "without the need to compromise basic safety standards for the mother and child."[30] Later the paper refers to situations in which there is "conflict between the patient's desires and the health interests of the fetus."[31]

In a similar fashion, while expressing sympathy for the notion of permitting autonomy to pregnant women, Bayles suggests that the "medical approach" to birth "considers only physical safety in judging outcomes. Other values are not considered". Although he is quite willing to give considerable weight to these "other values," he nevertheless assumes that they do conflict with safety: "Physical health does not always outweigh other considerations. Psychological and social values can outweigh risks to physical health."[32] And while taking quite the opposite view of the weighing of safety and psychological needs, John A. Robertson also believes that they are likely to be incompatible: "A woman's interest in an aesthetically pleasing or emotionally satisfying birth should not be satisfied at the expense of the child's safety."[33]

The belief in a conflict between safety and psychological values is, of course, entirely consistent with the traditional dualistic view of human persons that pits body against mind. In the birthing context, the body/mind split is perhaps most clearly exemplified in the use of regional anesthesia, which separates the laboring woman's experience from the activities of her body and turns her into "a more or less impartial observer of the [birth] scene."[34]

Once again, however, it is necessary to question the assumption that there is a conflict here. In fact, there is some evidence to indicate that safety and psychosocial needs are not generally incompatible with each other. For example, the psychological state of the pregnant woman can affect the physical state of the fetus and thus the well-being of the newborn. Measures promoting physical safety may affect the woman's psychological condition in a positive way. Yet at the same time undue emphasis on safety through the use of technology may bring about a disturbed state in the pregnant woman, and studies suggest that if the mother is extremely fearful or unhappy, the fetus will be adversely affected.[35] There is a very close relationship between the safety aspects of birth and the psychological aspects of the birthing experience; they are, in fact, interdependent. Hence attention to the quality of the birthing experience—that is, to the psychosocial elements of the birth environment—may enhance rather than conflict with or detract from the safety of the birth.

No doubt safety is generally thought to be a more important consideration than psychosocial concerns simply because survival is a precondition for the satisfaction of other needs. However, as was argued in chapter 3, this obvious empirical fact does not of itself imply that sheer survival, ongoing life, is a more important moral concern than the quality of that life. And it does not imply that matters pertaining to safety can be assessed and promoted independently of considerations pertaining to the psychological and social aspects of human life. In fact, safety considerations cannot even be described and evaluated independently of the social context that defines what constitutes safety and how it is to be achieved.

This latter claim is an important one and reflects further on what was said earlier about the alleged conflict between the fetus and the pregnant woman. Antifeminist and nonfeminist writers often appear to think that considerations of safety pertain only to the fetus, whereas considerations of the quality of the birthing experience are relevant only to the pregnant woman and are likely to benefit only her. But the argument just adduced shows that measures to enhance the quality of the birthing experience—measures that may be obtained through close attention to the needs and desires of the pregnant woman—can benefit the fetus and are in its interest as well as in the interests of its mother. In other words, both can be helped by promoting a happy and stress-free birth experience. As a result, it seems plausible to suppose that pregnant women are not in fact deluded when they believe that they are genuinely seeking what is good, not only for themselves but for their fetuses.

Values and Goals in Childbearing

The emphasis by nonfeminist and antifeminist writers on an alleged conflict between safety and psychosocial needs appears to be connected with two other basic beliefs. The first concerns the nature of risk-taking in childbirth, and the second concerns the significance of childbearing. To examine both of these requires some thought about the values and goals of childbirth.

A recurrent ideal cited in nonfeminist and antifeminist literature on birth is the health of the baby and the mother. From this point of view, "a 'successful' pregnancy is one which results in a physically healthy baby and mother as assessed in the period immediately following birth."[36] Bayles, for example, describes "the ethically ideal childbirth" as involving "a vaginal delivery with a healthy mother and infant."[37] The OMA Discussion Paper says that in the traditional system of provision of reproductive care by physicians, the physician's goal was "to facilitate the birth of a healthy baby"; hospitals attempted to "ensure efficient functioning of the hospital and safety of patients."[38] (This in itself is an interesting priority of values!)

As Bayles himself readily acknowledges, this quest for a healthy baby and mother is translated, in practice, into an

all-out attempt to "make the best of the worst possible outcome, no matter what the likelihood of its occurring."[39] For
example, while claiming that "the chances for a successful
labor and delivery are certainly 98 out of 100 or greater,"[40] one
physician states that if one is "interested in taking that 2%
chance [of an unsuccessful birth outcome], then fetal monitoring is unnecessary. [But] if one is interested in optimizing
the chances for *every* fetus, fetal monitoring is *essential*."[41] The
quest is most clearly exemplified in the medical establishment's insistence that home birth is dangerous and that all
births should take place in a hospital. The Ontario Medical
Association asserts categorically that "planned home births
involve increased and avoidable risks to the health of the
mother, foetus and newborn infant"; it therefore opposes
without reservation all planned home births.[42] The American
College of Obstetricians and Gynecologists has a similar
position.[43]

Planned home births, however, have an impressive safety
record,[44] comparing very favorably with hospital births in
terms of both mortality and morbidity rates. Hence the fact
that there is a low rate of unforeseeable risk in any birth (for
instance, as a result of cord prolapse or postpartum hemor-
rhage[45]) does not morally justify approaching all births as if
they involved the highest degree of risk.

Probably 20 per cent of births are to mothers with no high-
risk factor identifiable before delivery, yet about 10 per cent
of perinatal deaths are to such mothers. To ensure that these
unpredictable dangerous births take place in consultant hospitals, obstetricians recommend that all births should take
place there, for they claim that the chances of a successful
outcome are then improved. However valid the claim may
be in individual cases, the available statistical evidence does
not support it in general. It does not show that an increased
rate of hospitalization promotes the objective of reducing
overall mortaity.[46]

Similarly, the low rate of unforeseeable risk to pregnant
women and their fetuses of riding in automobiles does not
justify enforced banishment from cars![47] It is impossible to

eliminate all risks completely from human activities; an attempt must be made to make a realistic assessment of and preparation for possible dangers and, where possible, to reduce or compensate for them.

The fact that there may be an unforeseen negative outcome of one particular woman's birth choice—for example, in favor of home birth—does not by itself demonstrate that *all* similar choices are therefore unjustified. More important still, the occurrence of an unforeseen negative outcome is not even sufficient to show that the specific choice itself was unjustified. To see this, imagine the following analogous case. An individual decides to take her family for a car ride. The weather is fine, road conditions are good, the woman drives carefully and defensively. Nevertheless an accident occurs and an occupant of the car is injured. The fact that an injury occurred does not show that the decision to take the car ride in the first place was unjustified. Given all of the foreseeable information at the time, and given the appropriate precautions the driver took, the car ride was an entirely justified activity. Similarly, if a low-risk mother chooses home birth and takes all appropriate precautions for the circumstances of the birth, then the fact that an unforeseen injury occurs is not sufficient to show that her choice was unjustified.

No studies exist to support the justification of universal hosptalization, and existing studies of the safety of home versus hospital are often misused by the medical profession.[48] Furthermore, as Paul Thompson points out,

> hospital birth, while reducing a number of risks which are present in home birth, introduces new risks and increases remaining risks. And . . . it is not immediately obvious that the negative outcomes of the new risks introduced by hospital birth are more desirable than those of the risks of home birth which have been eliminated or reduced.[49]

Assessments both of what constitutes a benefit and of what constitutes a benefit substantial enough to warrant taking a risk to achieve it are value judgments.[50] Moreover, there is good evidence to suggest that contemporary medical practice creates what is regarded as a risk by defining certain conditions—such as having had three previous births—as high risk.[51] Hence the error in positions such as that of the OMA is that they fail to recognize that the mere acknowledgment of the possible existence of a risk does not by itself entail a particular course of action; a further evaluation of the significance of the risk is necessary, and such an evaluation is a moral, not a medical, judgment. Moreover, in light of the implausibility of assuming that pregnant woman and fetus are in conflict, it is not even very obvious that risks and benefits can or should be assessed separately for each of them.[52]

Part of the concern for the avoidance of risk in childbirth may be related to what has been called "public pressure" on doctors to ensure that every child is born in perfect health. The OMA Discussion Paper claims, "Neonatal outcomes that were accepted as normal or inevitable even a few years ago are not felt to be unacceptable to the public."[53] This statement assumes that higher morbidity and mortality rates were considered by parents to be "normal" and "inevitable" in the past, and it implies that the public is now raising its formerly low expectations. But it seems likely that even in the past the parents of a child who died or turned out to be handicapped found nothing normal or inevitable in those outcomes. Furthermore, the growing commodification of reproduction has contributed to the tendency to see procreation as commodity production: to raise our standards of what are considered to be acceptable offspring, and to extend those standards back in time to the period before birth. But the causes of these rising standards are to be found not in sudden consumer-oriented pressure from parents but in the social conditions that make the holding of these standards seem more realistic.[54]

> Not only the survival, but particularly the mental health of children has become increasingly important to families. Couples are aware that the costs of caring for a defective child can be ruinous to a family and, on the other hand, they want each child of theirs to be as nearly perfect as possible in order to take its place in an achievement-oriented society that makes education and mental ability a prerequisite of social mobility. . . . As psychologists discover increasingly subtle forms of "minimal brain damage" in schoolchildren,

damage often attributed to birth trauma, the search for the best delivery is accelerated.[55]

Even Sheila Kitzinger, a childbirth educator usually very sensitive to the pressures on pregnant women, remarks, "if a woman is only going to have a few children, or one, how much more desirable it is that she makes a good job of it!"[56]

Who ought to make decisions about the evaluation of risk in childbirth, and how should those decisions be made? I suggest that they should be made by the pregnant woman herself, through a process that places the childbirth event within the more general context of her life. Childbearing is not something that merely happens to women, but is a process in which women are (or can be) actively engaged. "Birth cannot simply be a matter of techniques for getting a baby out of one's body,"[57] and childbirth is not just a type of production.[58] Although hospitals do not reward, encourage, or even recognize competence in giving birth,[59] there is a very important conceptual and experiential difference between giving birth and being delivered. "When the *mother* is seen as delivering, then the attendant is assisting—aiding, literally attending. But when the *doctor* is delivering the baby, the mother is in the passive position of *being delivered*."[60]

It therefore seems unduly pessimistic to claim, as does Bayles, that "there does not appear to be any way to justify one attitude toward risk rather than another."[61] Evaluation of possible risk in childbirth, and of the importance of achieving a healthy baby and mother, requires situating the birth event within the wider circumstances of the mother's life. This is not to say that the familiar antifeminist belief in a conflict between safety and psychosocial needs must be reinstated. Instead it is necessary to reconstruct, from the point of view of the laboring woman, the very nature of what have been called "psychosocial needs" and "psycho-social interests."[62] Is it correct to say that the pregnant woman seeks to "personally grow and experience to the fullest a basic aspect of [her] femininity"? Or that "childbirth is an opportunity for personal development and growth"?[63] Or, as Bayles remarks, that "women generally want childbirth to be a rewarding personal experience"?[64]

Although written from viewpoints ostensibly sympathetic

to pregnant women, these statements are sadly inadequate descriptions of the full experience and significance of childbearing to the women who live it. As Mary O'Brien so vividly notes, there is a conspicuous inattention in "male-stream thought" to birth,[65] at least to birth as it is experienced by the laboring woman, rather than as it is experienced by her male attendants. That inattention perhaps partially explains the poverty of some theoreticians' descriptions of the birth experience.[66] What is missing is a sense of childbirth as a transitional episode in a woman's life, a transformative event[67] that—particularly but not only in the case of a first birth[68]— functions as both the culmination of pregnancy and a rite of passage[69] from one life situation to another. It should not be abstracted from other life experiences and treated as an isolated medical event.[70] Even childbirth preparation classes designed, at their best, to permit women more control over and participation in their deliveries often focus upon the birth as it if were an independent and self-sufficient event, unconnected with the years of nurturing a new little person who is produced through the woman's labor. But as Kitzinger, herself a mother of five, describes it:

> The experience of bearing a child is central to a woman's life. Years after the baby has been born she remembers acutely the details of her labor and her feelings as the child was delivered. One can speak to any grandmother about birth and almost immediately she will begin to talk about her own labors. It is unlikely that any experience in a man's life is comparably vivid.[71]

The suggestion that the childbearing experience is central to a woman's life[72] need not be at all incompatible with a feminist perspective on birth. It is of course necessary to avoid prescribing, as so many writers have in the past,[73] what childbirth *must* be like, or how it *must* be experienced,[74] and to avoid describing it romantically as a necessarily transcendent, quasi-mystical experience. The point being made is not that a woman is incomplete without experiencing birth, nor that childbearing is women's natural work, nor even that childbirth is always a happy event.

Instead what is being pointed to is the simple fact that childbirth is, or can be, if not skewed in its meaning by a medical reconstruction, a powerful, self-affirming, and memorable event whose meaning is not isolated but resonates throughout all of the woman's subsequent experiences as a woman and as a mother.[75] Since women now tend to have fewer children and have few, if any, opportunities to participate in other women's births, childbirth is for most of those who undertake it a journey into the unknown. Giving birth is a chance to come to know oneself and one's strengths, and to weave that knowledge into a more general understanding of the significance of one's life. Insofar as a "rewarding personal experience" (to use Bayles's phrase) is sought by pregnant women, that experience arises not just from the relatively brief events surrounding birth but from the mother-baby relationship and from the integration of motherhood into the woman's life pattern.[76]

Hence the conclusion must be that, in general, decisions about the birth of her baby belong primarily to the pregnant woman herself, for whom the process is not some isolated medical emergency but a vital part of the living of her life. And although it is impossible to specify uniformly what all births ought to be like, it can at least be said that they should not be founded upon the belief that the pregnant woman's interests conflict with those of her fetus, or that safety requirements must conflict with psychological needs. Ordinarily childbearing need not and should not require sacrifices of the pregnant woman.

Notes

1 Shelly Romalis, "Natural Childbirth and the Reluctant Physician," in *Childbirth: Alternatives to Medical Control*, ed. Shelly Romalis (Austin: University of Texas Press, 1981), p. 69.
2 For example, Doris Haire, "The Cultural Warping of Childbirth" (Seattle, Wash.: International Childbirth Education Association, 1972); Suzanne Arms, *Immaculate Deception: A New Look at Women and Childbirth in America* (Boston: Houghton Mifflin, 1975); Con-

stance A. Bean, *Labor and Delivery: An Observer's Diary* (Garden City, N.Y.: Doubleday, 1977); Yvonne Brackbill, June Rice, and Diony Young, *Birth Trap: The Legal Low-Down on High-Tech Obstetrics* (St. Louis: C. V. Mosby, 1984), chaps. 1 and 2; Germaine Greer, *Sex and Destiny: The Politics of Human Fertility* (London: Secker & Warburg, 1984), chap. 1.

3 For example, Margot Edwards and Mary Waldorf, *Reclaiming Birth: History and Heroines of American Childbirth Reform* (Trumansburg, N.Y.: The Crossing Press, 1984); Ann Oakley, "Wise Woman and Medicine Man: Changes in the Management of Childbirth," in *The Rights and Wrongs of Women*, ed. and introduction by Juliet Mitchell and Ann Oakley (Harmondsworth, England: Penguin Books, 1976); Datha Clapper Brack, "Displaced—The Midwife by the Male Physician," in *Biological Woman—The Convenient Myth*, ed. Ruth Hubbard, Mary Sue Henifin, and Barbara Fried (Cambridge, Mass.: Schenkman, 1982), pp. 207–226; Sheila Kitzinger, *Women as Mothers* (Glasgow: Fontana Books, 1978), chaps. 5 and 6; Adrienne Rich, "The Theft of Childbirth," in *Seizing Our Bodies: The Politics of Women's Health*, ed. Claudia Dreifus (New York: Vintage Books, 1977), pp. 146–163; Margarete Sandelowski, *Pain, Pleasure, and American Childbirth* (Westport, Conn.: Greenwood Press, 1984); Dorothy C. Wertz, "Man-Midwifery and the Rise of Technology," in *Birth Control and Controlling Birth: Women-Centred Perspectives*, ed. Helen B. Holmes, Betty B. Hoskins, and Michael Gross (Clifton, N.J.: The Humana Press, 1980), pp. 147–166; Richard W. Wertz and Dorothy C. Wertz, *Lying-In: A History of Childbirth in America* (New York: Schocken Books, 1977).

4 Hilary Graham and Ann Oakley, "Competing Ideologies of Reproduction: Medical and Maternal Perspectives on Pregnancy," in *Women, Health and Reproduction*, ed. Helen Roberts (London: Routledge & Kegan Paul, 1981), pp. 50–74; Romalis, "Natural Childbirth and the Reluctant Physician," pp. 63–91.

5 See Adele E. Laslie, "Ethical Issues in Childbirth," *Journal of Medicine and Philosophy* 7 (1982): 179–195, for a discussion of moral issues arising in connection with hospital births.

6 Barbara Katz Rothman, *Giving Birth: Alternatives in Childbirth* (Harmondsworth, England: Penguin Books, 1984), p. 277.

7 OMA Committee on Perinatal Care, "Ontario Medical Association Discussion Paper on Directions in Health Care Issues Relating to Childbirth" (Toronto, 1984). Although the paper is said not to represent present OMA policy (p. 1), it can be taken as representative of standard medical views on childbearing and on the relationship of the pregnant woman to her fetus.

8 Ibid., p. 12.

9 Thanks to Marguerite E. Ritchie for raising this point (private communication, 4 March 1986).

10 John A. Robertson, "Procreative Liberty and the Control of Con-

108   *Ethics and Human Reproduction*

ception, Pregnancy, and Childbirth," *Virginia Law Review* 69 (April 1983): 456.

11 Judith Jarvis Thomson, "A Defense of Abortion," in *Moral Problems: A Collection of Philosophical Essays* 2nd ed., ed. James Rachels (New York: Harper & Row, 1975), p. 103.

12 Sheila Kitzinger, "The Social Context of Birth: Some Comparisons between Childbirth in Jamaica and Britain," in *Ethnography of Fertility and Birth*, ed. Carol P. MacCormack (London: Academic Press, 1982), p. 183.

13 For a complete discussion, see Brackbill et al., *Birth Trap*, pp. 1–38, and Haire, "The Cultural Warping of Childbirth."

14 Ronald R. Rindfuss, Judith L. Ladinsky, Elizabeth Coppock, Victor W. Marshall, and A. S. Macpherson, "Convenience and the Occurrence of Births: Induction of Labor in the United States and Canada," in *Women and Health: The Politics of Sex in Medicine*, ed. Elizabeth Fee (Farmingdale, N.Y.: Baywood, 1982), pp. 37–58.

15 Janice Armstrong, "The Risks and Benefits of Home Birth" (unpublished paper, 1982), p. 10.

16 A. D. Jones and C. Dougherty, "Childbirth in a Scientific and Industrial Society," in MacCormack, *Ethnography of Fertility and Birth*, p. 280.

17 Brackbill et al., *Birth Trap*, pp. 3–4.

18 Armstrong, "Risks and Benefits of Home Birth," p. 2.

19 C. P. MacCormack, "Biological, Cultural and Social Adaptation in Human Fertility and Birth: A Synthesis," in *Ethnography of Fertility and Birth*, pp. 18–19.

20 Rothman, *Giving Birth*, p. 278, Rothman's emphasis.

21 Robertson, "Procreative Liberty," p. 452, my emphasis.

22 It is not unlikely that this approach could be extended to earlier periods of prenatal life, where it could be applied to fetal surgery, for example.

23 Sara Ann Ketchum, "The Moral Status of the Bodies of Persons," *Social Theory and Practice* 10 (Spring 1984): 32, Ketchum's emphasis.

24 David Stewart and Lewis E. Mehl, "A Rebuttal to Negative Home Birth Statistics Cited by ACOG," in *21st Century Obstetrics Now!* I, 2nd ed., ed. Lee Stewart and David Stewart (Chapel Hill, N.C.: NAPSAC, 1977), p. 29.

25 "OMA Discussion Paper," p.12.

26 "Home Birth: Consumer Choice and Restrictions of Physician Autonomy," *Journal of Business Ethics* 6 (1987): 76.

27 But, as will be argued in chapter 8, those rights are not unlimited.

28 Michael D. Bayles, *Reproductive Ethics* (Englewood Cliffs, N.J.: Prentice-Hall, 1984), p. 80.

29 "OMA Discussion Paper," p. 12.

30 Ibid., p. 22.

31 Ibid., p. 23.

32 Bayles, *Reproductive Ethics*, p. 80.

33 Robertson, "Procreative Liberties," p. 453; compare p. 458.

34 Sheila Kitzinger, *The Experience of Childbirth* 3rd ed., (Harmonds-worth, England: Penguin Books, 1972), p. 21; compare Kitzinger, *Women as Mothers*, p. 161.

35 Arms, *Immaculate Deception*, pp. 130–135.

36 Graham and Oakley, "Competing Ideologies of Reproduction," p. 54.

37 Bayles, *Reproductive Ethics*, p. 83.

38 "OMA Discussion Paper," p. 9.

39 Bayles, *Reproductive Ethics*, p.80.

40 Henry Klapholz, "The Electronic Fetal Monitor in Perinatology," in Holmes et al., *Birth Control and Controlling Birth*, p. 167.

41 Ibid., p. 173, my emphasis.

42 "OMA Discussion Paper," p. 30.

43 Richard H. Aubry, "The American College of Obstetricians and Gynecologists: Standards for Safe Childbearing," in Stewart and Stewart, *21st Century Obstetrics Now!*, p. 20.

44 Brackbill et al., *Birth Trap*, pp. 59–61; Gerard Alan Hoff and Lawrence J. Schneiderman, "Having Babies at Home: Is It Safe? Is It Ethical?" *Hastings Center Report* 15 (December 1985): 21.

45 Armstrong, "Risks and Benefits of Home Births," p. 4.

46 Marjorie Tew, "The Case against Hospital Deliveries: The Statistical Evidence," in *The Place of Birth*, ed. Sheila Kitzinger and J. A. Davis (Oxford: Oxford University Press, 1978), p. 65.

47 Compare Thompson, "Home Birth: Consumer Choice," pp. 75–78.

48 Stewart, "The Case for Home Birth," pp. 221–223.

49 Paul Thompson, "Childbirth in North America: Parental Autonomy and the Welfare of the Fetus," unpublished paper, Toronto, Ontario (1984): 5.

50 Ibid., p. 10.

51 Barbara Katz Rothman, "Awake and Aware, or False Consciousness," in Romalis, *Childbirth: Alternatives to Medical Control*, p. 177.

52 As some recommend: e.g., Hoff and Schneiderman, "Having Babies at Home," p. 24.

53 "OMA Discussion Paper," p. 15.

54 Edwards and Waldorf, *Reclaiming Birth*, pp. 107–108.

55 Wertz and Wertz, *Lying-In*, pp. 241–242.

56 Kitzinger, *The Experience of Childbirth*, p. 13.

57 Ibid., p. 24.

58 Rich, "The Theft of Childbirth," p. 162.

59 Greer, *Sex and Destiny*, p. 17.

60 Rothman, *Giving Birth*, p. 174, her emphasis.

61 Bayles, *Reproductive Ethics*, p. 81.

62 "OMA Discussion Paper," p. 33.

63 Ibid., pp. 22, 24.

64 Bayles, *Reproductive Ethics*, p. 83.

65 Mary O'Brien, *The Politics of Reproduction* (Boston: Routledge & Kegan Paul, 1981), pp. 20–21.

110   *Ethics and Human Reproduction*

66 Such inattention is evident throughout twentieth-century discussions of birth; see, for example, Edwards and Waldorf, *Reclaiming Birth*, pp. 42, 86.
67 Compare Sheila Kitzinger, *Giving Birth: The Parents' Emotions in
   Childbirth* (New York: Schocken Books, 1971), pp. 17–21.
68 "First childbirth has a capacity that other births do not have to
   brand reproduction with a lasting meaning for the mother, to
   influence all other reproductive experiences. And it is a turning
   point, a transition, a life crisis: a first baby turns a woman into a
   mother, and mothers' lives are incurably affected by their
   motherhood; in one way or another the child will be a theme for
   ever." Ann Oakley, *Becoming a Mother* (New York: Schocken
   Books, 1979), p. 24.
69 Kitzinger, "The Social Context of Birth," pp. 182–184; Jones and
   Dougherty, "Childbirth in a Scientific and Industrial Society,"
   pp. 280–282.
70 Graham and Oakley, "Competing Ideologies of Reproduction,"
   pp. 52, 54; Oakley, *Becoming a Mother*.
71 Kitzinger, *The Experience of Childbirth*, p. 17.
72 As Adrienne Rich points out (*"The Theft of Childbirth"*, p. 152), at
   times Kitzinger takes this claim too far—when, for example, she
   refers to births as "perhaps the most important moments of their
   [women's] lives" (Kitzinger, *The Experience of Childbirth*, p. 20).
73 Wertz and Wertz, *Lying-In*, pp. 188–189.
74 Lester Dessez Hazell's moving "Truths about Birth" remind us
   that each birth is unique (Lester Dessez Hazell, "Spiritual and
   Ethical Aspects of Birth: Who Bears the Ultimate Responsibility?"
   in Stewart and Stewart *21st Century Obstetrics Now!*, p. 259).
75 Kitzinger, *Giving Birth*, p. 31; Graham and Oakley, "Competing
   Ideologies of Reproduction," p. 54.
76 Graham and Oakley, p. 54; Rich, "The Theft of Childbirth,"
   pp. 161–162. If, for example, she returns to work after she has
   ostensibly recovered from the birth, "she is not the same worker
   who left to bear a child. Asking her to continue as if nothing had
   happened is absurd" (Greer, *Sex and Destiny*, p. 13).

6 *Surrogate Motherhood*

Depending on the circumstances, a surrogate mother can be praised as a benefactor to a suffering couple (the money is hardly adequate compensation) or condemned as a callous user of offspring to further her selfish ends.[1]

The arguments as to the social and moral appropriateness of this new kind of sale simply reiterate the view of female will found in discussions of prostitution: does the state have a right to interfere with this exercise of individual female will (in selling use of the womb)?[2]

The previous chapters focused mainly on the embryo/fetus and some actual and potential treatments of it in the context of pregnancy, abortion, and birth. In this chapter the emphasis is primarily on some of the ways in which reproductive technology affects women. I examine the moral and conceptual aspects of the practice of surrogate motherhood.

I shall call into question what seem to be generally accepted assumptions about surrogate motherhood and suggest that the practice may be morally troubling for reasons not always fully recognized by other writers on this issue. These reasons go beyond the fairly obvious consequentialist misgivings about its effects on the persons—particularly the child—involved.[3] For example, there is concern for how the child might be affected by learning that its gestating mother conceived and carried it with the deliberate intention of giving it up. Adopted children in later life very often feel a longing to search for their genetic parents; would the child born to a surrogate want to seek her out? And should that child be permitted access to his or her surrogate mother? A concern for the well-being of the child produced by a surrogate is entirely justified, and later chapters will discuss some general questions about the effects on children of the social uses of reproductive technology. But the focus in this chapter is upon the surrogate mother herself.

Surrogate motherhood is typically resorted to when the female member of a married couple is unable—for a variety of reasons—to bear a child. I am primarily interested in the commercial forms of surrogate motherhood, not in those far rarer cases in which a woman bears a child for a friend or relative.[4] In the former case what has been called the "commissioning couple"[5] pays a fee to a surrogate who is artificially inseminated with the husband's sperm, gestates the child, and surrenders it to the couple. Usually the husband's name will be listed on the infant's birth certificate;[6] the infertile wife, however, must formally adopt the child in order to become its legal mother.[7] In another possible form of surrogacy, the surrogate gestates an embryo is not the product of her own ovum but was produced through in vitro fertilization of another woman's egg, or was obtained through the process of uterine lavage. Such a form raises issues comparable to those in standard surrogacy cases but may be complicated further by the fact that the child that is produced is not genetically related to the gestating mother.

What does surrogate motherhood suggest about the social use of human reproductive faculties, about women's relationship to their bodies, and about the interrelationships of males and females? Part of the reason for the failure to acknowledge these questions fully lies in the frameworks used to discuss the practice. Hence my general aim here is to reexamine those frameworks and subject them to critical analysis. I want to reveal what surrogate motherhood really is. And in so doing, I am not disclosing some hidden essence of the practice but, rather, am indicating how we most reasonably should look at it.

There are currently at least two different points of view about surrogate motherhood, which I call the free market model and the prostitution model.[8] The free market model is clearly nonfeminist in nature, whereas the prostitution model has arisen out of feminist analyses. Of the two, the prostitution model is better. But it shares with the free market model certain assumptions about reproductive labor and reproductive choice, assumptions that turn out to be highly implausible and only obscure our understanding of what surrogate motherhood really is. It is essential, then, to criticize the nonfeminist free market model, to expose the limitations of the prostitution model, and to build upon the insights garnered by previous feminist analyses of surrogate motherhood.

The Free Market Model

According to the free market model, surrogate motherhood is at best a desirable, useful, and indeed necessary service that uncoerced women may offer for purchase by childless but fertile men and their infertile wives.

This approach is defended by John A. Robertson, who regards surrogate motherhood as one type of "collaborative reproduction"—that is, reproduction in which "[a] third person provides a genetic or gestational factor not present in ordinary paired reproduction."[9] Other types include adoption and the use of artificial insemination by donor (AID). According to Robertson, there are few, if any, important social or moral differences among the various forms of collaborative reproduction.[10] Indeed, in some respects resort to surrogate motherhood may be preferable to agency adoption because it is

an alternative to the nonmarket, agency system of allocating children for adoption, which has contributed to long queues for distributing healthy white babies. This form of independent adoption is controlled by the parties, planned before conception, involves a genetic link with one parent, and enables both the father and the mother of the adopted child to be selected in advance.[11]

Robertson lists other supposed benefits of surrogate motherhood, such as the alleviation of suffering and the satisfaction of the desires of the infertile.[12] But it is clear that for Robertson, the major value of the use of a surrogate is that it involves the uncoerced exercise of economic choice. The commissioning couple obtains the type of child they want[13] and at the time they choose. The couple freely decides to invest their money in their preferred form of consumer good: a child. As one adoptive mother of a baby born to a surrogate said, "My God, people spend more on a Mercedes than we spent on Alexander. It's an alternative for people who want infants."[14]

Of course, since the cost of hiring a surrogate mother is now $22,000 to $25,000[15] and increasing, this service is not, in fact available to all. Robertson calls it "a consumption item for the middle classes." Its limited accessibility is not, he claims, unjust to poor couples, because it does not leave them worse off than they were before.[16] Michael D. Bayles also uses this defense and mentions some others. He says that the price will drop if many women decide, because of the attractive fees, to become surrogates, and more children will become available for adoption. "In general," says Bayles,

> one should not accept limitations on otherwise permissible activities because poor people cannot afford them, but should try to raise the income of the poor or subsidize the activities so that poor people can afford them.[17]

The suggestion seems to be that the state should subsidize access to the services of surrogate mothers for those infertile couples who would otherwise not be able to pay for them.

Furthermore, the surrogate, like the commissioning couple, also exercises free choice, according to Robertson. Equality of opportunity has been extended: like the sperm vendor, a woman is now free to sell her reproductive capacities.[18] She chooses, in effect, a particular type of temporary (though by no means part-time!) job. Robertson states that surrogates "choose the surrogate role primarily because the fee provides a better economic opportunity than alternative occupations."[19] Thus Jane Doe chooses to be a surrogate mother rather than a waitress, let's say, because the pay for the former is (or appears to be) better. High school guidance counselors take note:

female students should be alerted to the existence of this new employment opportunity.

It should be remarked at this point that there might be some question as to how rewarding the payment for surrogate mothering really is. Much of the money paid by the couple goes toward lawyers' fees, medical and travel expenses, and insurance; surrogate mothers usually receive about $10,000.[20] This means that a woman who becomes pregnant at the very first attempt at artificial insemination would earn around $1.50 per hour for her full-time 24-hour-per-day "job" as a pregnant woman.

Nevertheless, says Robertson, the payment of a fee (such as it is) is crucial to the surrogate mothering contract, for "few surrogates will volunteer for altruistic reasons alone." A ban on fees is not necessary to protect the surrogate from coercion or exploitation, since the surrogate has made "a considered, knowing choice, often with the assistance of counsel, before becoming pregnant."[21] Bayles elaborates this suggestion. Poor women, he says, are not exploited in being offered attractive payments to be surrogates. After all, "other people are attracted by large fees to become lawyers or physicans." (This comment clearly assumes that surrogacy is a sort of career, however temporary.) It is true that poor uneducated women might not have many alternative forms of employment, but this fact is not a good reason to ban this form of opportunity. In fact, he says, it would be unjust to deprive them of the opportunity, providing their decision to become a surrogate is an informed one.[22] Another philosopher expresses this idea more bluntly: "Given a choice between poverty and exploitation, many people may prefer the latter."[23]

Robertson does not fail to recognize some potential problems in surrogate motherhood. These problems mainly concern the possibility of psychological suffering of the parties to the contract between the surrogate and the commissioning couple, harms to the child, the artificial manipulation of the natural process of reproduction, and difficulties resulting from noncompliance with the contract. Robertson apparently regards such problems as just a manifestion of the pains of the human condition: they are not unique to surrogate motherhood. Furthermore, they can be significantly diminished by providing good medical and legal services.

Robertson summarizes his discussion of possible problems in surrogate motherhood in a most significant statement. "The morality of surrogate mothering," he says, "depends on how the duties and responsibilities of the role are carried out, rather than on the mere fact that a couple produces a child with the aid of a collaborator."[24] For Robertson what is important is "not what we do—but how we do it."[25] No further analysis of "what we do" in surrogate mothering is needed. All that is required is reasonable "public scrutiny, through regulation of the process of drawing up the contract rather than its specific terms."[26]

The Prostitution Model

At the very least the free market model for surrogate motherhood seems naive. Among its problems are the assumptions that the commodification of babies is morally acceptable; that the high cost to the commissioning couple along with the low fee to the mother is not unjust; that surrogate mothers choose freely to sell their services at a fair price and are therefore not the victims of exploitation; that the practice of surrogate motherhood requires only legal regulation in order to prevent problems; and that *what* surrogate motherhood is does not require further analysis. Such an approach is nonfeminist because it is almost oblivious to the way in which women themselves might experience surrogacy; and although it pays lip service to the possibility of injustice, it is blind to the real nature of the coercion and exploitation involved in this practice.

The second point of view on surrogate motherhood, which I have called the prostitution model, at first sight is quite different from the first, for it calls into question at least some of the assumptions made by the free market model. It is usually advanced by feminist writers, but it is nowhere as fully expressed and developed as the free market model. Instead it is necessary to piece it together from a variety of rather brief commentaries.

According to this second point of view, surrogate

motherhood is a type of deliberate exploitation of women's reproductive capacities and in that way is akin to prostitution.[27]

An outline of this type of analysis is provided by Mary Kay Blakely, in a short paper whose very title, "Surrogate Mothers: For Whom Are They Working?" invites an examination of underlying assumptions about surrogate motherhood. She suggests that the practice is governed by racist and sexist beliefs.[28] Surrogate motherhood, she says, raises issues concerning ownership of children, "the conceit of patriarchal genetics,"[29] infertility as a failing in women, and finally "guilt and money, and how women earn both."[30] But these comments just hint at a feminist analysis, and Blakely herself never answers the provocative question in the title of her paper.

In response to Blakely's paper, another writer[31] states that recognition of a woman's right to control her own body and to make decisions about childbearing does not imply a license to exploit one's body. Surrogate mothers may feel a sense of fulfillment at least partly because childbearing has been, historically, almost the only realm for which women gain recognition.[32] Thus although women should have a "right to choose" in regard to surrogate motherhood, "society's endorsement of this choice as a valid female occupation" would be a mistake because it would serve as an affirmation of the tradition of fulfillment through childbearing.

A possible answer to the question, "for whom are surrogates working?" is provided by Susan Ince. In her investigation of the operation of a surrogate motherhood broker, she found that the infertile wife, who is the raison d'être of the surrogate industry, is "notably absent" from the surrogate motherhood relationship. The company investigated by Ince urged each "girl" to find ways to include the biological father (the husband of the infertile woman) in her pregancy and birth, for example, by sending a "nice note" to the father after conception, and later, a tape of the baby's heartbeat.[33] Furthermore, the contract used by the company makes it clear that it is the father who is the purchaser; it is he to whom the child-product belongs and to whom it must be delivered.[34] The preeminence of the father over his infertile wife is emphasized by the fact that her consent is not usually required for his participation in the surrogate motherhood arrangement. (This contrasts with the regular procedures governing the use of artificial insemination by donor: consent of the husband is ordinarily required before a woman is artificially inseminated.) Indeed, the chief beneficiary of surrogacy appears to be the father, who receives a child conceived from his sperm and enjoys the titillation of surrogate reproduction. His wife, on the other hand, may be driven by a variety of pressures to acquiesce in the arrangement—pressures such as lack of alternatives to child-rearing and fear of social ostracism and emotional and economic abandonment by her husband.[35] Thus Ince's analysis suggests that the true employer of the surrogate is not the so-called commissioning couple but only the male who provides the sperm.

That suggestion renders more plausible the claim that surrogate motherhood is like prostitution. The comparison is used briefly by Mary B. Mahowald, who also challenges the assumption of the free market model that women freely choose the job of surrogate mother. Expressing concern about women's right to self-determination regarding their own bodies, she writes,

> Most prostitutes are driven to their "trade" by economic and emotional pressures largely beyond their control; and surrogacy? What either practice says about society is more telling than what it says about the individual. Accordingly, we might more appropriately critique the social conditions that make these options genuine and unavoidable for individual women, than worry about the legal complaints arising from their practice.[36]

Finally, Andrea Dworkin has also written about surrogate motherhood in the course of a longer discussion of prostitution. She argues that the scientific separations of sex from reproduction and of reproduction from sex now "enable women to sell their wombs within the terms of the brothel model."[37] Thus reproduction can become the sort of commodity that sex is now. All reproductive technologies "make the womb extractable from the woman as a whole person in the same way the vagina (or sex) is now."[38] A surrogate mother is,

Dworkin says, a "reproductive prostitute."[39] It might be added that insofar as they profit from the sale of a woman's reproductive services, the lawyers and doctors who recruit the surrogate and match her with a commissioning couple are also very like pimps.

The Two Models: Similarities and Critique

The nonfeminist free market model and the feminist prostitution model of surrogate motherhood appear to be rather different. The former states that surrogate motherhood is a freely chosen arrangement between two or more human beings operating to the potential benefit of all concerned. The latter sees surrogate motherhood as akin to prostitution, a type of exploitive employment by men into which the women involved enter not freely but out of economic necessity or social coercion. Consequently the two viewpoints are sharply divided as to the moral justification of the practice—the free market model regards it as acceptable, the prostitution model as morally questionable—and also as to social policy, with the free market model seeing surrogacy as in need only of legal regulation, whereas the prostitution model sees it as necessitating a dramatic restructuring of society so that women will not be forced into being surrogate mothers.

Nevertheless, despite these apparent differences, closer examination of the two viewpoints on surrogate mothers reveals that they share several assumptions in common. The first concerns the idea of reproductive labor, which is expressed in this context by treating surrogate motherhood as a job; the second concerns the concept of reproductive choice.

In a very literal sense the surrogate mother is engaging in reproductive labor: her body is doing the work necessary to produce a human being. Moreover, she is being paid for this work. Hence surrogate motherhood appears to be, or to be like, a job. This is an assumption shared by both the free market model and the prostitution model, and even by the women themselves.[40] Just as, for example, a music teacher might sell her pedagogical services privately to individual students, or a lawyer might sell her legal services to clients, or a prostitute might sell her sexual services to customers, the surrogate mother sells her reproductive services to the commissioning couple or, more accurately, to a man, or possibly to a series of individual men. The practice of surrogacy thus extends the commodification of reproduction from the sale of reproductive products such as sperm to the sale of reproductive services such as gestation. In the typical case hiring a surrogate seems to be something like taking raw materials to a worker who then provides the labor (and perhaps some natural resources of her own) to create a finished product.

To treat surrogate motherhood as a job appears only too consistent with other traditional uses of women's reproductive labor. For as feminist writers have pointed out, under ordinary circumstances such labor is either a species of volunteer work, which women supposedly undertake for sheer love of it, or, in less congenial circumstances, a type of slavery.[41] Thus the fee paid to the surrogate mother at least appears to put reproductive labor on a more equal footing than it usually possesses with other forms of paid labor.

But *if* surrogate motherhood is to be regarded as a job, then we are forced to accept the peculiar implications that follow from it. For example, consider this: The free market model assumes that the surrogate is employed by the commissioning couple; the prostitution model suggests that she is employed by the man who provides the sperm. But closer investigation makes it at least as plausible to say that the surrogate is self-employed.

Surrogate motherhood is similar in several respects to a small-scale owner-operated business. The woman, after all, operates out of her own home; she provides the equipment for carrying out the labor; and her earnings are controlled (or limited) by the amount of work she is willing to do (that is, by the number of babies she is willing to produce). I would even venture that if the government found out about her income, it would require her to pay taxes directly to the state.[42] The surrogate motherhood brokers who bring buyers and sellers together are not the employers of the woman; they explicitly disavow any responsibility for adverse outcomes,[43] and they do not pay the woman for her services. But then, neither are the couple, or the biological father, the employer of the woman, any more than a lawyer's clients or a music teacher's pupils are their employers.

Thus *if* surrogate motherhood is a job involving the selling of reproductive labor on a private basis, then an answer at least as plausible as any other to Blakely's question, "for whom is the surrogate working?" is herself.

Now of course I do not really want to claim that surrogate mothers are self-employed. I simply want to explore the implications that follow from treating surrogate motherhood as a job. They reveal that there is an error in seeing surrogate motherhood as being or being like a job involving the selling of one's reproductive services. For if the surrogate mother is self-employed, then we are led to regard her as an individual whose activities must be regulated in order to protect those who hire her services, the potential child, and the general public from any possible dangers or failure of responsibility in her exercise of her vocation.[44] Indeed, legislation to govern surrogate motherhood has already been proposed which is designed to safeguard lawyers, doctors, the commissioning couple, and the potential baby by providing legal and financial penalties to be exacted if the mother should abort, engage in negligent behavior, or fail to surrender the child, in violation of the terms of her contract.[45] The idea that the surrogate mother is self-employed thus leads to a concern for the licensing of surrogates; for setting appropriate fees;[46] for requisite training, qualifications, screening, advertising, insurance, contracts, and penalties for noncompliance. Moreover if surrogate motherhood is a job, then it appears that the only worry about the women involved—if there is one at all—must be whether it is a good job. Our concern will be directed toward improving their working conditions, raising their income, providing insurance and workers compensation, perhaps even offering a pension plan, and so on.

But all of these concerns entirely lose sight of part of what seems to be implicit in and correct about the feminist critique of surrogate motherhood: namely, that the surrogate mother is *herself* in need of protection from the lawyers, doctors, and infertile couples who wish to make use of her services. The assumption that surrogate motherhood is or is like a job essentially misrepresents the power relations that are defined by the practice. The immediate locus of power in the surrogate arrangement is a necessarily rather wealthy man who pays the fee and provides the sperm, and the person, usually a male lawyer, who represents him and receives a commission for his services. But the wider network of control is constituted by the authority relations defined in patriarchy, in the context of which reproduction is usually labor done by women for men. It seems highly unlikely that in becoming a surrogate mother a woman is invested with power and independence that she would otherwise not possess in the exercise of her reproductive capacities. As in the case of prostitution, the mere payment of a small fee in no way changes the possibility that she is a victim of exploitation, and the nature of the exploitation is not such that an increase in fees or improved working conditions will change it.

In order to give more substance to this contention, I shall turn to analysis of the second item on which the two models of surrogate motherhood agree. Both of them assume that individuals should, perhaps within certain limits, have the freedom to choose what kind of job to take (whether, let's say, to become a secretary or a waitress, or whether to choose self-employment as a doctor or as a surrogate mother). And becoming a surrogate mother is assumed to be at least potentially one possible result of the exercise of that free choice— in particular, free choice concerning the use of one's reproductive capacities.

Of course, the two models disagree as to whether this freedom really exists in the case of surrogate motherhood: the free market model says it does; the prostitution model says it does not. And in this respect the prostitution model is, I would argue, correct. A question raised by the Canadian Advisory Council on the Status of Women about prostitution applies almost verbatim to surrogate motherhood:

> Can a person of minimal education and financial well-being be said truly to choose a way of life that is stigmatized by much of society, that is physically dangerous at times, that leaves her with little control over her earning power, and

that can cause her considerable legal complications?[47]

In one of the few psychological studies so far undertaken on the characteristics of women who apply to be surrogate mothers, it was discovered that 40 percent of the sample were unemployed or receiving some form of financial aid or both. Moreover, 72 percent of the women had an education level of high school graduation or less.[48] The researcher, Philip J. Parker, also found that a large majority of the group had been pregnant previously; when pregnant these women "felt more content, complete, special, and adequate and often felt an inner glow; some felt more feminine and attractive and enjoyed the extra attention afforded them."[49] In this sample, 35 percent of the women either had had a voluntary abortion or had relinquished a child for adoption, a fact that led Parker to surmise that these women "felt (often unconsciously) that surrogate motherhood would help them master unresolved feelings they had regarding a previous voluntary loss of fetus or baby."[50] (One might wonder here how "voluntarily" losing a child by surrendering it to the commissioning couple could help them master feelings about the previous voluntary loss of a fetus or baby.) Considering all of these factors, the candidates for surrogate motherhood seem not only to be motivated by very real financial need but also to be influenced by traditional role expectations about the importance of pregnancy and motherhood in women's lives.[51]

It is most ironic that after uncovering this information about applicants for surrogate motherhood, Parker emphasizes the importance of ensuring that every applicant is "competent" and is "voluntarily and freely making an informed choice, free of coercion and undue influence."[52] There is a fundamental contradiction between the fact that social conditions such as those delineated in Parker's study create the demand for surrogate motherhood and permit reproductive services to become a commodity, and the fact that the women involved are perceived as able to make a free choice.[53] Yet the free market proponents of surrogate motherhood are likely to use that alleged free choice to defend the practice by asking, rhetorically, what right the state has to deny a woman the exercise of her free will in selling her reproductive capacities.[54] As one feminist expresses it, "Men are controlling not only what choices are open to women, but what choices women learn to want to make."[55]

Perhaps the cause of the disagreement between the two models as to whether surrogate motherhood is the result of free choice is a failure to examine what reproductive choice means. Both models appear to assume that the main moral question about reproductive choice is whether or not it exists—in this context, whether the women who become surrogate mothers freely choose this use of their reproductive capacities. But the idea of reproductive choice is in need of further analysis: It is more complex than proponents of the two models appear to realize.

Barbara Katz Rothman has sounded some warnings about the meanings of reproductive choice. Examining the varieties of choices offered by reproductive technology—options for fetal monitoring, contraceptive use, abortion, prenatal diagnosis, and infertility treatments—Rothman argues that apparent expansions of choice often result in the loss of other choices because they become socially less acceptable, or in the existence of choices that women are paradoxically forced to make.[56] Thus reproductive choice sometimes turns out to be more apparent than real.

This kind of insight can be applied to surrogate motherhood. What options may be foreclosed for some women by the existence of the apparent choice of selling one's reproductive services? For individual women the existence of surrogate motherhood as an apparent choice may tend to obscure or override other possible interpretations of their lives. Just as the overwhelming presence of the role of housewife presented itself, until recently, as the only "choice" for women, so also surrogacy may appear to be the only possible escape route for some women with few resources and opportunities. A woman may reason, in effect, that if all else fails, she can still become a surrogate mother. If surrogate motherhood becomes a socially approved "choice", it will affect how women see both their relationships to their children and the use of their reproductive capacities, and it will further distort the social construction of women's reproductive roles.

So far what has been said about reproductive choice does

not go much beyond what feminists have said about it in other contexts. However, I want to suggest a second reason to reconsider the notion of reproductive choice in the context of surrogate motherhood: it can lead to an undiscriminating acceptance of the many ways in which women's reproductive capacities may be used. In endorsing an uncritical freedom of reproductive choice, we may also be implicitly endorsing all conceivable alternatives that an individual might adopt; we thereby abandon the responsibility for evaluating substantive actions in favor of advocating merely formal freedom of choice.[57] We must think very carefully about whether surrogate motherhood is a "choice" that should be recognized in this way.

This point implies a more fundamental reservation about the idea of reproductive choice in the context of surrogate motherhood: Is becoming a surrogate mother really the kind of thing one can freely choose? The question could perhaps be more clearly expressed by asking whether surrogate motherhood is genuinely a part of what we ought to *mean* by the exercise of reproductive choice. The problem is not merely that surrogate motherhood may not be freely chosen by those women who take it up. The problem is that there is a real moral danger in the type of conceptual framework that presents surrogate motherhood as even a *possible* freely chosen alternative for women.

This becomes apparent when we consider whether the practice of surrogacy would raise fewer moral questions if only middle-class, economically advantaged women became surrogate mothers. (And in fact some commentators have suggested that such women may be a substantial component of the applicants for surrogate motherhood.[58] One study of a very small sample of applicants found that nine of ten of the women "were of modest to moderate means"—although in many cases this turned out to mean that they were supported by a husband or boyfriend.[59]) No woman is compelled to become a surrogate mother at the point of a gun, and middle-class women are not, apparently, forced into it by economic expediency. Thus one writer suggests that such women are "motivated by sympathy and charity for the commissioning parents"; they therefore act freely and are not exploited.[60] But the absence of compelling economic conditions does not mean that it makes sense to say that a woman is making a free choice to be a surrogate and is thereby exercising a type of reproductive freedom.

Surrogate motherhood is not and cannot be merely one career choice among others. It is not a real alternative. It is implausible to suppose that fond parents would want it for their daughters. We are unlikely to set up training courses for surrogate mothers. Schools holding "career days" for their future graduates will surely not invite surrogate mothers to address the class on the advantages of their "vocation." And surrogate motherhood does not seem to be the kind of thing one would put on one's curriculum vitae.[61]

Surrogate motherhood is no more a real job option than selling one's blood or one's gametes or one's bodily organs can be real job options. Although an individual's blood, gametes, and organs *are* hers (and no one else's) to dispose of, all of these commercial transactions involve an extreme form of personal and bodily alienation. Surrogate mothering is "at the extreme end of the spectrum of alienated labour," for the surrogate mother must contract out of all of the "so-called 'normal' love, pride, satisfaction, and attachment in, for, and to the product of her labour."[62] In surrogate motherhood the woman gives up the use of her body, the product of her reproductive labor, and that reproductive labor itself to persons who pay to make them their own.[63] In so doing she surrenders her individuality, for becoming a surrogate mother involves receiving a fee not for labor that is the unique expression of one's personal abilities and talents but only for the exercise of one's reproductive capacities. As one applicant for surrogate motherhood aptly expressed it; "I'm only an incubator."[64]

Now some have claimed that reproductive labor is not impersonal: that some form of personal expression enters into it by means, for example, of choices as to what is consumed during pregnancy, the type of activities one engages in, and the moods and feelings one experiences. But while these factors can indeed affect the nature of the pregnancy and its outcome (that is, not only the health of the baby but the woman's own well-being), for the most part the course of pregnancy and even of childbirth is outside the control of the woman involved. This is emphasized by Mary O'Brien in a discussion of Marx's comparison of the architect and the bee.

> Mother and architect are quite different. The woman cannot realize her visions, cannot make them come true, by virtue of the reproductive labour in which she involuntarily engages, if at all. Unlike the architect, her will does not influence the shape of her product. Unlike the bee, she knows that her product, like herself, will have a history. Like the architect, she knows what she is doing; like the bee, she cannot help what she is doing.[65]

For this reason, the woman who engages in paid reproductive labor is permitted no moral significance as an individual. In fact, as Andrea Dworkin points out, when women are defined and used as a sex class, as they are when they are paid for their reproductive or sexual services, the individual woman becomes a fiction.[66] It is clear that within certain broadly defined limits—for example, being fertile, being white, being healthy, even being pretty—the women who work as surrogate mothers are interchangeable. Despite some superficial attention to finding the "right" woman—and indeed, sometimes the hiring father is encouraged to choose his woman on the basis of data supplied by the lawyer or agency[67]—the women involved are defined solely as gestators, without reference to their individual characteristics or potential.[68]

Surrogate motherhood is not and cannot be a freely chosen "job" because the practice is such that it recognizes no individual who can make the choice. The institution defines the individual woman out of existence. All that is left is what has been described as a "womb for rent." Although her body and its capacities are hers (and no one else's) to dispose of, the practice of surrogacy negates her as a person and thus renders free choice impossible. In surrogate motherhood, there can be no doubt, a commercial transaction take place, but it is not a transaction between equals, or even between potential equals. Although the woman involved may rightly be described as being freely chosen by a man, who pays her fee and who thus exercises a special type of reproductive choice, she does not freely choose him. The man who pays the fee and provides the sperm has merely leased for nine months a part of her body, together with its reproductive capacities, and has purchased outright the egg from which the baby grows. A woman can no more choose to be a surrogate mother than a room can choose to be leased, or a pet can choose to be bought. Surrogate motherhood is no more a job than being occupied, for a fee, is a job.

Thus while the nonfeminist analysis of the practice of surrogate motherhood is seriously in error, the feminist analysis also incorporates some false assumptions. A close examination of the practice leads to the rejection of two assumptions made both by those who praise and by those who condemn it—that is, by the free market model and by the prostitution model. Surrogate motherhood is not a job. And to become a surrogate mother is not the sort of thing that can plausibly be regarded as the exercise of reproductive choice.

Policy Implications

While in no way wanting to glorify some hypothetical form of "natural" motherhood, I nevertheless believe that this examination of what surrogate motherhood is—that is, within what framework or set of assumptions it should be understood—shows both that this practice is part of a broader context of morally and conceptually dubious assumptions about women's role in reproduction and that the commercial form of surrogate motherhood as it now exists is not the kind of social practice that should be fostered or benignly tolerated.

In regard to policy, it is illuminating to compare the very different recommendations about surrogacy made by two widely separated committees, the Ontario Law Reform Commission and the Committee of Inquiry into Human Fertilisation and Embryology (the Warnock Committee). These have already been referred to briefly in chapter 3, where restrictions upon the commodification of reproduction were discussed.

The Ontario Law Reform Commission's *Report on Artificial Reproduction and Related Matters* implicitly accepts the nonfeminist free market model of surrogate motherhood. It argues that "recourse to medical means of alleviating the effects of infertility or genetic impairment cannot conscionably be forbidden" and that prohibition of surrogacy arrangements "would result in recourse to clandestine private arrangements that would realize the worst fears of those who oppose this practice."[69] Hence any concerns about potential problems in surrogacy can best be addressed through legislation that would regulate but not prohibit such arrangements.[70]

Accordingly, the commission recommends a series of laws to govern all surrogacy contracts. First, the suitability of the parties—both the surrogate and the hiring couple—to participate in the arrangement would be evaluated by the appropriate courts in advance of conception.[71] At its birth there would be provision for testing the infant to assure that it is indeed the offspring of the hiring father.[72] A surrogate mother who refuses to transfer custody of her infant would be compelled to do so by court order.[73] In order to "reveal any financial exploitation of a surrogate mother by the prospective social parents," all payments for surrogacy arrangements would have to receive prior court approval. The commissioning couple would be responsible even for a handicapped child (although if they do not accept custody of it, the Children's Aid Society would intervene).[74] In the event of a spontaneous abortion, the surrogacy contract "might provide for the reimbursement of any expenses advanced in anticipation of a birth."[75] And it is further recommended that the parties to the contract should come to an agreement about other matters such as arrangements for the future of the child if one of the hiring parents dies or if they cease to live together as a couple; the right of the surrogate to future information about or contact with the child; restrictions upon the surrogate's activities prior to and after conception; and prenatal diagnostic screening.[76]

In the register of births only the social parents, not the surrogate, would be listed as the child's parents; the social parents would be recognized as the parents of the child for all legal purposes, including inheritance.[77] A surrogacy arrangement that fails to comply with the regulations would be unenforceable,[78] and there would be financial penalties for persons who participate in it.[79] However, "social parents who acquire custody of children pursuant to unapproved surrogate motherhood arrangements should be allowed to utilize existing procedures to establish their parentage in law after the fact."[80] Furthermore "there may be place for private agencies to arrange surrogate motherhood agreements," subject to supervision by the Ministry of Community and Social Services.[81]

It is evident that the Ontario Law Reform Commission's approach to the legalization and regulation of surrogacy substantially discounts any moral questions about the well-being and autonomy of the women who resort to this arrangement. Moreover despite an avowed aim to "protect the best interests of the child" produced through surrogacy,[82] the recommendations appear primarily to serve the hiring couple, particularly the father.

Of course, in addition to the two alternatives of prohibiting surrogacy outright or lending it legitimacy through state regulation, there is a further policy option: surrogacy contracts could simply be rendered legally unenforceable. This is the substance of the recommendation of the Warnock Committee. Its chief reason is "that people should treat others as a means to their own ends, however desirable the consequences, must always be liable to moral objection. Such treatment of one person by another becomes positively exploitative when financial interests are involved."[83] It therefore recommends that legislation render criminal the creation or operation of agencies, both profit-making and nonprofit, for the recruitment of surrogates or the making of surrogacy arrangements, and render criminally liable the actions of professionals who knowingly participate in a surrogacy arrangement. However, "private persons", including the mothers themselves, who participate in such arrangements, would not be subject to criminal prosecution.[84]

Although I do not rely upon the Warnock Committee's moral justification for their position on surrogacy, I regard their policy recommendations as justified. Certainly it is important to avoid "blaming the victim"—the surrogate herself—by regarding her as the criminal in the arrangement.

Legal responsibility must be placed on those whose entry into the arrangement is genuinely voluntary: the hiring couple, particularly the father, and the professionals and mercenaries who arrange the agreement.

If these contracts were rendered unenforceable, so that legal rights and responsibilities for the child are not transferable to the hiring couple but remain with the surrogate, and the courts cannot compel transfer of the child or payment of the fee,[85] the potential reward for entering into such contracts would be substantially diminished. Moreover, such legislation would apprise professionals of their responsibilities and prevent them from profiting from the sale of reproductive services. Advertising of surrogacy services and the recruitment of women as surrogates should also be prohibited. And if, as some think is inevitable, some persons nevertheless attempt to set up and participate in surrogacy arrangements,[86] there could be penalties for the professionals involved. Actual custody of any child that is thereby produced should be determined by its own well-being and not by the desires and intentions of the hiring couple.

Above all, such an approach to policy about surrogate motherhood would avoid lending a spurious legitimacy and state sanction to arrangements that deny the authenticity of the women who appear to choose to participate in them. In the long run, of course, it would be necessary to revolutionize the social framework that makes surrogacy seem a reasonable and morally appropriate "choice" for women. Only within a context in which reproduction is no longer labor performed by women for the benefit of men, and in which standard assumptions about the value of children, fertility, and a genetic link with one's offspring are reassessed, can the social conditions that create the demand for surrogate motherhood disappear.

Notes

An earlier version of part of this chapter entitled "Surrogate Motherhood" will appear in the *Canadian Journal of Philosophy* (forthcoming 1987); the material is used here with permission.

1 John A. Robertson, "Surrogate Mothers: Not So Novel after All," *Hastings Center Report* 13 (October 1983): 32.

2 Andrea Dworkin, *Right-Wing Women* (New York: Perigee Books, 1983), p. 182.

3 The usual approach to moral questions about the practice of surrogate motherhood is simply to list the possible problems that might arise within a surrogate motherhood arrangement. For examples of this kind of approach, see Robert T. Francoeur, *Utopian Motherhood: New Trends in Human Reproduction* (Garden City, N.Y.: Doubleday, 1970), pp. 102–106; and Council for Science and Society, *Human Procreation: Ethical Aspects of the New Techniques* (Oxford: Oxford University Press, 1984), pp. 66–70.

4 There may also be moral questions to be raised in regard to cases of apparently entirely altruisitic surrogacy. Does such a woman freely choose to be a surrogate? Does she derive any real benefit from it? And can the woman for whom she bears the child fill her need for a child in some other way?

5 This is the term used by the Committee of Inquiry into Human Fertilisation and Embryology in their *A Question of Life: The Warnock Report on Human Fertilisation and Embryology*, introduction and conclusion by Mary Warnock (Oxford: Basil Blackwell, 1985), p. 42.

6 Michael D. Bayles, *Reproductive Ethics* (Englewood Cliffs, N.J.: Prentice-Hall, 1984), p. 22.

7 See also Robertson, "Surrogate Mothers," p. 67.

8 There are others—such as Herbert T. Krimmel's view that surrogate motherhood is immoral primarily because of the motivations of the persons involved and the effects on the children produced—which I shall not discuss here. See "The Case against Surrogate Parenting," *Hastings Center Report* 13, no. 5 (October 1983): 35–39. Compare *Report of the Committee of Inquiry into Human Fertilisation and Embryology*, p. 45.

9 Robertson, "Surrogate Mothers," p. 28.

10 Bayles also compares the issues surrounding surrogate motherhood to those in AID (p. 23). Compare Alan B. Rassaby, "Surrogate Motherhood: The Position and Problems of Substitutes," in *Test-Tube Babies: A Guide to Moral Questions, Present Techniques and Future Possibilities*, ed. William Waters and Peter Singer (Melbourne: Oxford University Press, 1982), p. 103; and Suzanne M. Patterson, "Parenthood by Proxy: Legal Implications of Surrogate Birth," 67 *Iowa Law Review* 385 (1982): 390–391.

11 Robertson, "Surrogate Mothers," p. 28.

12 Compare Rassaby, "Surrogate Motherhood," p. 104.

13 For example, white, not black: "Almost every adopting white couple wants a healthy white baby, and the great majority of young, pregnant, white American women do not give up their babies for adoption." Cynthia Gorney, "For Love and Money," *California Magazine* (October 1983): 91.

14 Gorney, "For Love and Money," p. 155.
15 Margaret Munro, "'Rent-a-Womb' Trade Thriving Across Canada-U.S. Border," *The Montreal Gazette* (January 21, 1985): D–11.
16 Robertson, "Surrogate Mothers," p. 29.
17 Bayles, *Reproductive Ethics*, p. 26; Compare Rassaby, "Surrogate Motherhood," p. 103.
18 The Committee of Inquiry into Human Fertilisation and Embryology also cites this claim as a possible justification for surrogacy: "Carrying mothers . . . have a perfect right to enter into such agreements if they so wish, just as they have a right to use their own bodies in other ways, according to their own decision" (p. 45). Compare Council for Science and Society, *Human Procreation*, p. 66.
19 Robertson, "Surrogate Mothers," p. 29.
20 Munro, "'Rent-a-Womb' Trade Thriving," p. D–11.
21 Robertson, "Surrogate Mothers," pp. 32–33.
22 Bayles, *Reproductive Ethics*, p. 25.
23 Rassaby, "Surrogate Motherhood," p. 103. Compare William A. W. Walters and Peter Singer, "Conclusions—And Costs," in Walters and Singer, *Test-Tube Babies*, p. 138.
24 Robertson, "Surrogate Mothers," p. 32.
25 Ibid., p. 33.
26 Ibid., p. 34.
27 The analogy is not perfect. For example, prostitution appears to be *defined* by the presence of payment for (sexual) services, whereas the surrogacy arrangement—given the possibility of altruistic surrogacy—is not. I owe this observation to Jocelyn Downie.
28 Advertisements for prospective surrogates usually make it clear that applicants should be white. And the commissioning couple may "try again" for a boy if the pregnancy produces a female infant (Mary Kay Blakely, "Surrogate Mothers: For Whom Are They Working?" *Ms.* 11, no. 9 (March 1983): 18, 20). She could also have added class considerations. See Rosalind Pollack Petchesky, "Reproductive Freedom: 'Beyond A Woman's Right to Choose'," in *Women: Sex and Sexuality*, ed. Catharine R. Stimpson and Ethel Spector Person (Chicago: University of Chicago Press, 1980), pp. 92–116, for a discussion of class distinctions in the availability of other reproductive services, such as abortion and contraception.
29 Susan Ince states: "The need to continue patriarchal lineage, to make certain the child has the sperm and name of the buyer, is primary." "Inside the Surrogate Industry," in *Test-Tube Women: What Future for Motherhood?* ed. Rita Arditti, Renate Duelli Klein, and Shelley Minden (London: Pandora Press, 1984), p. 112.
30 Blakely, "Surrogate Mothers," p. 20.
31 Susan E. Nash, letter, *Ms.* 11, no. 12 (June 1983): 5.
32 Some confirmation for this appears in a recent brief discussion of

the motives of surrogate mothers. One woman wrote, "When I first heard of surrogate motherhood, my immediate thoughts were, 'Goodness, I could do that! I can't cook, I can't play tennis or do tapestries, but I am good at being pregnant and giving birth." Quoted in Carl Wood and Ann Westmore, *Test-Tube Conception* (Englewood Cliffs, N.J.: Prentice-Hall, 1984); p. 113.

33 Ince, "Inside the Surrogate Industry," p. 102.

34 Ibid., p. 112.

35 Gena Corea, *The Mother Machine: Reproductive Technologies from Artificial Insemination to Artificial Wombs* (New York: Harper & Row, 1985), p. 220.

36 Letter, *Hastings Center Report* 14 (June 1984): 43.

37 Dworkin, *Right-Wing Women*, p. 181.

38 Ibid., p. 187.

39 Ibid., p. 188.

40 Munro, "'Rent-a-Womb' Trade Thriving," p. D–11.

41 Elizabeth W. Moen, "What Does 'Control over Our Bodies' Really Mean?" *International Journal of Women's Studies* 2 (March/April 1979): 133.

42 I owe these ideas to Ted Worth.

43 Ince, "Inside the Surrogate Industry," p. 107.

44 This point of view is taken most noticeably by Bernard D. Hirsch in "Parenthood by Proxy," *Journal of the American Medical Association* 249 (22/29 April 1983): 2251–2252. See also Iwan Davies, who claims without offering any evidence that "the United States experience shows that some surrogates will take the money and then run to an abortionist." "Contracts to Bear Children," *Journal of Medical Ethics* 11 (June 1985): 63.

45 This seems to be reflected in surrogate motherhood contracts: the contract signed by the mother is often longer, and specifies more limitations, than that signed by the commissioning couple. "Nothing Left to Chance in 'Rent-A-Womb' Agreements," *The Toronto Star* (January 13, 1985). See also Theresa M. Mady, "Surrogate Mothers: The Legal Issues," *American Journal of Law and Medicine* 7 (Fall 1981): 351.

46 "One wonders . . . whether fair compensation for being a surrogate mother should be determined simply by market forces," William J. Winslade, "Surrogate Mothers: Private Right or Public Wrong?" *Journal of Medical Ethics* 7 (1981): 154.

47 Canadian Advisory Council on the Status of Women, *Prostitution in Canada* (Ottawa, March 1984): 84.

48 Philip J. Parker, "Motivation of Surrogate Mothers: Initial Findings," *American Journal of Psychiatry* 140, no. 1 (January 1983): 117.

49 Ibid., p. 118.

50 Ibid. In an interview with Gena Corea, Parker admitted that some women explicitly denied any connection between their previous abortion and their present desire to be a surrogate; nevertheless he

insisted that there was a connection (Corea, *The Mother Machine*, p. 239).

51 Compare the findings of Darrell D. Franks, "Psychiatric Evaluation of Women in a Surrogate Mother Program," *American Journal of Psychiatry* 138, no. 10 (October 1981): 1378–1379.

52 Philip J. Parker, "Surrogate Motherhood: The Interaction of Litigation, Legislation and Psychiatry," *International Journal of Law and Psychiatry* 5 (1982): 352.

53 Dworkin, *Right-Wing Women*, p. 182.

54 Ibid., p. 180; compare *Prostitution in Canada*, p. 69; Ince, "Inside the Surrogate Industry," p. 99; and Martha Hall, "Rights and the Problem of Surrogate Parenting," *The Philosophical Quarterly* 35 (October 1985): 423. I am grateful to J. E. Bickenbach for drawing the latter to my attention.

55 Corea, *The Mother Machine*, p. 233.

56 Barbara Katz Rothman, "The Meanings of Choice in Reproductive Technology," in Walters and Singer, *Test-Tube Women*, pp. 23–33. Compare Kathleen McDonnell, *Not an Easy Choice: A Feminist Re-Examines Abortion* (Toronto: The Women's Press, 1984), pp. 71–72, and Petchesky, "Reproductive Freedom," p. 101, on abortion as a "free" choice.

57 An unlimited advocacy of the further development of reproductive choice would seem to imply, for example, an unlimited "right" to choose the sex of one's children through selective abortion. See McDonnell, *Not an Easy Choice*, p. 79, and Petchesky, "Reproductive Freedom," p. 100.

58 John Robertson, "John Robertson Replies," *Hastings Center Report* 14, no. 3 (June 1984): 43.

59 Franks, "Psychiatric Evaluation of Women," p. 1379.

60 Hall, "Rights and the Problem of Surrogate Parenting," p. 423.

61 Lorraine Code, "Commentary on 'Surrogate Motherhood' by Christine Overall," (unpublished paper, Kingston, February 1985), p. 3.

62 Code, "Commentary on 'Surrogate Motherhood,'" p. 4. The effects on the woman of giving up her child—effects that are at least hinted at by women who change their minds about surrendering the baby once it is born—must be counted as part of the exploitation and psychological costs to the mother of the practice of surrogate motherhood.

63 Compare Mary O'Brien, *The Politics of Reproduction* (Boston: Routledge & Kegan Paul, 1981), pp. 58–59, on alienation and appropriation.

64 Parker, "Motivation of Surrogate Mothers," p. 118.

65 O'Brien, *The Politics of Reproduction*, p. 38.

66 Dworkin, *Right-Wing Women*, p. 182.

67 Munro, "'Rent-a-Womb' Trade Thriving," p. D–11.

68 It is worth noting that this loss of individuality will be exacerbated in the near future when embryo transfers become routine and the

surrogate mother contributes only her reproductive services to the production of the baby.

69 Ontario Law Reform Commission, *Report on Artificial Reproduction and Related Matters* II (Toronto: Ministry of the Attorney General, 1985), p. 232.
70 Ibid., p. 231.
71 Ibid., pp. 234–242.
72 Ibid., pp. 245–246.
73 Ibid., p. 252. In this recommendation there is no recognition of the possible psychological costs to the woman of being forced to surrender her child.
74 Ibid., p. 255.
75 Ibid., p. 257.
76 Ibid., p. 259.
77 Ibid., pp. 260–261.
78 Ibid., pp. 267–268.
79 Ibid., pp. 268–270.
80 Ibid., p. 271.
81 Ibid., p. 262.
82 Ibid., p. 260. But note that the commission lists as a *problem* in existing laws governing child custody, when they are used for the purposes of surrogacy, the fact that the status of the child is determined "according to the best interests of that child, which may not necessarily conform to the intentions expressed in the agreement between the adult parties" (p. 220).
83 The Committee of Inquiry into Human Fertilisation and Embryology, *A Question of Life*, p. 46.
84 Ibid., p. 47.
85 Compare Ontario Law Reform Commission, p. 220.
86 E.g., Iwan Davies, "Contracts to Bear Children," *Journal of Medical Ethics* 11 (June 1985): 62.

7 Infertility, Children, and Artificial Reproduction

What is artificial reproduction? In one sense, all of human reproduction may be said to be artificial, insofar as it is socially structured—for example, by definitions of who is permitted to have sexual relations with whom.[1] As Joseph Fletcher remarks,

> Any attempt to set up an antinomy between natural and biologic reproduction, one the one hand, and artificial or designed reproduction, on the other, is absurd. The real difference is between accidental or random reproduction and rationally willed or chosen reproduction.[2]

However, it seems useful to define artificial reproduction more narrowly as reproduction that takes place without sexual intercourse.[3] In this sense, then, the term includes such processes as artificial insemination by donor (AID) and in vitro fertilization (IVF).

The *overt* justification usually cited for the development of technologies of artificial reproduction is the treatment of the rapidly growing incidence of infertility. In other words, the reason most often offered for proceeding with the exploration of new forms of artificial reproduction is that it is necessary in order to respond to the needs and desires of those who are otherwise unable to become parents.

This justification is explicitly cited by Robert Edwards, who was the co-creator (in an important sense to be discussed later), with Patrick Steptoe, of the first in vitro baby. Edwards's argument is worth quoting in full, for it mentions many significant ideas about infertility:

I had no doubts about the morals and ethics of our work. I accepted the right of our patients to found their family, to have their own children. I was blessed, Patrick [Steptoe] was blessed, some of our most stringent critics were fortunate to have children of their own. It was a priceless asset. It was a gift, the relationship of parent to a developing human being. And almost within our grasp was the possibility of passing on this gift to couples who had suffered years of childlessness and frustration—who longed for children, who had indeed, as often as not, repeatedly undergone unsuccessful gynaecological operations in order to try to have children. The Declaration of Human Rights made by the United Nations includes the right to establish a family.

There were those who argued, "Why should infertility be cured when orphans and other children are desperately awaiting adoption?" Adoption is an excellent institution, but the argument implies the withdrawal of medical care from one group of people in order to solve the problems of another. Besides, many of our patients had tried to adopt children repeatedly and without success. Moreover, adoption is likely to become more difficult in the future with the spread of contraception and abortion, and with the rapid decline in the number of unwanted children. More and more couples would surely be pleading for the right to have their own child.[4]

In order to assess the general function and value of the new reproductive technology, it is important to explore some usually unexamined beliefs about infertility. In this chapter, therefore, I discuss the meaning of infertility and its connection with social attitudes toward children. In referring to the meaning of infertility I have in mind not merely how the term "infertility" is defined but also the broader personal and social significance it is accorded and the values that are associated with it. What is actually said about infertility by those who have been involved in studying and treating it (biomedical scientists and sociologists, mostly male and not discernibly feminist in their views) provides some revealing insights into the rationale for the use of reproductive technology.

Surprisingly, however, the topic of infertility has received relatively little attention from philosophers and feminists.[5] This lacuna is both significant and unfortunate, for how infertility is understood and evaluated matters. It has implications for whether and how the condition is treated, for attitudes toward children, and for social expectations of women. In other words, the concept of infertility is both normative and prescriptive. It assumes certain standards for normal social attitudes and interactions, and it implies appropriate behavior, especially for medical personnel and the women and men who are their patients. Questions about the meaning of infertility are implicitly ethical questions, and the answers to them provided by feminists, nonfeminists, and antifeminists are very different.

Infertility

According to physician Melvin L. Taymor, infertility

> implies a lack of fertility, or the inability to produce children. However, because fertility requires a variable time factor for establishment and development of the zygote, the definition for the term infertility, unlike other medical conditions, has a time element in its definition. The definition proposed by the American Fertility Society, and one that is widely accepted, states, "a marriage is to be considered barren or infertile when pregnancy has not occurred after a year of coitus without contraception."[6]

Infertility is generally perceived to be a problem. A widely quoted figure is that at least 15 percent of all married couples in North America and Europe are infertile.[7] In a couple, infertility can be a condition of the male, of the female, or of both.[8] It has been convincingly argued that a substantial amount of infertility is iatrogenic; that is, it results from other types of medical intervention: for example, contraceptives like the intrauterine device and depo-provera, the drug diethylstilbestrol given during fetal development,[9] and inadequate treatment of sexually transmitted diseases.[10]

The existence of iatrogenic infertility is a particularly bitter irony in light of the fact that infertility is regarded by many commentators as being something like a disease, the victims of which are in need of help from medical science. Is the language of disease and cure appropriate to the understanding of infertility? This question is raised by scientist Leon R. Kass, who asks whether the production of a baby by IVF could be accurately described as therapeutic treatment of infertility. He says, "Is the inability to conceive a disease, or merely the symptom of a disease? Can a couple have a disease?"[11]

To answer these questions, it is necessary to make use of the concepts of impairment and handicap. Infertility in women or men is an impairment—that is, a loss of function of (some aspects of) the procreative capacities. Infertility in a woman, for example, is the "inability to conceive after a year or more of sexual relations without contraception."[12] Thus the infertile woman lacks the capacity to conceive; her infertility is a departure from normal functioning, at least of females during their reproductive years. This impairment may be produced by intentional behavior (as in the case of surgical sterilization), by accidental circumstances (as in the case of environmental causes), or by disease (as in the case of endometriosis in women).

But furthermore, in some cases a disability may be interpreted or treated as being a handicap:

> Handicap is a value-judgment applied by others to an impaired-disabled person on the basis of failure to perform customary social roles; and of course, this value-judgment the impaired person may apply to him- or herself, or vigorously reject.[13]

Norms or values are built into the concept of handicap; a handicap is in part a socially constructed entity. Like a disease, it is defined as bad and undesirable, usually by both society at large and by the individual affected, and its presence ordinarily implies a need for treatment of some kind.[14]

The question whether infertility should be discussed in the

language of disease and cure becomes, then, a question of whether infertility is, or should be treated as, a handicap. What would be crucial in seeing it as a handicap is a negative perception of the impairment and its symptoms. But in the case of infertility, it is not clear that this is necessarily always present.

How infertility is evaluated depends upon the total context of the person's life. Sociologist Sally MacIntyre has discussed what she calls "two versions of reality": the social equations of marriage with motherhood and nonmarriage with nonmotherhood.[15] She points out that in married women, "pregnancy and childbearing are normal and desirable, and conversely a desire not to have children is aberrant and in need of explanation," whereas for single women, "pregnancy and childbearing are abnormal and undesirable and conversely the desire to have a baby is aberrant, selfish, and in need of explanation."[16] This suggests that infertility is more likely to be generally perceived as a problem for a married woman than for a single woman. This is confirmed by Leon Kass, for example, who argues:

> To consider it [infertility] a disease leads to a focus on an individual; yet infertility is a condition that is located in a marriage, in a union of two individuals. . . . More is at stake here than the correction of linguistic imprecisions; the error in language is not innocuous. To consider infertility solely in terms of the traditional medical model of disease . . . can only help to undermine, both in thought and in practice, the bond between childbearing and the convenant of marriage.[17]

Hence Kass seeks to *define* infertility as a condition that is located in a marriage, on the grounds that "even though the abnormality responsible is usually found in only one of the partners, their interaction is required to make the problem manifest."[18] Kass does not seem to recognize that the condition could also be "made manifest" in individuals who are not married or not heterosexual in orientation. Thus according to this view, an unmarried woman who is unable to conceive is not seen as having a problem; accordingly, she might not be viewed as having a handicap.

There may be, then, variations in the social perception of

infertility, depending upon the circumstances of the infertile individual. But there may also be variations in how the individuals themselves perceive their condition, and these are probably more important. Some writers refer to infertility as a state of being "involuntarily childless,"[19] and that gives us a clue. To be involuntarily childless is not the same as being infertile; childlessness and infertility are distinct, although of course related, problems. A woman might be fertile in the sense of having a capacity to conceive, and indeed to carry a pregnancy to term, and yet be involuntarily childless: she wants children but does not have them, perhaps because she is unable to find a sexual partner whom she wants to be the father of her child, or because she is prevented from engaging in sexual activity, as might happen in a restrictive culture, or because she is refused access to reproductive technology such as AID, or even because she has had a child and it was taken from her against her will. Nevertheless, the word "involuntary" is crucial here. Whether an infertile woman is married or single, she might regard her infertility as an advantage to be envied by those who must struggle with dangerous and/or inefficient methods of birth control, rather than as a disadvantage. If so, then her infertility in this case is not a handicap. Infertility is less likely to be a handicap if the person affected does not perceive it as a problem.

But of course the predominant perceptions of infertility, both on the part of individuals and on a general social level, are negative. And there can be no denying the anguish felt by many who are infertile.[20] One woman says, "It hurts to be infertile, to make the conscious and informed choice to have children and then to be denied."[21] Another describes her experience of infertility:

> There was a huge amount of disbelief, an unbelievable amount of grief. I was, as I later found out, clinically depressed. I did seek out psychiatric help for that problem. I was a wreck. I cried all the time. I felt guilty, lots of guilt. I felt that I had stuck my husband with this woman that would never give him the children that we had wanted. I felt asexual, I felt very neutered by the whole experience. I felt I had lost all my womanness. It was a pretty dreadful time.[22]

Since infertility is most often perceived as a problem, it is necessary to ask why it is perceived in this way, and what type of problem it is perceived to be. For some or perhaps even most women, part of the problem of infertility lies in the loss of powerful and fulfilling life experiences: the experiences of pregnancy and birth, which are valuable for their own sake. In their book on the experience of infertility, Naomi Pfeffer and Anne Woollett refer to women who "regret missing out on the experience of pregnancy and childbirth." For some, they suggest, "the key to their desire for motherhood lies in being pregnant and giving birth." Moreover, since pregnancy and childbirth are given a great deal of attention, it is not easy "to forego such an emotionally powerful experience and give up being at the centre of so much attention." Infertility is a problem in part because being pregnant and giving birth can become elements of personal history that give shape to one's subsequent life, contribute to one's understanding of oneself, and create bonds with the rest of the community, especially with other women.[23] Men, too, who are infertile themselves or whose wives are infertile forego the experiences of living with a pregnant woman, being aware of the gradual development of the embryo/fetus, feeling its movements within the woman's body, and anticipating and sharing in the birth of the child.

But the poignancy of infertility also lies in the fact that one will not have a child of one's own. What is the significance of this loss?

In Western society there is a curious ambivalence about children and parenthood. On the one hand, some writers have documented the pronatalist pressures on women to reproduce.[24] Even now, for married women, motherhood can scarcely be regarded as wholly an option. Those who are well educated are expected to be superwomen, to do it all: to pursue the brilliant and fulfilling career (or at least the demanding and exhausting job) as well as to bear and raise the requisite one or two children.[25] For women with less training and education there are few rewarding alternatives to motherhood. We may wonder, then, to what degree motherhood can be a real option; as Elisabeth Badinter says in her discussion of "mother love," "How are we to know if the legitimate desire for motherhood is not at least partly a mad response to social constraints (penalization of the unmarried and nonmothers, social recognition for the woman in her role as mother)?"[26] The desire for children is at least partly a manufactured one, a social creation.

The other side of the coin, however, is the general attitude toward children themselves.[27] Some have gone so far as to suggest that North Americans fear and hate children.[28] This may be an exaggeration; what is more certain is that this culture is in many ways not adapted for children, does not readily accommodate their special needs and interests, and deems it inappropriate for them to mingle too freely with adults. In our time, as in Queen Victoria's, children are all right in their place (and that place is a limited one); they may be seen but not heard—and perhaps even seen as little as possible, as is suggested by places like some apartment buildings and restaurants that prohibit the presence of children. Prejudice against children is socially acceptable. No one is shocked by a person who states that he does not like children, thereby condemning an entire class of people, whereas most today would be shocked by one who claimed that he did not like blacks, or even that he did not like women.

In spite of (or possibly because of) these conflicting attitudes toward children and toward women's reproductive capacities, in the Western world today the child is something like a commodity in the Marxist sense—that is, a product with an exchange value, a luxury item one might or might not want or need. Just as human gametes and the embryo/fetus are becoming commodities, so also are the products of procreation, human offspring. While apparently being valued for their own sake, children are regarded as a type of consumer good. According to prevailing social attitudes, one should acquire children only if one can afford them and they can be accommodated in one's "lifestyle."[29] Such a view is given its most cynical expression by Janet Radcliffe Richards, a philosopher who identifies herself as a "sceptical feminist" but whose views are most often antifeminist or nonfeminist at best. She says,

If we think of children as valued possessions of their parents (which is unquestionably one thing they are) . . . we should say that one couple chooses to spend its income on children, while [an]other chooses to spend its money on holidays or cars or antique furniture.[30]

If children are like a commodity, then, for those who desire that commodity (regardless of how the desire has been acquired), it will be important to obtain one's *own*. It is not enough to appreciate and enjoy children for their own sake; one must come to *possess* one or more. This idea is apparent in the passage by Robert Edwards quoted earlier. He refers to couples who had suffered "years of childlessness." He is not suggesting, of course, that these people did not have a chance to know children, to interact with them, work or play with them, teach them, or care for them. For all we know, the couples involved could include child care workers or teachers, pediatricians or playground supervisors, librarians or camp counselors, all of whom have ample opportunity to be with children. Or they might be none of these. The point is that it does not matter. What is important is not being with children but having them, having one's own. Children are a type of property.[31] The infertile, says Edwards, have been deprived of "the right to have their own children." To be infertile and childless is clearly not necessarily to have no chance to be with children, but rather to miss the chance to own a child.

If infertility is often (regarded as) a handicap, how should it be treated? Leon Kass points out that infertility "is not life threatening or crippling, nor does it lead to detectable bodily damage."[32] In this respect infertility does not much resemble diseases such as arthritis or cancer. Moreover the use of artificial reproductive technologies, Kass claims, is treatment only in a peculiar way.

> Providing a child by artificial means to a woman with blocked oviducts is not treatment (as surgical reconstruction of her oviducts would be). She remains as infertile as before. What is being "treated" is her desire—a perfectly normal and unobjectionable desire—to bear a child.[33]

The argument is echoed by William J. Daniel:

When medical or biological skill is turned from curing dys-function to enhancing function, its justification is less simple and obvious. . . . It is not wrong *per se* for the medical profession to go beyond the curing of disease to the "satis-faction of desires," but it must be acknowledged that it is going beyond its basic therapeutic role.[34]

Bernard M. Dickens states,

Inability to conceive may not necessarily render a woman unhealthy . . . and her disappointment in hopes of childbearing may be no different from that of an unpart-nered or lesbian woman. If pregnancy and childrearing serve emotional rather than physical or strictly psychiatric needs, in achieving a sense of fulfilment, self-esteem, and enhancement of human experience, they may appear cosmetic rather than therapeutic.[35]

Similarly, Snowden, Mitchell, and Snowden say that the pro-vision of AID to enable a healthy woman to become pregnant meets "a social need rather than a medical one."[36]

According to this view, then, the treatment of infertility by means of artificial reproduction cannot be justified in the same way that the treatment of diseases is justified. For aside from the fact that infertility is alleged to be not as damaging as other medical conditions, its treatment by means of artificial repro-duction does not cure the infertility. Instead, the treatment is a response to a need or desire in the patient.

Not surprisingly, this approach to the justification of treatment for infertility is vehemently rejected by Robert Edwards.[37] He argues,

a great many medical advances depend on the replacement of a deficient compound or an organ. Examples include insulin, false teeth, and spectacles: the clinical condition itself remains, but treatment modifies its expression. . . . In fact, most medical treatment, particularly of constitutional or genetic disorders, is similarly symptomatic in nature. Exactly the same argument applies to the cure of infertility:

should patients have their desired children, the treatment would have achieved its purpose.[38]

Ultimately, then, Edwards agrees with Kass and others like him that in providing artificial reproduction for the infertile, what is treated is not the underlying cause of the infertility— no cure, in any literal sense, is effected—but rather what is treated is the desire for a child. However, Edwards disagrees with Kass in regarding such treatment as entirely justified.

What seems significant to me, however, is precisely how this "desire for a child" is understood and responded to. The nature of the recommended treatment of infertility reveals much about the meaning that infertility is thought to have. Both Kass and Edwards misconstrue the real issue between them; as Samuel Gorovitz rightly says,

> We cannot oppose clinical IVF on the ground that it is the treatment of a desire, nor can we simply approve it on the ground, as Edwards suggests, that the treatment of desires is medically legitimate. Rather, we must face directly the question of whether the desire to have a child of one's own, when IVF is the only available means, is one of the desires that warrants medical response.[39]

It has been argued that it is absurd for the "public purse" to pay for psychiatric treatment of the depression and anxiety caused by infertility but not to pay for the treatment of infertility itself.[40] Yet to acknowledge the suffering of the infertile does not immediately imply how they should be helped. Like many others who write about infertility, Kass and Edwards, both nonfeminist in outlook, fail to consider adequately the social origins of the desire for a child, the nature of the desire, and the many ways in which it might be responded to.

For example, in the first quotation at the beginning of this chapter Edwards rejects adoption as the solution to the problem of infertility.[41] His objection to it is ostensibly pragmatic; as he says elsewhere,

> Adoption can satisfy the desires of some infertile couples, but fewer children are available today for adoption because

of contraception, abortion, and the widespread acceptance of the illegitimate child, and many infertile couples have been unsuccessful in their attempts to adopt.[42]

But it would probably be more accurate to say that fewer children *of the right sort* are available for adoption. Healthy white babies are in short supply; older nonwhite children and children with various handicaps are available, but of course in a commodity-oriented society these children are often not considered desirable, even (or especially), by the infertile.[43]

Similarly, in considering the argument that infertile couples should adopt children rather than resort to IVF, another writer remarks,

> there seems to be little ethical about thrusting children who are strangers upon couples who want the chance to create biological children of their own. . . . [I]t may not be in the children's best interest to be adopted by the infertile couples who would prefer in vitro fertilization.[44]

Indeed, this claim receives some confirmation from a study of couples using AID. Such couples almost universally regarded adoption as a second best alternative to the use of AID. According to the authors, "The couples' primary need was to have a baby of their own and they saw adoption almost entirely as a means of alleviating their childlessness and meeting their own needs, rather than as a means of meeting the needs of a child."[45] In general, artificial reproduction is not designed to serve the best interests of the children it produces.

Thus in their acknowledgment of the undoubted emotional pain suffered by the infertile, these writers do not seriously contemplate other forms of contact and interaction with children as "therapy" for the desire on the part of the infertile for a child. Instead what is thought important in the "therapy" is to give the infertile their *own* child,[46] and for that purpose the technologies of artificial reproduction are indispensable.

I have already pointed out the general idea of ownership associated with parenting children. Now we see that in the treatment of infertility, ownership is specifically interpreted in terms of genetic ties with the child.[47] Emphasis is placed on the idea that the child must be the product of one's own ovum or sperm. This emphasis is conveyed, for example, in Patrick Steptoe's discussion of the case of Lesley Brown, who became the mother of the first in vitro baby. Steptoe remarks that Lesley Brown's husband, John, was fertile; in fact, he had a fourteen-year-old daughter by a previous marriage. However, Mrs. Brown's fallopian tubes were blocked; so if she were not helped by means of the IVF technique, "it was evident that Mrs. Brown would be childless forever."[48] Through this dramatic statement, Steptoe reveals his assumption that her husband's child could not possibly be regarded as becoming Lesley Brown's child.[49]

Similarly, surrogate mother broker Noel P. Keane lists as one important reason that surrogate motherhood will "surpass adoption methods for infertile couples" the fact that use of a surrogate means that "there is a genetic connection between at least one parent and the baby."[50] R. Snowden and G. D. Mitchell say that a perceived advantage of AID over adoption is that the former appears to "reduce uncertainty about the genetic background of the child to be introduced into the family"; the AID baby is "less of a risk" than an adopted one.[51] Finally, Robert Edwards argues that IVF has what he calls an "ethical advantage" over the use of AID for couples whose infertility results from a low sperm count in the male. This latter claim is extraordinary, considering the pain involved to the woman in the process of recovering eggs for IVF and the expenses incurred by the whole procedure.[52] But according to Edwards, the big advantage of IVF is that it enables the man with a low sperm count to "conceive his own child" and thus not to have to become, as AID requires, a father to a baby "unrelated" to him (although it would be his wife's child).[53] The perceived hardship of such a prospect is confirmed by Barbara Eck Menning, who says that in using AID, "many women feel that it is 'selfish' to achieve a pregnancy without the genetic contribution of the husband."[54]

Indeed, the need for a genetic connection with one's offspring seems to be of particular importance to men. Its special significance is suggested by the fact that for couples who are carriers of genetic diseases, the solution to their problem is seen to lie in the use of prenatal diagnosis and abortion rather than in providing AID for the women. "The problem is maintaining genetic paternity. If that were not so, then artificial insemination with noncarrier donor sperm would be readily accepted."[55] Rothman suggests that for men, parenthood means genetic parenthood; so many fathers do so little child-rearing that social fatherhood is less significant to men. "What makes a man really the father of a child in this society, if not genetics?"[56] Moreover, in their study of couples using AID, Snowden, Mitchell, and Snowden remark,

> A few of the more thoughtful husbands were disturbed that the continuity of reproduction, of ancestor and descendant, had for them come to an end. Husband 902 said, "My major hang-up really was based on this rather metaphysical notion of genetic immortality. What depressed me most of all, and overwhelmed me mentally, was this idea that at this point my genetic channel stops. That's the end. And that was the most chilling thing that I had to take on board." Children were seen as continuity with the future, a way in which parents would live on in future generations, almost as a means of achieving immortality. These husbands saw the finality of their infertility as a kind of genetic death, and AID did not cure this problem for them.[57]

Hence according to many male writers, the real value of technologies of artificial reproduction is that they enable infertile individuals to have their own children in this genetic sense, and this tends to be regarded as the only valid treatment of the desire for a child. If the child is like a commodity, then its exchange value, for infertile parents, is represented by the cost of its production by means of the relevant reproductive technology. IVF enables both husband and wife to have their "own" child.[58] AID enables a woman to have her "own" child, although it is not her husband's "own." When a woman gestates an embryo that is the in vitro product of the fertilization of a donor egg by her husband's sperm, the child produced is not her "own" child, although it is her husband's; his paternity is left intact.[59] And the practice of hiring a surrogate mother, who is artifically inseminated, enables a man to buy his "own" child, although it is not his wife's "own." By making it possible for the infertile to have their own offspring, reproductive technology appears to reinforce one aspect—the genetic link—of the parent-child relationship,[60] while simultaneously promoting the severence of that link for other individuals such as surrogate mothers and those who provide reproductive products.

Thus just as infertility is in part thought to be a problem because it entails missing the chance to own a child, so also the treatment for infertility is thought to require giving the patient her or his own child, in the genetic sense, and any other form of therapeutic response is regarded as second best. The assumption here seems to be that the genetic link with a child is paramount, equaling or even surpassing the value of what has been called "social parenthood,"[61] that is, the rearing of the child. The meaning of infertility is such that the importance of social interaction with children and responsibility for children who are not one's own is overridden by notions of possession and genetic relatedness. What is important is not merely to have a child but to have a child who is one's own.

The Genetic Link

The question is whether these values are justified; that is, whether the genetic link with one's offspring is really so important as to justify the use of more invasive forms of artificial reproduction instead of using those that are less invasive, or resorting to adoption—or even, more radically, finding other ways in which to be with and relate to young human beings.

It is notable, first of all, that almost all of the writers so far quoted who stress the alleged importance of a genetic link with one's offspring are male; hence this emphasis may reflect men's experience with reproduction more than women's. It is worth considering whether a biological link with children is as important to women as it seems to be to men. With the development of the technology of egg donation, there may very soon be oppportunities to evaluate, separately from the experience of pregnancy and birth, the meaning for women of genetic ties to their children. In fact, women who seek to use reproductive technology may do so not so much because they want their children to be *theirs* but because they desire the experiences of pregnancy and childbirth, the joy of caring for a newborn, the control over the child's early life experiences, and the continuity and wholeness of raising a person who grew within one's own body. From their point of view, then, the problem with adoption—especially the adoption of an older child—is not necessarily that the child is not genetically related but, rather, that these experiences must be foregone.

Nevertheless, it cannot be concluded that a genetic link with one's offspring has, or should have, no moral value at all. The problem is to determine just what significance it should be accorded.

Unlike many other male writers, Michael D. Bayles argues that the desire for genetic offspring is probably irrational, or at least not as important as often thought.[62] The desire to beget, he says, could be fulfilled merely by donating gametes that are successfully used in conception by other persons. No further experience beyond the making of the donation is involved in such an action, which for women would likely occur under anesthesia. "Moreover, one must discount the satisfaction one would have from knowing that one's donation was used, because that satisfaction is dependent on one's having the desire. That is, one would not have the satisfaction unless one had the desire, so it cannot be a reason for having the desire." A desire is irrational if its fulfillment fails to contribute to one's life experiences; hence since begetting offers minimal or even no experience, the desire to beget for its own sake is irrational.[63]

In defending these claims Bayles distinguishes between begetting, bearing, and rearing children, distinctions that the new reproductive technologies certainly encourage and enable us to make. But his comparable distinction of the *desire* to beget from the *desire* to bear or to rear children is more problematic. The three may be theoretically distinguishable but they are not, in all probability, distinct in people who want to have children. It is unlikely that many people merely want to beget for its own sake; to have one's own genetic offspring is

desired, as Bayles himself recognizes, because it "might contribute to the value of bearing and rearing."[64] In other words,
women usually want not only to beget but to bear and rear
their own offspring.

Nevertheless, says Bayles, there is no real difference
between bearing and rearing one's own child or that of another
person, except perhaps the thought that the child is or is not
one's own. "Many people have raised children in the
erroneous belief that the children were their genetic offspring
when they were not, so the only difference seems to be the
belief."[65] And adoptive parents enjoy child-rearing as much as
do natural parents. It is merely cultural conditioning that
makes people believe that rearing their own genetic offspring
is preferable.

While it is easy to be sympathetic to what appears to be
Bayles's purpose—namely to cast serious doubt on the
insistence upon the necessity of a genetic link to one's
offspring—his grounds for doing so are open to question. If
Bayles were correct, then women giving birth in a hospital
could just as well (provided there were no administrative
hurdles) take home any baby born around that time, and it
would make no difference to either the women's or the babies'
lives. But it is surely false to claim that there is no experiential
difference, other than the belief itself, between bearing and
rearing one's own child or that of another person.

The undeniable fact that some people have incorrectly
believed that a child whom they were raising was genetically
related to them does not show that there is no other experiential difference between bearing and raising one's own child
and bearing and raising someone else's. There are logically
four possible child-rearing situations: raising a genetically
related child whom one believes to be genetically related to
oneself (still probably the most usual case); raising a child who
is not genetically related but whom one mistakenly believes to
be genetically related to oneself (the situation cited by Bayles);
raising a genetically related child whom one mistakenly
believes not to be genetically related to oneself (presumably a
rare situation but imaginable if a husband, say, were unjustifiably suspicious of his wife's sexual activities); and raising a
child who is not genetically related and whom one believes not

to be genetically related to oneself (the usual case with an adopted child). It cannot be supposed that the only difference between these four scenarios is simply the belief, whether true or false, held in each case by the parent.

According to Bayles, to place importance upon the genetic relationship is to imply "that adoptive parents cannot have as valuable experiences of child rearing as natural parents, which seems false."[66] But to say that rearing a child not genetically related is *not the same as* rearing a child who is does not imply that raising adoptive children is a less valuable experience. It is simply a different experience.[67] And this is at least suggested by those parents who choose both to have their own genetic offspring and to adopt others, a practice that suggests that they find value in both types of child-rearing.

In rearing one's genetically related offspring, very real experiences are involved in discerning and appreciating the similarities between oneself and one's children. A parent can also enjoy witnessing her own parents' talents or personality emerging in her children. There is a sense of continuity and history created by the genetic tie.

Bayles, however, has an answer to this. It is quite likely, he says, because of its combined genetic inheritance, that one's "own" offspring will be very different from oneself. No personal immortality is achieved through offspring; "each individual is unique . . . ; no one is the incarnation of someone else."[68] But what he fails to recognize is that this very fact contributes to the joys of rearing one's own children. It is true that one can achieve no real immortality in one's children; nevertheless in them one can see the similarities to oneself and one's own family and to the child's other parent and that family. The child's special individuality arises partly from the ways in which she both continues some of the characteristics of her parents and grandparents and yet is quite different from any of them.

Bayles denies this. "As a subclass of the desire to have genetic offspring, the desire to have genetic offspring with a specific person is also irrational."[69] Not only does it make no difference whether a child is genetically related to oneself; it also makes no difference whether a child is related to one's partner. But an example can illustrate the falsehood of this view. Suppose a woman who desires to have a child with her partner of many years is unable to conceive. Such a woman could, of course, attempt to resolve "her" infertility problem by a variety of means: artificial insemination by donor, self-insemination with sperm provided by a cooperative male friend, or sexual intercourse with a man other than her husband.[70] Although steps such as these are certainly empowering for the woman involved, Bayles is wrong to assert that it should not make any difference to the woman who the biological father of her child is.

In order to see this, suppose now that before the woman is able to make use of any of these alternative means for achieving pregnancy, she falls victim to rape by a stranger and becomes pregnant as a result. We should hardly expect her to feel grateful that she is now going to have a baby and indifferent as to who that baby is. She *might* be very happy to be pregnant at long last, but it is just as likely that she would not be. The context makes a difference; and part of the context is the identity of the fetus and the identity of its biological father. In addition to the fact that the fetus is the product of a violent act, what is important is that it is neither the much-loved result of sexual activity with a man whom she has chosen nor the outcome of deliberate insemination, but is instead the fetus of a stranger for whom she feels repugnance. Surely not wanting that fetus—in fact, wanting it aborted—is not irrational on the woman's part.[71]

Nevertheless, despite the apparent inadequacies in Bayles's argument, the doubts that animate him—doubts about the reasonableness of the desire to beget for its own sake—are important. Although his claims fail to do justice to the varying experiences of rearing children, they serve to raise questions about the significance of the desire to have one's own offspring in the genetic sense. Bayles is correct to insist that such a desire is socially constructed. Its power appears to depend upon social conditions; for example, as will be argued shortly, the availability of reproductive technology such as IVF contributes to the strength of the desire.

On the one hand, then, a genetic link to one's children may be of genuine importance, and it may affect the experience of nurturing those children. In this respect the desires of infertile women are comprehensible and reasonable. On the other hand, it is essential not to overvalue the genetic link—that is, to endow it with almost exclusive significance—exclusive of all the other positive aspects of child-rearing and enjoying the company of children. Nor should the emphasis on a genetic link be confused with the desire of many women to experience pregnancy and childbirth and to care for a child who is under her care from its earliest beginnings. A child is not valuable just insofar as she is genetically related to oneself, and an adopted daughter or son is not a second-best substitute for the real thing. Moreover, contrary to some arguments, surrogate motherhood is not more morally reprehensible in those cases (the majority) in which the surrogate supplies the ovum as well as her gestational services.[72] Finally, the human importance of a genetic link to one's offspring does not, by itself, in any way provide an unanswerable justification for the use of artificial reproduction. For not only are there other beneficial ways of responding to the desire for children, but also there are additional facts about the treatment of infertility by means of artificial reproduction that render it of questionable value for women.

Reproductive Control

Artificial reproduction may enable the infertile woman to have her "own" child; but what also deserves emphasis is that it is a doctor or scientist, almost always male, who in an important sense "gives" it to her, and this fact serves to reinforce some of the prevailing meanings of infertility.[73] Infertility specialists and reproductive technologists appear strongly motivated to arrogate women's reproductive capacities.

This use of technology represents a powerful version of what Mary O'Brien refers to as the male appropriation of women's reproductive power: "Women are willfully alienated by men from their own reproductive labour power."[74] Artificial reproduction typically involves the taking over of two hitherto exclusively female "moments" (to use O'Brien's term) in the reproductive process—that is, ovulation and conception—and the outright negation of the shared reproductive moment—copulation.[75] By virtue of these processes men like Edwards and Steptoe become the "creators" of babies like Louise Brown. In regard to this appropriation Germaine Greer remarks,

> The surgeon's motivation for devoting time and concentrated energy to defeating sterility is not simply a desire for fame and money; the satisfaction in causing a woman to bear is much more profound than can be supplied by either. It is the most seductive extension of his regard for his own power to father. . . . The successful fertility specialist is the technological version of the polygynous patriarch.[76]

Some evidence for the accuracy of Greer's description lies in the words of a male gynecologist who treats infertility in women. He states that his patients are not always "aware of the impact [of infertility] on their *physician's* psyche."

> Nobody likes month after month of failure; it's not good for anyone's ego. If the nurse says to me that Mrs. X is on the phone to talk to me and she is one of my long-standing nonsuccesses, I realize immediately that she's calling to tell me she got her period again. . . . Sometimes I get so upset that my reaction is: "I don't want to talk to her; you talk to her." It may take me a day or two to get myself together enough to call her, console her, and set up next month's program.[77]

In a similar vein, Leon Kass describes reproductive technology as meaning that "some *men* [*sic*] may be destined to play God, to recreate other *men* in their own image."[78] He adds that the power of reproductive technology "rests only metaphorically with humankind; it rests in fact with particular *men*—geneticists, embryologists, obstetricians."[79] Through the use of reproductive technology these men "who extract eggs, culture them, transfer embryos, surgically birth babies, or control the dials on the artificial womb will have a more continuous reproductive experience than men have ever before had."[80]

The production of Louise Brown by Edwards and Steptoe is a marvellous example of male control, by means of artificial reproduction, of the reproductive process in infertile women and men. Edwards has been described as an "egg snatcher"[81] because of his use of human ovarian tissue and eggs in the development of in vitro techniques—apparently without the knowledge or consent of the women from whom they were removed in the course of gynecological surgery. His partner, Patrick Steptoe, controlled the process of production of Louise Brown by, for example, deliberately choosing to withhold from her parents throughout the pregnancy his knowledge of her sex, knowledge acquired through amniocentesis four months before her birth. He also chose not to forewarn, or permit the mother to forewarn, the baby's father of the impending cesarean delivery. Alerting him only at the last minute, Steptoe then delivered the baby surgically while the mother was totally anesthetized. The earliest photographs of the baby are revealing: Lesley and John Brown, her genetic and social parents, are nowhere in sight; the baby is shown with Steptoe and Edwards, the two men who created her, and Jean Purdy, the woman who assisted them.[82]

It appears that the treatment of infertility by means of artificial reproductive technologies contributes to and reinforces a role of passive, uninvolved quiescence particularly on the part of the female patients. For them the treatment of infertility means that producing a child is not something one does but something that is done to one. A woman is a baby-producing machine, and an infertile woman is a machine that does not work properly and needs to be assisted. In this context, then, the meaning of infertility is that it is a failing, an inadequacy, and the specialists are the "technological fixers" who will save women from their own nonfunctional bodies by giving them the longed-for product, a baby.[83] As Hilary Rose and Jalna Hanmer point out, the work of IVF specialists such as Edwards and Steptoe "is explicitly designed to enable women, otherwise barren, to fulfill their biological destiny. . . . [T]heir work, using the language of helping women, is in fact deeply conservative in terms of preserving the woman's role."[84]

The technologies themselves may be said to sustain the very needs for them. Barbara Katz Rothman writes,

All of the new treatments for infertility have also created a new burden for the infertile—the burden of not trying hard enough. . . . If there is always one more doctor to try, one more treatment around, then the social role of infertility will always be seen in some sense as chosen: they chose to give up. Did taking away the inevitability of their infertility and substituting the "choice" of giving up truly increase their choice and their control?[85]

The development of artificial reproduction to treat infertility reinforces the feelings of failure and helplessness associated with the condition. It may in fact exacerbate what has been called "the moral pressure to have children."[86]

The development of procedures such as IVF can help a very few fortunate individuals with specific types of infertility and can satisfy some women's deep desires for the experiences of pregnancy, birth, and caring for a newborn. But the context in which the technology is provided and promoted also encourages us to interpret the desire for those experiences as merely a desire for genetically related offspring, and to see the infertile as persons who are handicapped and in dire need of help. Moreover, instead of assisting those whose infertility cannot be overcome to adjust to and accept the fact that they do not have children[87]—or, better still, instead of encouraging all of us to feel concern and responsibility for all children[88]—it drives home the idea that an individual is not complete, not a real woman or a real man, without her or his "own" genetically related child, and that childless persons should explore every possible means of obtaining one.

The discussion in this chapter has shown that the meaning of infertility in the context of the justification of artificial reproduction is closely related to certain attitudes toward children and parenting. Despite the many questions I have raised about the social responses to infertility, I do not claim that all current ideas about infertility and the special treatments it is accorded by means of artificial reproduction must be abandoned entirely. My point is just that they should be seen for what they are. Having become aware of the significance of infertility we can then consider whether alternative perceptions of and responses to it might be more appropriate.

I can agree with William J. Daniel that an individual infertile woman might not be much helped by this. As he says, "Her need is real enough to her, and the object of it, surely, is a good one: the having of a baby."[89] It is impossible to condemn the truly human desire to love and care for a young human being; such a desire is as valid as the human desire to work, to learn or to play. But in the long run the well-being not only of those who are infertile but also of children themselves, and of all those who care for and about them, may best be promoted through a reexamination of the beliefs and values that create and sustain that need for a baby.

Notes

An earlier version of part of this chapter, entitled "Artificial Reproduction and the Meaning of Infertility," appeared in *Queen's Quarterly* 92 (Autumn 1985): 482–488. The material is used here with the permission of the journal.

1 R. Snowden, G. D. Mitchell, and E. M. Snowden, *Artificial Reproduction: A Social Investigation* (London: George Allen & Unwin, 1983), p. 3; Jenny Teichman, *Illegitimacy: A Philosophical Examination* (Oxford: Basil Blackwell, 1982), p. 5.

2 Joseph Fletcher, *Humanhood: Essays in Biomedical Ethics* (Buffalo: Prometheus Books, 1979), p. 88.

3 Snowden et al., *Artificial Reproduction*, p. 5.

4 Robert Edwards and Patrick Steptoe, *A Matter of Life: The Story of a Medical Breakthrough* (London: Hutchinson, 1980), pp. 101–102.

5 For example, in Michael D. Bayles, *Reproductive Ethics* (Englewood Cliffs, N.J.: Prentice-Hall, 1984); Rita Arditti, Renate Duelli Klein, and Shelley Minden, eds., *Test-Tube Women: What Future for Motherhood?* (London: Pandora Press, 1984); William A. W. Walters and Peter Singer, eds., *Test-Tube Babies: A Guide to Moral Questions, Present Techniques and Future Possibilities* (Melbourne: Oxford University Press, 1982); Helen B. Holmes, Betty B. Hoskins, and Michael Gross, eds., *The Custom-Made Child? Women-Centered Perspectives* (Clifton, N.J.: Humana Press, 1981).

6 Melvin L. Taymor, *Infertility* (New York: Grune & Stratton, 1978), p. 10.

7 Gina Bari Kolata, "Early Warnings and Latest Cures for Infertility," *Ms.* (May 1979): 85; Alison Hearn, "Infertility: A Choice

Denied," *News/Nouvelles: Journal of Planned Parenthood Federation of Canada* 4 (September 1983): 8; Paul J. Keller, "Introduction," in *Female Infertility*, ed. Paul J. Keller (New York: Karger, 1978), p. 1; Boston Women's Health Book Collective, *The New Our Bodies, Ourselves*, 3rd ed. (New York: Simon and Schuster, 1984), p. 420.

8 Taymor, *Infertility*, pp. 6, 11. See *The New Our Bodies, Ourselves*, pp. 421–452, for a discussion of the causes of infertility.

9 Merle J. Berger and Donald J. Goldstein, "Infertility Related to Exposure to DES In Utero: Reproductive Problems in the Female," in *Infertility: Medical, Emotional and Social Considerations*, ed. Miriam D. Mazor and Harriet F. Simons (New York: Human Sciences Press, 1984), pp. 157–168.

10 Adele Clark, "Subtle Forms of Sterilization Abuse: A Reproductive Rights Analysis," in Arditti et al., *Test-Tube Women*, pp. 199–200; Gena Corea, *The Mother Machine: Reproductive Technologies from Artificial Insemination to Artificial Wombs* (New York: Harper & Row, 1985), pp. 144–165.

11 Leon R. Kass, "Babies by Means of In Vitro Fertilization: Unethical Experiments on the Unborn?" *New England Journal of Medicine* 285 (18 November 1971): 1176.

12 *The New Our Bodies, Ourselves*, p. 419.

13 David Thomas, *The Experience of Handicap* (London: Methuen, 1982), p. 7.

14 Talcott Parsons, "Definitions of Health and Illness in the Light of American Values and Social Structure," in *Concepts of Health and Disease: Interdisciplinary Perspectives*, ed. Arthur L. Caplan et al. (Reading, Mass.: Addison-Wesley, 1981), p. 70.

15 Sally MacIntyre, "'Who Wants Babies?' The Social Construction of 'Instincts,'" in *Sexual Divisions and Society: Process and Change*, ed. Diana Leonard Barker and Sheila Allen (London: Tavistock, 1976), p. 159.

16 Ibid., pp. 159–160.

17 Kass, "Babies by Means of In Vitro Fertilization," pp. 1176–1177. Compare Leon R. Kass, "Making Babies—The New Biology and the 'Old' Morality," *The Public Interest* 26 (Winter 1972): 20.

18 Kass, "Babies by Means of In Vitro Fertilization," p. 1177.

19 Kolata, "Early Warnings," p. 85.

20 See Barbara Eck Menning, "The Psychology of Infertility," in *Infertility: Diagnosis and Management*, ed. James Aiman (New York: Springer-Verlag, 1984), pp. 17–29; Carolyn Coman, "Trying (and Trying and Trying) to Get Pregnant," *Ms.* (May 1983): 21–24; Germaine Greer, *Sex and Destiny: The Politics of Human Fertility* (London: Secker and Warburg, 1984), pp. 46–47; Taymor, *Infertility*, pp. 94–96; Edwards and Steptoe, *A Matter of Life*, p. 121; Isabel Bainbridge, "With Child in Mind: The Experience of a Potential IVF Mother," in Walters and Singer, *Test-Tube Babies*, pp. 119–127; Miriam D. Mazor, "Emotional Reactions to Infertility," in Mazor and Simons, *Infertility: Medical, Emotional and Social*

Considerations, pp. 23–25; Naomi Pfeffer and Anne Woollett, *The Experience of Infertility* (London: Virago Press, 1983).

21 Barbara [Eck] Menning, "In Defense of In Vitro Fertilization," in Holmes et al., *The Custom-Made Child?* p. 264; Compare Elizabeth Fuller, *Having Your First Baby after Thirty* (New York: Dodd, Mead, 1983).

22 Jill Eisen, "Drawing the Line: Reproductive Technology," transcript of CBC Ideas 17 and 24 March 1986, p. 1.

23 Pfeffer and Woollett, *The Experience of Infertility*, p. 127.

24 See Ellen Peck and Judith Senderowitz, eds., *Pronatalism: The Myth of Mom and Apple Pie* (New York: Thomas Y. Crowell, 1974); Corea, *The Mother Machine*, pp. 169–170; Martha E. Gimenez, "Feminism, Pronatalism and Motherhood," in *Mothering: Essays in Feminist Theory*, ed. Joyce Trebilcot (Totowa, N.J.: Rowman & Allanheld, 1983), pp. 287–314.

25 Gimenez, "Feminism, Pronatalism, and Motherhood," p. 308.

26 Elisabeth Badinter, *Mother Love: Myth and Reality* (New York: Macmillan, 1982), p. 316.

27 Greer, chap. 1, "A Child Is Born," in *Sex and Destiny*, pp. 1–30.

28 Letty Cottin Pogrebin, *Family Politics: Love and Power on an Intimate Frontier* (New York: McGraw-Hill, 1983), pp. 42 ff.

29 Clark, "Subtle Forms of Sterilization Abuse," p. 190; Barbara Katz Rothman, "The Products of Conception: The Social Context of Reproductive Choices," *Journal of Medical Ethics* 11 (1985): 188.

30 Janet Radcliffe Richards, *The Sceptical Feminist: A Philosophical Inquiry* (Harmondsworth: Penguin, 1980), p. 294; compare p. 295.

31 Barbara Katz Rothman, "How Science Is Redefining Parenthood," *Ms.* (July/August 1982): 158. See Janet Farrell Smith, "Parenting and Property" (in *Mothering*, pp. 199–212), for a discussion of the concept of children as property.

32 Kass, "Babies by Means of In Vitro Fertilization," p. 1176.

33 Ibid., p. 1177. Compare "Making Babies," p. 26, and Leon R. Kass, "'Making Babies' Revisited," *The Public Interest* 54 (Winter 1979): 54.

34 William J. Daniel, "Sexual Ethics in Relation to IVF and ET: The Fitting Use of Human Reproductive Power," in Walters and Singer, *Test-Tube Babies*, p. 72.

35 Bernard M. Dickens, "Reproduction Law and Medical Consent," *University of Toronto Law Journal* 35 (Summer 1985): 284.

36 Snowden et al., *Artificial Reproduction*, p. 160.

37 Edwards and Steptoe, *A Matter of Life*, p. 112; R[obert] G. Edwards, "The Current Clinical and Ethical Situation of Human Conception In Vitro," in *Developments in Human Reproduction and Their Eugenic, Ethical Implications*, ed. C. O. Carter (New York: Academic Press, 1983), pp. 91–92.

38 R[obert] G. Edwards, "Fertilization of Human Eggs in Vitro: Morals, Ethics and the Law," *Quarterly Review of Biology*, 50th Anniversary Special Issue (1976): 376. Compare Mary Warnock, *A*

Matter of Life: The Warnock Report on Human Fertilisation and Embryo-logy (Oxford: Basil Blackwell, 1985), p. 9.

39 Samuel Gorovitz, *Doctor's Dilemmas: Moral Conflict and Medical Care* (New York: Macmillan, 1982), p. 177.

40 Peter Singer and Deane Wells, *The Reproduction Revolution: New Ways of Making Babies* (Oxford: University of Oxford Press, 1984), p. 67; Warnock, *A Matter of Life*, p. 10.

41 For a less pessimistic view, see Robert H. Glass and Ronald J. Ericsson, *Getting Pregnant in the 1980s: New Advances in Infertility Treatment and Sex Preselection* (Berkeley: University of California Press, 1982), p. 7, and Pfeffer and Woollett, *The Experience of Infertility*, pp. 126–133.

42 Edwards, "Fertilization of Human Eggs in Vitro," p. 375.

43 Singer and Wells, *The Reproduction Revolution*, p. 59; R. Snowden and G. D. Mitchell, *The Artificial Family: A Consideration of Artificial Insemination by Donor* (London: Unwin Paperbacks, 1983), pp. 29, 34–35; Ontario Law Reform Commission, *Report on Human Artificial Reproduction and Related Matters* I (Toronto: Ministry of the Attorney General, 1985), pp. 15–16.

44 Lori B. Andrews, "Ethical Considerations in In Vitro Fertilization and Embryo Transfer, ed. Don P. Wolf and Martin M. Quigley (New York: Plenum Press, 1984), pp. 407–408. Compare Singer and Wells, *The Reproduction Revolution*, pp. 59, 61.

45 Snowden et al., *Artificial Reproduction*, p. 86.

46 Compare Dickens, "Reproduction Law and Medical Consent," p. 284.

47 Kass, " 'Making Babies' Revisited," p. 44.

48 Edwards and Steptoe, *A Matter of Life*, p. 142.

49 Gena Corea points out that a number of successful IVF mothers have already had children before the IVF procedure—often from a previous marriage. See *The Mother Machine*, pp. 145, 171.

50 Noel P. Keane, "Surrogate Motherhood: Past, Present and Future," in *Difficult Decisions in Medical Ethics*, ed. Doreen Ganos, Rachel E. Lipson, Gwynedd Warren, and Barbara J. Weil (New York: Alan R. Liss, 1983), p. 163.

51 Snowden and Mitchell, *The Artificial Family*, p. 30.

52 Corea, *The Mother Machine*, pp. 120–121.

53 Edwards, "The Current Clinical and Ethical Situation of Human Conception In Vitro," p. 95.

54 Menning, "The Psychology of Infertility," p. 24. Compare Snowden et al., *Artificial Reproduction*, p. 85.

55 Barbara Katz Rothman, *The Tentative Pregnancy: Prenatal Diagnosis and the Future of Motherhood* (New York: Viking/Penguin, 1986), p. 233. See also p. 234.

56 Rothman, *The Tentative Pregnancy*, p. 236.

57 Snowden et al., *Artificial Reproduction*, p. 135.

58 Glass and Ericsson, *Getting Pregnant in the 1980s*, p. 98.

59 Rothman, *The Tentative Pregnancy*, p. 237.

60 The Ontario Law Reform Commission appears to think that the mere fact that a parent is genetically related to a child makes the parent more familiar to it and, in contrast to adoption, supposedly eliminates the necessity of evaluating the parent's fitness to raise the child (*Report on Human Artificial Reproduction and Related Matters* II, p. 234).

61 Rothman, "How Science Is Redefining Parenthood," p. 154. Noel Keane gives the example of a fifty-nine-year-old man who wants to hire a surrogate so that he will be able to leave his estate to his "own," genetically related child, rather than leaving it to his less closely related nieces and nephews. See Noel Keane, "Surrogate Motherhood: Past, Present and Future," in Ganos et al., *Difficult Decisions in Medical Ethics*, p. 163.

62 Bayles, *Reproductive Ethics*, p. 129.

63 Ibid., p. 13.

64 Ibid.

65 Ibid.

66 Ibid.

67 See Louise Cannon Lazare, "The Adoptive Parents' Experience: A Personal Narrative," in *Infertility: Medical, Emotional and Social Considerations*, pp. 108–125; and Teichman, *Illegitimacy*, pp. 117–118.

68 Bayles, *Reproductive Ethics*, p. 14.

69 Ibid., p. 41.

70 See Barbara Katz Rothman, *Giving Birth: Alternatives in Childbirth* (Harmondsworth: Penguin, 1982), pp. 122–125.

71 It is significant that Bayles is willing to say that the desire of "some fully informed women" to bear for its own sake is not irrational (Bayles, *Reproductive Ethics*, p. 14). Such a claim could easily serve as the ideological prop for antiabortion or prosurrogacy arguments.

72 Herbert T. Krimmel, "The Case against Surrogate Parenting," *Hastings Center Report* 13 (October 1983): 35.

73 Kass, "Making Babies," p. 46.

74 Mary O'Brien, *The Politics of Reproduction* (London: Routledge & Kegan Paul, 1981), pp. 58–59.

75 Somer Brodribb, "Reproductive Technologies, Masculine Dominance and the Canadian State," Occasional Papers in Social Policy Analysis no. 5 (Toronto: Ontario Institute for Studies in Education, 1984), p. 2.

76 Greer, *Sex and Destiny*, p. 73.

77 Robert L. Madison, "Foreword," in *Having Your First Baby after Thirty*, p. x, my emphasis.

78 Kass, "Making Babies," p. 19, my emphasis.

79 Ibid., p. 45, my emphasis.

80 Corea, *The Mother Machine*, p. 290.

81 Genoveffa Corea, "Egg Snatchers," in Arditti et al., *Test-Tube Women*, pp. 41–42. Compare Corea, *The Mother Machine*,

pp. 101–104, and Kass, "Making Babies," pp. 30–32.

82 Edwards and Steptoe, *A Matter of Life*, pp. 163, 180, and facing p. 97.

83 Rothman, "How Science Is Redefining Parenthood," p. 158.

84 Hilary Rose and Jalna Hanmer, "Women's Liberation: Reproduction and the Technological Fix," in *Ideology of/in the Natural Sciences*, ed. Hilary Rose and Steven Rose (Cambridge, Mass.: Schenkman, 1980), p. 133.

85 Barbara Katz Rothman, "The Meaning of Choice in Reproductive Technology," in Arditti et al., *Test-Tube Women*, pp. 31–32.

86 Jeremy Laurance, "The Moral Pressure to Have Children," *New Society* 61 (5 August 1982): 216–218.

87 For a discussion of resolutions of feelings about infertility, see Menning, "The Psychology of Infertility," p. 21, and Barbara Eck Menning, "RESOLVE: Counseling and Support for Infertile Couples," in *Infertility: Medical, Emotional and Social Considerations*, pp. 53–60, and Pfeffer and Woollett, *The Experience of Infertility*, pp. 24, 137–147.

88 Pfeffer and Woollett, *The Experience of Infertility*, pp. 134–136, 143.

89 Daniel, "Sexual Ethics in Relation to IVF and ET," p. 73.

8 Reproductive Rights and Access to the Means of Reproduction

The examination in chapter 7 of the meaning of infertility showed that infertility is often perceived as a handicap requiring treatment. Do the infertile have a *right* to that treatment, particularly if it involves the use of artificial reproduction? The pursuit of an answer to that question requires attention to larger problems about the social structuring of human reproduction: problems concerning whether there is in general a right to reproduce or not to reproduce, and problems about how access to the various means of reproduction should be determined.

A Right to Reproduce? Or Not to Reproduce?

The belief in a right to reproduce, a belief that is perhaps not always clearly articulated by those who hold it, is not only evidenced in strong reluctance by courts and social agencies to remove children from their parents unless it is absolutely necessary, but is also apparent in the controversy that surrounds the enforced sterilization of the mentally retarded.[1] Some such belief also seems to be behind the views of those who attack state regulation of in vitro fertilization and surrogate motherhood,[2] and of those who defend a system of private adoption.[3]

Gena Corea records her suspicion that the use of the language of rights in connection with reproductive technology may be an attempt by antifeminist "reproductive engineers" to obscure "the impact of reproductive engineering on women as a class."[4] Such a language is withdrawn, she says, when it interferes with patriarchal control of women's reproduction;[5] and it is certainly not applied in other arguably more crucial contexts, such as equal protection under the law and equal pay for equal work.[6] Moreover, as Rosalind Pollack Petchesky points out, "Rights are by definition claims staked within a given order of things"; they fail to challenge the existing social structure, the social relations of production and reproduction.[7]

Nevertheless, the language of rights has also been adopted by some feminists. Responding to the practice of barring access to reproductive technology to lesbians and single heterosexual women, they have argued that there is a general right to reproduce possessed, if not by all human beings, then at least by all women. Somer Brodribb, for example, in her paper, "Reproductive Technologies, Masculine Dominance and the Canadian State," unfortunately seems to assume that there is a logical relationship between the right not to reproduce and the alleged right to reproduce, for she recommends, "Following the principle that any woman who wants a baby has a right to one, no one should have the obligation to bear a child."[8]

Now there is undoubtedly a sound basis for claims to a right of women *not* to reproduce, for this means the entitlement not to be compelled to bear children against one's will—forced reproductive labor, as it were—and it requires, at the least, access to contraception resources and abortion services.[9] Without them women are the victims, through biological "destiny," of a sort of reproductive slavery.

To say that women have a right not to reproduce is to say that there is no obligation to reproduce. Consider a case in which a man and woman marry with the express agreement that the woman will bear a child.[10] If the woman then refuses to have offspring, she will cause unhappiness and disappointment in her spouse. But as many critics have pointed out, the utilitarian concern for creating as much happiness in the world as possible, either in existing persons or in persons who will exist in the future, cannot be a sufficient justification for an obligation to produce a child who will have a pleasant life.[11]

There might be a case in which it would be very good of the woman to reproduce, just as there might be a case in which it would be very good of her to donate an organ to another, but in either case "it is something that cannot be legitimately required of her."[12] It cannot be said that any woman is morally obligated, against her present will, to procreate. The essential reason is that such an obligation would be a form of involuntary servitude:[13] it would involve an alienation of her body from the person herself.[14] She cannot have an obligation to donate the services of her body for the sake of another person's project, even if she previously entered into an agreement to do so.

Although there are ample grounds for defending a right not to reproduce, we should not assume that there is any ethical, political, or logical symmetry between that right and an alleged right to reproduce. Contrary to what some have claimed,[15] the right not to reproduce neither implies a right to reproduce nor follows from a right to reproduce.

Moreover, *if* there is a right to reproduce, then such a right must necessarily be limited in nature. For as Hugh LaFollette points out, "even if people had a right to have children, that right might also be limited in order to protect innocent people, in this case children."[16] Thus the alleged right is not unconditional but would have to be hedged with qualifications, just as people's other rights—to free speech, to drive, and so on—are not unconditional but are dependent on not causing harm and/or on possessing a certain level of competence.

Furthermore, the claim to a right to reproduce may be understood in either a strong or a weak sense. In its weak sense it would simply mean "the opportunity or liberty to decide when and how many children one will have"; it implies "an obligation on everyone or governments not to limit people's liberty to procreate."[17] Thus in the weak sense, the right to reproduce is the right not to be interfered with, or, in old-fashioned language, "the right to found a family" and to be protected from racist marriage laws, forced sterilization, and coercive birth control programs.[18] This seems to be the form of the right that is referred to in the Universal Declaration of Human Rights. According to Bernard M. Dickens, the Declaration does not . . . require any person, government, or other authority to offer services to assist the infertile to overcome their disability. Futher, it seems to refer to individuals' rights to use their own initiatives to have their own biological children, rather than to the right to donate sperm or ova to assist the infertile directly or indirectly to become responsible for rearing the biological children of others in their homes.[19]

A stronger sense of the right to reproduce would imply the entitlement to be given all necessary assistance to reproduce,[20] using any technique of reproduction. In this sense having children, it has been claimed by some, is a right to which one is entitled by virtue of behing human. "Because fertile married persons have the right to add children to the family, infertile married persons must have it as well: a legal distinction based on the natural lottery of physical equipment is not reasonable."[21] One is entitled to have offspring that are the product of one's own gametes, "to separate the genetic, gestational, or social components of reproduction and to recombine them in collaboration with others."[22]

One argument for the existence of such a right has been based upon an appeal to the concept of privacy,[23] which was one of the main grounds for the American Supreme Court's landmark 1973 abortion decision, *Roe* v. *Wade*. It has been argued that the legal "right of privacy to be free from governmental intrusion"[24] into decisions about childbearing entitles infertile couples—who could not otherwise have their own child—to the use of IVF and embryo transfer. Such a claim has also been made on behalf of a right of access to the services of a surrogate mother.[25] This reproductive privacy has been regarded as being analogous to the privacy to which people are entitled in regard to their sexual activities.[26]

But the concept of privacy may well be applicable in the case of abortion simply because it supports the right *not* to reproduce. Yet it cannot be assumed that the justification based on privacy of services supporting the right not to reproduce implies a justification of services supporting a right to reproduce.

To claim the right to reproduce in this stronger sense would

require the acceptance of certain implications about which
feminists should have serious reservations. Although this
right is sometimes explicated as a right not to be prevented
from gaining access to and using techniques for artificial reproduction,[27] it has even wider implications. It shifts the burden
of proof onto those who have moral doubts about the morality
of technologies such as IVF and practices such as surrogate
motherhood. For it suggests that a child is somehow owed to
each of us, as individuals or as members of a couple, and that it
is indefensible for society to fail to provide all possible means
for obtaining one. For example, it would seem to imply that
fertile men married to infertile women are entitled to the
services of surrogate mothers,[28] and that surrogate mothers
should be legally compelled to surrender their children after
birth. It also suggests that if a man offers his sperm to fertile
women and they all reject him, then his right to reproduce has
been violated.[29] It implies that any person who wants to do so
is entitled to adopt a child. It could be used as a basis for
requiring fertile people to donate gametes and embryos to
assist the infertile. And it might be used to found a claim to
certain kinds of children—for example, children of a desired
sex, appearance, or intelligence.

The strong version of the claim to a right to reproduce could
therefore contribute to the treatment of children as commodities and to the misappropriation of women's reproductive
capacities. Hence there is no "claim on society to provide
expensive technology to give me a family, any more than
society is obliged to find me a mate."[30] The fact that each of us
has a right not to reproduce, and perhaps also that no one has a
right to prevent another from reproducing, does not imply
that one has a right in the strong sense to reproduce—that is, a
right to be assisted to reproduce.

I would guess that the assumption made by feminists who
assert a right to reproduce in this latter strong sense is that
such a claim must be made in order to protect women against
unjustified discrimination in the provision of reproductive
services. They are concerned about the general disregard for
and ignorance of the experiences and needs of infertile
women[31] and about the possibility of state-imposed limitations on their access to treatment for their "disease." Such

limitations appear to be the price of sacrificing a right to reproduce in the strong sense. If appeal to such a *right* is abandoned, then we seem to be committed to holding that having children is a *privilege* that must be earned through the possession of certain personal, social, sexual, and/or financial characteristics. The provision of reproductive technology then appears to become a luxury service the access to which must be controlled by means of criteria used to screen potential candidates.[32]

Undoubtedly forms of screening for parenthood are occurring in many contexts in Western society. That is, one or more sets of criteria are employed to determine who will and who will not be permitted to become parents. This process of screening now occurs, most obviously, in the institution of adoption. But it is also a part of the determination of eligibility for access to reproductive technology such as in vitro fertilization, artificial insemination by donor, and surrogate parenting by means of embryo transfer. (Interestingly, criteria of eligibility for parenthood are apparently employed for some forms of reproductive technology and not for others. For example, "surgical repair of a woman's fallopian tubes is now undertaken . . . without physicians or others asking whether she is married, is suited for motherhood or, for instance, has a history of child abuse."[33])

In general, for most processes of artificial reproduction the criteria of eligibility include such characteristics as sexual orientation, marital status, and consent of the spouse. Because access to these processes is costly, economic status also has become, at least indirectly, a criterion of eligibility. Further criteria have also been used—for example, the number of existing offspring[34] and the absence of physical disabilities.

Can screening for parenthood in these ways be justified? To answer that question, it is first necessary to evaluate the reasons that have been offered so far to justify various forms of screening. Then, instead of laying claim to a right to reproduce in the strong sense, feminists can attack unjustified discrimination in access on its own grounds and attempt to understand the relevance of that discrimination to the patriarchal control of women. In the next sections I demonstrate this approach by concentrating in particular upon the ways in which sexuality and marital status have been used to determine access to artificial reproduction. Feminists need not be pushed into agreeing that the new reproductive technology is a privilege for the special few; access to the means of reproduction is neither a right in the strong sense nor a privilege to be defended by screening.

Sexuality and Access to Reproductive Technology

As some commentators never tire of pointing out, the various forms of modern reproductive technology permit the complete separation of reproduction from sex, a possibility that may be deliberately sought, as in the case of contraceptive use, or merely a by-product, as in some treatments of infertility.[35] More or less effective contraception permits heterosexual activity without the hazards of reproduction. But even more significantly, forms of artificial reproduction such as artificial insemination by donor and in vitro fertilization permit reproduction without the hazards of heterosexual activity.[36]

Not all of those who write about artificial reproduction have been convinced of its independence from the taint of sexuality. For example, in the recent past some concern was expressed (mostly by male commentators) that a woman who receives AID might by guilty of adultery,[37] on the ground that adultery is just any act that results in illegitimate conception.[38] But the expression of that worry appears to have subsided, and the consensus seems to be that these technologies constitute a modern-day form of the immaculate conception.[39]

Nevertheless the apparently growing technological separation of the biological processes of reproduction and sex should not dupe theorists into supposing that in the uses of artificial reproduction there are no important connections between attitudes toward sexuality and attitudes toward procreation, and between the practices that regulate both of them. In fact, the reproductive choices we make and are permitted to make still remain closely connected to attitudes toward sexuality and sexual expression. The social uses of reproductive technology thus have two apparently contradictory functions: while they disengage sexual activity from procreation in important respects, they simultaneously reconnect sexual expression with reproduction in ways that reinforce the patriarchal control of women's bodies.

Infertility is usually regarded as a handicap; there is a social stigma on the infertile. And since infertility may result from certain sexually transmitted diseases,[40] from the use of some contraceptives such as the intrauterine device, and from botched abortions, infertility may also be seen as a type of punishment justly administered to those who transgress accepted gender norms for sexual and reproductive activity— another case of blaming the victim.[41] For example, Leon R. Kass asks rhetorically "whether it makes sense for a Federally-funded baby to be the wage of aphrodisiac indiscretion"; he believes that government-funded IVF services and research unfairly "rescue" those whose "unrestricted sexual activity" during adolescence resulted in infertility.[42] Furthermore, a recent proposal has suggested that access to artificial reproduction be limited to those who are not "responsible" for their infertility (i.e., those whose infertility is caused by disease and not by elective sterilization[43]—which is sought, presumably, to permit more carefree sexual expression).

According to those who are in the business of developing or providing reproductive technology, its preferred use is for women who demonstrate certain limited forms of sexual activity. Ordinarily they must be heterosexual, but only within a marriage or a "stable" union.[44] For example, a sociological study of AID unequivocally recommends that "artificial reproduction should only take place where a couple responsible for nurturing the child are married."[45] Similarly, while not requiring that a couple be married, the Warnock Report explicitly assumes that a couple seeking access to reproductive technologies would inevitably be heterosexual.[46] Thus women who are independent of men as regards their living arrangements and/or their sexual activity are excluded from access to the technology, and this exclusion is held to be justified. This social use of reproductive technology both reinforces, at least indirectly, the connection of standard heterosexuality with reproduction and disengages other forms of sexual life expression from procreation.

The justification for the requirement that potential consumers of reproductive technology be heterosexual and married is usually couched in terms of concern for children or, more ambiguously, "the family."[47] Here is a representative example of such a justification, offered in some detail in a report by the British Council for Science and Society:

> In so far as the social norm clearly associates childbearing with family life and parents who are married, this practice [of providing AID for single women and lesbians] is abnormal. . . . AID to single women will increase the social problems of child-care and welfare, and the encouragement of lesbian families can be seen as a threat to normal family life, to say nothing of both instances failing to provide a nurturing father-figure. The imbalance of interests in these cases suggests that the practice should be discouraged.[48]

Notice first that this argument assumes, without offering corroboration, that there are *many* single and/or lesbian women who would seek access to methods of artificial reproduction such as AID, and that their sheer numbers would raise special concerns. Yet the existing evidence actually suggests that their numbers would be fairly small.[49] On the other hand, if their numbers are not small, it is necessary to consider whether the prospect really poses a serious ethical and social danger. The argument claims that providing artificial reproduction methods to single women would increase problems of "child-care and welfare."[50] But in fact there is no evidence that large numbers of very poor, indigent, unemployed women, who are struggling with the minimal conditions of personal survival, would necessarily seek the technologies of artificial reproduction. It might be speculated instead that it is more likely to be relatively secure, employed women who would want access to them. In either case, however, if large numbers of women do want to use the technologies, and problems of "child-care and welfare" were to arise, it is always open to the society in which they occur to provide better forms of socially assisted child care and medical care, and ultimately to change the social context that makes rearing children a severe economic problem for many women. It should not be assumed, on an a priori basis, that raising a child without a man must inevitably be a financial burden shouldered by the mother alone.

Second, the sincerity of the concern, in reports such as the one quoted, for a family for every child is called into question by their usually very negative evaluation of lesbian families. Although willing to refer to a lesbian couple as a family, the report quoted clearly does not regard it as a "normal" family. In a similar fashion, a case study of a lesbian couple seeking AID refers to lesbianism as a "problem" and a lesbian woman's desire for a child as a "dilemma." The reception of a gynecologist to their request for AID is described as follows: "He pointed to Jill's family life and Roman Catholic background, and stated that he did not consider their relationship a stable one in which children could be reared." (The relationship actually was of five years' duration at the time of the couple's request for AID.)[51]

Such a family may of course not be statistically normal (what family now is?), but the study fails to adduce any evidence for its abnormality in any other sense likely to affect the child's well-being, which is the purported concern. The only explicitly alleged problem that is cited in the report I first quoted is the absence of a "nurturing father-figure." It would be interesting to know what is meant here by nurturance and whether in this argument the kind of nurturance allegedly provided by "father-figures" is thought to be different from that provided by mothers. Certainly it appears implausible to suppose that all intact "normal" heterosexual families include a "nurturing father-figure." As a philosopher and not a social scientist I must be modest in the claims I make on this issue. But I would at least say that if by "nurturance" what is meant is concern and care for, involvement in, and cherishing of the developing life of the child, then the degree of nurturance provided by many fathers is not immediately evident. While it can scarcely be disputed that children need and deserve nurturance, it is not clear that "father-figures" always provide it.

Therefore it is simply begging the question to claim, as some have, that "as a general rule it is better for children to be born into a two-parent family, with both father and mother."[52] The mere presence of a father in the home seems unlikely to protect a child from abuse, and in fact somewhat more fathers than mothers are responsible for physical violence directed against their children.[53] But in any case, even if it were conceded that most fathers are exceedingly nurturant, there is no a priori reason to suppose that such nurturance cannot also be provided by women, and it is unjust to rule out, in an a priori fashion, the possibility that individual women and female couples can provide it.

The reference in the report to "father-figures" also suggests a concern about the importance to children of specifically male role models. In the case study cited earlier, one participant remarks,

> I do not think we can abandon the concept that a child normally develops out of an experience in which there is a male person, usually father, and a female person, usually mother, and that it is the interaction in that situation which does a great deal to fit him to eventual masculinity and her to feminity [sic].[54]

And the authors of a book on AID remark, "once a stable marriage relationship is no longer a necessary precondition for AID then the social and psychological implications of babies being born in households where no males are present, have seriously to be considered."[55]

But the concern expressed in the examples just cited begs the question that feminists would raise: Is the type of modeling provided by most males essential in child-rearing? Is there some component of child-rearing that only males are capable of providing? One writer claims, "there are advantages to having both masculine and feminine influences on the child's development regardless of the child's sex."[56] But such a claim appears to assume without question both that models of traditional masculinity and traditional femininity are valuable in child-rearing, and that only parents of the "appropriate" sex can and do provide them. Those who point to the alleged necessity of male role models are taking for granted, without argument, that masculine behavior, attitudes, beliefs, and values ought to influence our children.

Yet another reason often cited for depriving women of

access to reproductive technology on the basis of their sexuality is that the resultant offspring will suffer ostracism because of their mother's sexual orientation. For example, "Given the structure of our society, it is easier and more practical to bring children into the traditional two-parent family . . . [because] the child is less likely to be subjected to denigration by his peers."[57] One critic goes even farther and suggests that lesbians who seek AID are "us[ing] the child as a catalyst to change society."[58] He argues that one should not deliberately put a child, who must in any case face the usual problems involved in growing up, in an environment in which extra problems, pertaining to the deviance of his parent, will be encountered.

Corea has pointed out that the notion that "every child should have a father" is an underlying value both in standard child custody proceedings and in the defense of the provision of artificial insemination.[59] This approach, of course, uses the sheer existence of the status quo to defend the status quo and then accuses those who wish to depart from the status quo of exploiting their children as a means to revolutionary change. This tactic is particularly unjust because it ignores the feminist criticism that the problems lesbian mothers face stem not from their inherent nature as women but from the heterosexist social context. A feminist analysis does not assume the moral validity and historical invariance of existing social arrangements.

One writer on artificial reproduction remarks that "it makes a difference whether artificial insemination [or IVF] is refused to a person simply because of that person's sexual orientation or because of the potential harm of that sexual orientation to the child who will be born. The latter is probably justifiable, the former may not be."[60] But what is also unjustifiable is to assume that there is inevitably a connection between the sexual orientation of the parent and potential harm to the offspring. If a woman changes her sexual orientation from heterosexual to lesbian, does she thereby become a worse parent? Would a child born to a lesbian parent be better off if it had never existed? Fitness to parent cannot and should not be evaluated on an a priori basis; at most it can be assessed only from individual case to individual case.

The Council for Science and Society sees the encouragement of lesbian families as "a threat to normal family life," but it has just been argued that the offspring themselves have not been shown to be endangered. Who or what, then, is threatened by providing access to reproductive technology to those who are not in suitable heterosexual relationships?

An answer is provided, perhaps inadvertently, by Michael D. Bayles. Although Bayles believes that the "ethical prohibition of AID for lesbians cannot be justified," he nevertheless cites a possible concern about providing AID for lesbians: "One might fear that their sexual preference would be transferred to their children. Female children might grow up hating males, and male children might grow up sexually confused."[61] Indeed, if one accepts the view that the family "provides the social milieu where children are brought up from infancy to *accept* the fundamental values of society,"[62] then one might well fear that lesbian and single heterosexual parents would fail to inculcate fundamental patriarchal values. For, as sociologists Snowden, Mitchell, and Snowden remark, a child born outside marriage is "at risk" in the sense that "there is no framework within which social control can be exercised over the responsibilities society has for the child."[63] As a result, one physician questions "very seriously whether it is ever psychologically advantageous to entrust the upbringing of a baby or toddler to any woman who is not currently loved by a man for her own sake."[64]

Bayles does not endorse this sort of concern, but merely to describe it is to lend it some dignity. It assumes that same-sex sexual orientation is like a contagious disease that can be transmitted to one's offspring. The fear of contagion appears also to animate an anonymous representative of the British Royal College of Obstetricians and Gynecologists, who has been quoted as observing, "if donors knew their sperm was going to lesbians, one can't help wondering if they would think this was a good thing."[65] Hence it has also been suggested that one legal question about AID is whether it can be said "that the donor has donated his sperm for use for any purpose including inseminating a lesbian or single woman, or, even if there are not express and hence binding restrictions on use, would some usually be implied by the law and would these include a term that the sperm was only to be used to impregnate heterosexual and married women."[66]

Significantly, however, heterosexual orientation is not in a similar fashion typically regarded as contagious in the way that a disease is, since its transmission is not regarded as a threat. In any case, the notion of transmission at work here seems flawed, since it would fail to explain why so many homosexual individuals had heterosexual parents. Why did these parents fail to transmit their sexual orientation to their offspring?[67]

But the major concern here is more wide-ranging than just a concern about producing homosexual offspring: "Female children might grow up hating males, and male children might grow up sexually confused." This worry is echoed in the case study on providing AID to lesbian couples. One participant asks, "Could the demand for AID from Lesbians arise from protest against hostile irrational attitudes against them as a group, to make up for a feeling that society is unjust to them, or as a basic hostility to men or to the traditional male pattern of society?"[68] The idea that the sexual orientation of lesbians is the result of, or is reducible to, hating men is not a new one. It is almost impossible for nonfeminists and antifeminists to see lesbianism as a positive choice for women.[69] But as one lesbian feminist explains, "I don't want to be a lesbian by default, the women I care for, I love because they are women, not because they are not men."[70]

The real threat, then, posed by lesbians and single heterosexual women who seek access to artificial reproduction is perceived as being directed against men, against the patriarchal control of women's sexual and reproductive capacities. One book, for example, while obliquely recognizing that some women may want "liberation from male dominance," describes the independent woman as wanting to "manage her own affairs single-mindedly without having to consider another's interests" and to "raise a child of her own in the way she wishes."[71] For such a woman, the book warns, "AID could become a means of dispensing with marriage and the inconvenience of a husband and, of course, with a father too."[72] The perceived selfishness of this woman would also extend to her children: she is envisaged as entrusting her child to "nursemaids, nursery schools, housekeepers, and so forth."[73] The implication, surely, is that such a woman is too selfish to consider other individuals', particularly men's, interests because she regards such individuals as "inconvenient." Hence one writer asks, rhetorically, "Can the American social conscience accept a woman who feels she has no need of a husband or a father for her children?"[74]

As Mary O'Brien so wisely points out, paternity is not a natural relationship to a child but is rather a socially created right to appropriate a child.[75] Marilyn Frye suggests that "the progress of patriarchy *is* the progress toward male control of reproduction, starting with possession of wives and continuing through the invention of obstetrics and the technology of extrauterine gestation. Giving up that control would be giving up patriarchy."[76] A careful evaluation of their arguments shows that in the final analysis nonfeminists and antifeminists are troubled about giving lesbians and single heterosexual women access to reproductive technology because they fear that it would result in a partial disruption of patriarchal power, disruption brought about by the severance of marriage and motherhood and the separation from men of certain women and their reproductive capacities.[77] They therefore anticipate and seek to prevent this possibility by reinforcing the connection between heterosexuality and procreation and by condemning the forgoing of any links between artificial reproduction and other expressions of sexuality.

As I suggested earlier, feminists need not oppose this point of view by claiming a general right to reproduce; it is necessary instead to reveal the poor reasoning used in its defense and to expose its antifeminist and misogynist roots. A member of the Ontario Law Reform Commission claims, "To accept and encourage resort to the artificial reproduction technologies by persons outside a stable marital union under the existing legal regime, in my view, is to sow the seeds of injustice, hardship, and social disorder."[78] Perhaps what he vaguely recognizes is that the assumption of reproductive control by independent women could indeed have revolutionary implications.

The Requirement of Spousal Consent

The deep and abiding concern for the maintenance of male control over women's sexual and reproductive capacities helps to explain the existence of another significant criterion for women's access to reproductive technology: the consent of cerain men—in particular, for married women, the consent of their husbands. It is a criterion applied in a manner that appears superficially to be inconsistent but that can be wholly explained by reference to the requirements of patriarchal dominance.

First, it is notable that a woman seeking AID from a physician or clinic ordinarily has no choice as to who her donor will be; the physician himself makes the selection.[79] Moreover if she is married, she is usually required to have her husband's consent for the procedure.[80] While subscribing to the principle that "the freedom of the individual to take what steps he [*sic*] could [in being treated for infertility or establishing a family] had to be respected,"[81] the Warnock Report explicitly recommends "that the formal consent in writing by both partners should, as a matter of good practice, always be obtained before AID treatment begins."[82] (Notice that if and when a single woman is provided with AID she has the advantage over a married woman in this one respect.) This requirement exists in spite of the fact that the problem of infertility is not hers but his; he permits her recourse to AID, although she could just as well have become pregnant through sexual intercourse with another man.[83]

The requirement of consent in the case of AID appears to be related to the practice in some hospitals of requiring (often contrary to the law) the spouse's permission when a woman seeks sterilization or abortion.[84] A case has also been reported in which a hospital would not perform surgery to clear a woman's blocked fallopian tubes without her husband's consent.[85]

In contrast to the requirements for AID, a man who hires a surrogate mother ordinarily has the opportunity to choose the woman who will receive his sperm, and since the contract is between only him and the surrogate, in effect he does not have to have his wife's consent to the procedure. But the surrogate mother herself, if she is married, is often expected to have her husband's consent to her being a surrogate, whereas the wife of a sperm donor in most jurisdictions does not have to consent to his being a donor.[86]

Some writers have been seriously concerned about the implications of a woman's obtaining AID without the knowledge or consent of her husband. For example, one writer asks whether AID children conceived without the knowledge or "permission" of the mother's husband should be regarded as legitimate. "This would place obligations of a legal nature upon the mother's husband which he might well consider unjust", she remarks. And she adds, "No doubt AID could prove grounds for divorce if it were adjudged to be 'unreasonable behaviour.'"[87] Another writer suggests that such a wife might be sued for divorce on the grounds of mental cruelty.[88]

Michael D. Bayles claims that "the consent of a woman's husband to AID is ethically required if he is to have parental responsibilities";[89] as a matter of policy, he suggests, "husbands of women artificially inseminated by donors should have parental rights and responsibilities if and only if they gave consent for AID."[90] These claims derive from what he calls a "fundamental ethical principle": "No one should involuntarily have parental responsibilities," a principle that "prohibits completely involuntary parenthood."

But while it can easily be agreed that a married woman who undergoes AID or other forms of reproductive technology should so inform her husband and obtain his agreement, it is difficult to concur that his consent is a *necessary* condition for his wife's receiving AID, or that if she fails to obtain that consent he should have no moral or legal responsibility for the resulting child. Of course, in accordance with what was said earlier about reproductive rights, the woman does not in general have a right to be given access to AID—that is, a right to some man's sperm. Yet it seems morally unjustified to grant another person the power to deny AID to her, and that is precisely what the requirement of spousal consent does. This requirement implicitly assents to the myth of the conniving female who uses her reproductive capacities to manipulate a male; to compensate, it accords great respect to the male's reproductive choice. But it utterly denies any recognition of the woman's reproductive freedom; such an approach confirms rather than challenges existing social inequities between women and men.

It might be argued that if women are entitled to choice about whether or not they reproduce, men are as well. Yet it is false to assume that men and women are in exactly the same situation in this respect. For a woman, reproductive freedom means the right not to be forced to give her body for the production of another human being, the entitlement to bodily integrity and self-determination. For a man there can be almost no equivalent of the forced reproductive labor to which women have been subject.

Nevertheless a concern for male reproductive autonomy might carry some weight were it not for the fact that failure to consent is linked to exemption from responsibility for the resulting offspring. For this condition disregards the welfare of the potential child, whose interests are probably not well served by providing a moral and legal escape hatch from responsibilities for the person who should be his social father.

In order to see this, consider the most difficult case (an imaginary one), that of a genuinely conniving female. A woman practices contraception (e.g., by taking contraceptive pills) with the full knowledge and consent of her husband. Then, without obtaining his consent or even informing him, she stops taking the pills. She subsequently becomes pregnant after intercourse with her husband. Without a doubt this man has not voluntarily consented to becoming a parent; he may have ardently desired to remain childless. His wife's unilateral action is unjustified; she ought to have at least discussed her decision with her husband. Perhaps the violation of spousal cooperation and good faith is even sufficient to justify his leaving her.

The most obvious observation about this case is that the wife's action does not entitle the husband to require that she obtain an abortion in order to maintain his reproductive liberty, for such a requirement would be a violation of her bodily autonomy. But in addition, it is not at all clear that the husband should automatically be relieved of all moral and legal responsibility for the child. In the rather clear-cut case of deliberate deception that I have postulated here, it might seem reasonable to say that the husband has no obligations to the resulting child. But in engaging in sexual intercourse, every man should understand that there is almost always a possibility, perhaps in some cases remote, that pregnancy will result, and men should accept the responsibility associated with taking that chance. Furthermore, given a widespread pattern of failure by divorced men to fulfil their financial obligations to their offspring, in general it is also not wise to provide men a loophole ("She tricked me") for avoiding responsibility for their biological offspring. For the imagined case is not a typical one: It is false to assume that women are in general duplicitous; and most instances of "unplanned" pregnancy presumably do not occur through the woman's deliberate deceit. Therefore this case indicates that a lack of opportunity to make a reproductive choice cannot always automatically absolve one of parental responsibility.

It might be thought, however, that the important feature of the AID consent requirement is that the child who is produced is not biologically the child of the woman's husband. Here it would seem that the husband cannot be held responsible because it was no act of his that resulted in the pregnancy. Of course, to a philosopher such as Bayles this cannot be significant, since, as we saw in chapter 7, Bayles also believes that the desire for genetic offspring is irrational. But even if, as I have argued, such a desire is not necesarily irrational, it still could not justify automatically permitting the husband to repudiate an AID child born without his "permission." This is most obvious if we imagine that the husband somehow does not discover until, say, five or ten years after the birth of the child that the child was conceived through AID. In such a case we would surely not want to absolve the man of any moral and legal responsibilities for the child.

The most difficult problem would arise if the husband discovers, not years later but during the wife's pregnancy, that conception occurred by means of AID without his consent. Unlike the last case, in this instance he has not yet developed a history of responsibility to the child, for no child yet exists. But relieving him of all moral and legal responsibility is still not necessarily in the best interest of the child who will be born in a few months. So although it might be important to allow the husband the opportunity for some legal recourse in this sort of situation, the possibility of such a case still does not of itself provide sufficient grounds for *automatically* relieving him of responsibility. Moreover the possibility of such a case is not sufficient to show that a married woman should be required to have the consent of her spouse before obtaining AID, for the requirement would still violate the woman's reproductive autonomy. Hence in general there seem to be a number of good reasons not to require a married woman to seek her husband's consent for AID.

Parental Screening

In the last two sections discussion was confined to the criteria for access to artificial reproduction, particularly artificial insemination by donor. Nevertheless it is not correct to assume that parental screening does not take place in other contexts; a covert form of parental screening occurs now and has always occurred in connection with reproduction. By means of the following practices the state helps to determine, both directly and indirectly, who will and who will not be parents[91]—that is, who will and who will not have access to the means of reproduction: (1) imposing social restrictions on sexual activity—for example, through the stigma of illegitimacy and regulations governing marriage;[92] (2) providing or failing to provide both contraceptive information and resources and abortion counseling and services; (3) instituting compulsory sterilization for those judged unfit to reproduce; and (4) providing or failing to provide parent support services such as paid maternity leave, child care services, and family allowances. Regardless of what the expressed goal may be of a state's population policy, all of these devices serve to select who will and who will not become parents.

These observations show that the issue of parental screening must be situated within the larger context of the social regulation of reproduction and child-rearing. The reason for screening for parenthood is to legitimate some forms of procreation and parenting and proscribe others. The way in which the state screens potential parents implicitly says a lot about such things as what kinds of parents are desirable, what sort of parent-child relationships should be developed, and what kinds of people children should turn out to be. Ultimately, then, screening for parenthood is the unavoidable expression of the sorts of very fundamental concerns any society must have about the kinds of people its citizens will be.

Hence existing practices of parental screening cannot be assessed on a piecemeal basis. The procedures by which it is decided who will adopt, who will have access to artificial reproduction, who will be permitted to conceive or abort or contracept, are part of a far-reaching system. To evaluate parental screening we must decide what is important. What value do we place upon fertility and upon children? What kinds of parenting do we want to encourage? Should procreation be a burden or a benefit for the women who engage in it? Is a biological connection of paramount importance in a family, so that to have one's "own" genetic child is essential? What is more important: the welfare of children, for their own sake, or the supposed "right" of a person to be a parent?

An antifeminist approach to parental screening is provided by Janet Radcliffe Richards. In a discussion of who should bear the cost of children, she takes the view that "the state" does not necessarily want children:

> It is not always obvious that other people are as anxious to have children as their producers blithely assume. . . . There are actually very few women whom the public at large views with anxiety lest they should take their graces to the grave and leave the world no copy.[93]

As a result she is inclined to think that the state's alleged need for children cannot be used to justify social support for children,[94] and it certainly cannot be used to justify the existence of such services as paid maternity benefits or free day care.[95]

But such a view fails to distinguish between children as individual, unique persons and children as future members of the society's work force.[96] It is unfortunately all too true that many people do not want chilren—their own or anyone else's—as individuals; as I argued in chapter 7, children seldom seem to be recognized or valued for their own sake. On the other hand, unless he is a hermit, even the most vehement child-hater will have to want at least some minimum number of children (whoever they are) to be created and grow to adulthood, since these future adults will help to maintain and produce the goods and social services he will need to survive when he becomes an elderly citizen. This fact explains how it is posssible for a society to be both antichild in its culture and also pronatalist in its social policies: children are not wanted—indeed, may be positively disliked—for who they are but are instead sought because of what they will be able to do in future for the society.[97]

Richards argues that if the state *does* benefit from the production of children, any exploitation of the women who produce them can be avoided simply by ensuring that women can "compete freely for everything else." If enough children are produced in such a "fair system," then not only is the state under no obligation to pay women anything more for the children; *"it certainly should not pay anything more."*[98] If not enough children are produced, then the state could "put its resources into making childbearing more attractive." "The only thing the state need do is decide how many children it wants, and provide incentives until people voluntarily produce enough."[99]

This is the crassest possible view of the state's role in screening for parenthood. Not only is it unjustifiably naive in its assumption that all injustice is removed simply by enabling women to compete, as men do, for opportunities, employment, and services, but it also fails to say anything about the justice and/or beneficence of the kinds of arrangements that might be used to provide incentives for childbearing. It is not, of course, "people" of both sexes who produce children; it is women. How might women be persuaded to "produce"? Would it be desirable to provide "incentives" to every woman to have four, six, eight children if the state determined that that number were needed? Would it be desirable to pay surrogates to produce babies? Would it be desirable to establish special baby farms where women could seek lucrative employment as breeders? None of these schemes is at all incompatible with Richards's view of the state's role in regard to child-rearing. Her arguments give us a glimpse of a true brave new world of reproduction. And they show indirectly that a genuinely desirable system of parental screening must first take into account the genuine experiences, desires, needs, and talents of the women who create children.

Despite her insouciance as regards the effects on women of parental screening, Richards is willing to concede that the needs of the children themselves must be met. The state must support them for that reason, so whether we like it or not, she says, parents will benefit from the state support of their children; and this is true in spite of the fact that such a benefit may produce overpopulation in the future.[100]

Richards's reluctance to have parents receive state benefits for having children seems mean-spirited, but for once her main concern is not misplaced. In shaping social policy for reproduction a second major concern ought to be the well-being of the offspring.[101] Their well-being, it seems, should be one of the prime determinants of the kinds of criteria to be employed in screening prospective candidates for reproductive technology.

Licensing Parents

It may then appear that the relevant concerns in determining access to reproductive technology will be characteristics of prospective parents that promote competence in child-rearing: for example, such nebulous but significant characteristics as the capacity for nurturance, tolerance, and love, the ability to encourage, stimulate, and develop children, and the person's intentions and goals in seeking offspring.

Why not then follow Hugh LaFollette's recommendation that we "license" parents? LaFollette argues that "any activity that is potentially harmful to others and requires certain demonstrated competence for its safe performance" should be regulated,[102] and parenting clearly fulfils these criteria. He considers and replies carefully to a variety of objections to the proposal, including the claims that denial of a licence could seriously harm a person, that competency tests might not be accurate, that tests for screening parents might intentionally or unintentionally be misused, and that a program of licensing parents could not be fairly enforced. He also recognizes that there might be skepticism as to whether most of the desiderata for parents can be effectively evaluated: Is it possible to devise tests that will accurately predict competence in child-rearing? LaFollette replies that the aim of licensing should not be to license only the best parents but merely to exclude the very bad ones—that is, those who would abuse their children.[103] Furthermore he cites evidence suggesting that adoptive parents are less likely than biological parents to mistreat their children and argues that this suggests that we have already achieved a successful form of licensing.[104]

Many other practical objections to the licensing proposal have been raised,[105] but these are not the significant problem in assessing it. Given that screening of parents does and will occur, as I have argued, the question is whether the system of prior restraint proposed by LaFollette is appropriate.

At the very least it might be objected that licensing would contribute to the attitude that children are the property of their parents. LaFollette himself is highly critical of that attitude,[106] but it is arguable that successfully licensed parents might well think of children as a prize they have earned.

Even more important, such a system requires applicants to demonstrate (at least minimal) competence; hence such persons are assumed incompetent until proved competent. Such an assumption is quite legitimate for such skills as driving, and unfortunately it may not be unjustified for many prospective parents in a society such as ours with its lack of opportunities to practice caring for children, its allocation of responsibility for parenting almost exclusively to women and not to men, its high rate of child abuse, its dislike of children as individuals, its emphasis on acquiring one's "own" children, and its indifference to the fate of children not one's own. Such existing social conditions and values appear to create the need for a system of prior restraint.

These observations about the present social context for child-rearing indirectly suggest a more appropriate response to LaFollette's proposal: not to institute a system of licensing but rather to change the conditions and values that otherwise seem to make necessary the prior restraint of some potential parents. This would involve developing feelings of responsibility for all children, not just our "own"; rejecting the notion that a genetically related child is superior to one that is not; providing social supports for many varieties of families and contexts for parenting; respecting and appreciating children as the individuals they are and not for what they represent or will become; creating a climate in which adults and children have many opportunities to work and play together, so that adults will have the experience and practical education relevant to rearing children and children will benefit from not being ghettoized; and expecting as a matter of course that men as well as women will nurture children.

In other words, what is necessary is a child-positive society, a society governed by feminist rather than by patriarchal principles. Contrary to the claim of one infertility specialist, who said that legislation for artificial reproduction "must place the couple and donors first,"[107] and that of another, who claims, fetishistically, that we should "protect the integrity of artificial reproduction itself,"[108] I am suggesting that all of our policies and practices pertaining to reproduction must give top priority to the authentic experiences of women and the real needs of children.

Notes

An earlier version of part of this chapter, entitled "Sexuality, Parenting, and Reproductive Choices," will appear in *Resources for Feminist Research/Documentation sur la recherche féministe* 16 no. 2 (forthcoming 1987), and is used here with permission.

1 E.g., Margot Joan Fromer, *Ethical Issues in Health Care* (St. Louis: C. V. Mosby, 1981), pp. 200–202; Margaret A. Somerville, "Birth Technology, Parenting and 'Deviance,'" *International Journal of Law and Psychiatry* 5 (1982): 128–129.

2 See Noel P. Keane, "Surrogate Motherhood: Past, Present and Future," in *Difficult Decisions in Medical Ethics*, ed. Doreen Ganos, Rachel E. Lipson, Gwynedd Warren, and Barbara J. Weil (New York: Alan R. Liss, 1983), p. 157.

3 Evelyn E. Ferguson, "'The Real Cabbage Patch Kids': An Examination of the Canadian Private Adoption System," Occasional Papers in Social Policy Analysis no. 2 (Toronto: Ontario Institute for Studies in Education, 1984).

4 Gena Corea, *The Mother Machine: Reproductive Technologies from Artificial Insemination to Artificial Wombs* (New York: Harper & Row, 1985), p. 313; see also p. 134.

5 Ibid., pp. 144–145.

6 Ibid., p. 183, note 1.

7 Rosalind Pollack Petchesky, *Abortion and Women's Choice: The State, Sexuality, and Reproductive Freedom* (Boston: Northeastern University Press, 1984), p. 7.

8 Somer Brodribb, "Reproductive Technologies, Masculine Dominance and the Canadian State," Occasional Papers in Social Policy Analysis no. 5 (Toronto: Ontario Institute for Studies in Education, 1984), p. 22.

9 Daniel Callahan, "Ethics and Population Limitation," in *Ethics and Population*, ed. Michael D. Bayles (Cambridge, Mass.: Schenkman, 1976), p. 25.

10 Fromer, *Ethical Issues in Health Care*, p. 172.

11 See, for example, D. S. Hutchinson, "Utilitarianism and Children," *Canadian Journal of Philosophy* 12 (1982): 61–73. In "Survival of the Weakest," in *Moral Prolems in Medicine*, ed. Samuel Gorovitz et al. (Englewood Cliffs, N.J.: Prentice-Hall, 1976), pp. 364–369, Richard M. Hare argues that we do have such obligations. There is extensive philosophical discussion of our obligations to future generations. See, for example, Derek Parfit, "Rights, Interests, and Possible People," in Gorovitz et al., *Moral Problems in Medicine*, pp. 369–375; Jan Narveson, "Moral Problems of Population"; Peter Singer, "A Utilitarian Population Principle"; and Derek Parfit, "On Doing the Best for Our Children," all in Bayles, *Ethics and Population*, pp. 59–115; and Trudy Govier, "What Should We Do about Future People?" in *Moral Issues*, ed. Jan Narveson (Toronto: Oxford University Press, 1983), pp. 398–413.

12 Hutchinson, "Utilitarianism and Children," p. 73.

13 Petchesky, *Abortion and Women's Choice*, pp. 378–379.

14 Hutchinson, "Utilitarianism and Children," p. 71.

15 John A. Robertson, "Procreative Liberty and the Control of Conception, Pregnancy, and Childbirth," *Virginia Law Review* 69 (April 1983): 416, 417.

16 Hugh LaFollette, "Licensing Parents," *Philosophy and Public Affairs* 9 (1980): 186.

17 Michael D. Bayles, "Limits to a Right to Procreate," in *Having*

Children: Philosophical and Legal Reflections on Parenthood, ed. Onora O'Neill and William Ruddick (New York: Oxford University Press, 1979), p. 14.

18 William J. Daniel, "Sexual Ethics in Relation to IVF and ET: The Fitting Use of Human Reproductive Power," in *Test-Tube Babies*, ed. William Walters and Peter Singer (Melbourne: Oxford University Press, 1982), p. 73.

19 Bernard M. Dickens, "Reproduction Law and Medical Consent," *University of Toronto Law Journal* 35 (Summer 1985): 256. However, Dickens cites two Covenants that may, he says, be interpreted to accord rights of access to "laboratory conception."

20 Robertson, "Procreative Liberty," pp. 406, 408–420; Lori B. Andrews, "Ethical Considerations in In Vitro Fertilization and Embryo Transfer," in *Human In Vitro Fertilization and Embryo Transfer*, ed. Don P. Wolf and Martin M. Quigley (New York: Plenum Press, 1984), p. 407.

21 Robertson, "Procreative Liberty," pp. 406, 428, 430–433; Elizabeth Fuller, *Having Your First Baby after Thirty* (New York: Dodd, Mead, 1983), p. 28.

22 Robertson, "Procreative Liberty," pp. 410.

23 See Bartha Maria Knoppers, "Women and the Reproductive Technologies," in *Family Law in Canada: New Directions*, ed. Elizabeth Sloss (Ottawa: Canadian Advisory Council on the Status of Women, 1985), p. 215; Somerville, "Birth Technology," p. 129; Ontario Law Reform Commission, *Report on Human Artificial Reproduction and Related Matters* I (Toronto: Ministry of the Attorney General, 1985), p. 43.

24 Lori B. Andrews, "Legal Issues Raised by In Vitro Fertilization and Embryo Transfer," in *Human In Vitro Fertilization and Embryo Transfer*, p. 11; and Andrews, "Ethical Considerations in In Vitro Fertilization and Embryo Transfer," p. 407.

25 Keane, "Surrogate Motherhood," p. 159.

26 *Report of Human Artificial Reproduction and Related Matters* I, pp. 42–43.

27 An example may be found in *Fertility and Sterility* 46 Supplement 1 (September 1986): 4S–6S, 23S.

28 Keane, "Surrogate Motherhood," p. 157.

29 Pall Ardall, Review of *Ethics and Population*, ed. Michael D. Bayles, *Dialogue* 19 (1980): 166.

30 Daniel, "Sexual Ethics in Relation to IVF and ET," p. 73.

31 See Naomi Pfeffer and Anne Woollett, *The Experience of Infertility* (London: Virago Press, 1983), p. 2.

32 R. Snowden and G. D. Mitchell, *The Artificial Family: A Consideration of Artificial Insemination by Donor* (London: Unwin Paperbacks, 1983), pp. 54–55.

33 *Report on Human Artificial Reproduction and Related Matters* I, p. 110.

34 Linda S. Williams, "Who Qualifies for In Vitro Fertilization? A

Sociological Examination of the Stated Admittance Criteria of Three Ontario IVF Programs" (Paper delivered at the Conference of the Canadian Sociology and Anthropology Association, 7 June 1986), pp. 6–7.

35 Iwan Davies, "Contracts to Bear Children," *Journal of Medical Ethics* 11 (1985): 61; George J. Annas, "Redefining Parenthood and Protecting Embryos: Why We Need New Laws," *Hastings Center Report* 14 (October 1984): 50; Leon R. Kass, "Making Babies: The New Biology and the 'Old' Morality," *The Public Interest* 26 (1972): 49; Daniel, "Sexual Ethics in Relation to IVF and ET," p. 77; Michael D. Bayles, *Reproductive Ethics* (Englewood Cliffs, N.J.: Prentice-Hall, 1984), p. 115.

36 R. Snowden, G. D. Mitchell, and E. M. Snowden, *Artificial Reproduction: A Social Investigation* (London: Allen & Unwin, 1983), pp. 4–7; Robertson, "Procreative Liberty," p. 407.

37 Fromer, *Ethical Issues in Health Care*, pp. 141–143; Harvey W. Freishtat, "Legal Implications of AID," in *Infertility: Medical, Emotional and Social Considerations*, ed. Miriam D. Mazor and Harriet F. Simons (New York: Human Sciences Press, 1984), p. 139.

38 Corea, *The Mother Machine*, p. 39.

39 Ian Brown, "High-Tech Conception," *The Toronto Globe and Mail* (1 February 1986): A10.

40 Germaine Greer, *Sex and Destiny* (London: Secker & Warburg, 1984), pp. 58–61.

41 Harriet F. Simons, "Infertility: Implications for Policy Formulation," in Mazor and Simons, *Infertility: Medical, Emotional and Social Considerations*, p. 65.

42 Leon R. Kass, "'Making Babies' Revisited," *The Public Interest* 54 (Winter 1979): 55 and footnote 14.

43 Edward Keyserlingk, quoted in *The Toronto Star* (5 October 1983).

44 Knoppers, "Women and the Reproductive Technologies," p. 216; Corea, *The Mother Machine*, p. 145; Brodribb, "Reproductive Technologies," pp. 15–16; Kathleen A. Lahey, "Alternative Insemination: Facing the Conceivable Options," *Broadside* 8, no. 1 (1986): 8–10; Anibal A. Acosta and Jairo E. Garcia, "Extracorporeal Fertilization and Embryo Transfer," in *Infertility: Diagnosis and Management*, ed. James Aiman (New York: Springer-Verlag, 1984), p. 217.

45 Snowden et al., *Artificial Reproduction*, p. 169.

46 Mary Warnock, *A Question of Life: The Warnock Report on Human Fertilisation and Embryology* (Oxford: Basil Blackwell, 1985), p. 10.

47 Annas, "Artificial Insemination," pp. 50 and 51.

48 Council for Science and Society, *Human Procreation: Ethical Aspects of the New Techniques* (Oxford: Oxford University Press, 1984), pp. 60–61. Compare H. Allan Leal, "Vice Chairman's Dissent," in *Report on Human Artificial Reproduction and Related Matters, II*, p. 288.

49 *Report on Human Artificial Reproduction and Related Matters* I, p. 21
    and II, p. 158. An entirely different assumption is made in
    another study, which compares "the vast majority of [married]
    couples" who use AID to the "more unusual fringe cases of
    AID"—that is, single women and lesbians (Snowden et al., *Artificial Reproduction*, p. 59).
50 Compare Snowden et al., *Artificial Reproduction*, p. 169.
51 "Case Conference—Lesbian Couples: Should Help Extend to
    AID?" *Journal of Medical Ethics* 4 (1978): 91.
52 Warnock, *A Question of Life*, p. 11. Compare *Report on Human
    Artificial Reproduction and Related Matters* II, p. 158. Some questions might be raised here about what is *meant* by "mother" and
    "father": for example, are these terms intended in the sense of
    the social parents or in the sense of the genetic parents?
53 Alfred Kadushin and Judith A. Martin, *Child Abuse: An Interactional Event* (New York: Columbia University Press, 1981),
    pp. 10, 287.
54 "Case Conference—Lesbian Couples," p. 93.
55 Snowden et al., *Artificial Reproduction*, p. 13.
56 Fromer, *Ethical Issues in Health Care*, p. 143.
57 Ibid., p. 143.
58 "Case Conference—Lesbian Couples," p. 93.
59 Corea, *The Mother Machine*, p. 52.
60 Somerville, "Birth Technology," p. 133.
61 Bayles, *Reproductive Ethics*, p. 18.
62 Snowden et al., *Artificial Reproduction*, pp. 168–169, my
    emphasis.
63 Ibid., p. 169.
64 Dr. Kenneth Soddy, quoted in Jenny Teichman, *Illegitimacy: A
    Philosophical Examination* (Oxford: Basil Blackwell, 1982), p. 120.
65 Quoted in Snowden and Mitchell, *The Artificial Family*, p. 118.
66 Somerville, "Birth Technology," p. 135. Interestingly, the same
    assumption underlies questions raised by Somerville about
    homosexual sperm donors: "What if there is some inherited
    predisposition to homosexuality, should we exclude such donors
    or at least warn the female recipient of the sperm of this characteristic of the donor? Would it be acceptable to insist on married
    donors in order to reduce the chance that the donor is homosexual?" (p. 127).
67 See "Case Conference—Lesbian Couples," pp. 92–93.
68 Ibid., p. 95.
69 Marilyn Frye, *The Politics of Reality: Essays in Feminist Theory*
    (Trumansberg, N.Y.: The Crossing Press, 1983), p. 98; and
    Adrienne Rich, "Compulsory Heterosexuality and Lesbian Existence," in *Women: Sex and Sexuality*, ed. Catharine R. Stimpson
    and Ethel Spector Person (Chicago: University of Chicago Press,
    1980), p. 63.
70 Dianne Grimsditch, in *Love Your Enemy? The Debate Between Heter-*

osexual Feminism and Political Lesbianism (London: Onlywomen Press, 1981), p. 20.

71 Compare Fromer, *Ethical Issues in Health Care*, p. 156.

72 Snowden and Mitchell, *The Artificial Family*, pp. 118–119.

73 Ibid., p. 119.

74 Fromer, *Ethical Issues in Health Care*, p. 143.

75 Mary O'Brien, *The Politics of Reproduction* (Boston: Routledge & Kegan Paul, 1981), pp. 54–55.

76 Frye, *The Politics of Reality*, p. 102, Frye's emphasis.

77 Compare Jalna Hanmer, "Reproductive Technology: The Future for Women?" in *Machina Ex Dea: Feminist Perspectives on Technology*, ed. Joan Rothschild (New York: Pergamon Press, 1983), p. 183; and Brodribb, "Reproductive Technologies," p. 5.

78 Leal, "Vice Chairman's Dissent," p. 288.

79 George J. Annas, "Artificial Insemination: Beyond the Best Interests of the Donor," *Hastings Center Report* 9 (August 1979): 14.

80 Freishtat, "Legal Implications of AID," p. 143; Knoppers, "Women and the Reproductive Technologies," p. 216; Brodribb, "Reproductive Technologies," pp. 3–10.

81 Warnock, *A Question of Life*, p. xiv.

82 Ibid., p. 25.

83 Barbara Katz Rothman, "How Science Is Redefining Parenthood," *Ms.* (July/August 1982): 154–155.

84 Dickens, "Reproduction Law and Medical Consent," pp. 266–267, 274.

85 Somerville, "Birth Technology," p. 138.

86 The exception is France. See Knoppers, "Women and the Reproductive Technolgies," note 25, p. 228. Freishtat suggests that it would be wise in all cases to obtain the consent of the donor's wife ("Legal Implications of AID," p. 143).

87 Teichman, *Illegitimacy*, p. 32, 33. Compare Fromer *Ethical Issues in Health Care*, p. 143.

88 Robert B. Munroe, "The Right to Be a Parent: A Legal Perspective," in *Medical Ethics and Human Life*, ed. John E. Thomas (Toronto: Samual Stevens, 1983), p. 168.

89 Bayles, *Reproductive Ethics*, p. 16.

90 Ibid., p. 18.

91 Elizabeth W. Moen, "What Does 'Control over Our Bodies' Really Mean?" *International Journal of Women's Studies* 2 (1979): 137–138.

92 Greer, *Sex and Destiny*, p. 80; Brodribb, "Reproductive Technologies," p. 20.

93 Janet Radcliffe Richards, *The Sceptical Feminist: A Philosophical Inquiry* (Harmondsworth: Penguin, 1980), p. 300.

94 Ibid., p. 304.

95 Ibid., pp. 317–318.

96 Surprisingly, Richards is able to recognize this distinction at another point in her arguments. See ibid., pp. 302–303.

97 Moen, "What Does 'Control over Our Bodies' Really Mean?" pp. 129–143.
98 Richards, *The Sceptical Feminist*, p. 303, Richards's emphasis.
99 Ibid., p. 304. For a partial assessment of this approach to population regulation, see Bayles, "Limits to a Right to Procreate."
100 Richards, *The Sceptical Feminist*, pp. 312–314.
101 *Report on Human Artificial Reproduction and Related Matters* II, p. 154.
102 LaFollette, "Licensing Parents," p. 183.
103 Ibid., p. 190.
104 Hugh LaFollette, "A Reply to Frisch," *Philosophy and Public Affairs* 11 (1981): 183.
105 See Lawrence E. Frisch, "On Licentious Licensing: A Reply to Hugh LaFollette," *Philosophy and Public Affairs* 11 (1981): 173–180.
106 LaFollette, "Licensing Parents," p. 196.
107 J. Scott, quoted in Linda L. Long, "Artificially Assisted Conception," *Health Law in Canada* 5 (1985): 102.
108 Annas, "Redefining Parenthood and Protecting Embryos," p. 52.

9 *Conclusion*

Chapter 1 began by asking whether prenatal diagnosis is insurance for healthy offspring or a dangerous form of eugenics, whether surrogate motherhood is a valuable service or a type of reproductive prostitution, whether fetal sex preselection fosters reproductive choice or gynecide, and whether the surgical recovery of eggs is a good source of experimental material or outright theft from women. These contrasting ways of posing ethical questions about reproduction illustrate the dichotomy between, on the one hand, a nonfeminist or antifeminist approach to reproductive ethics and, on the other hand, a feminist approach. The thesis of this book has been that a feminist approach to understanding issues in human reproduction is more insightful: it uncovers topics that are otherwise neglected, challenges received opinions about reproduction, and sheds light upon the true nature and implications of reproductive technology and the social uses to which it is put. In this final chapter I shall summarize the recurrent themes of a feminist approach to reproductive ethics, describe their policy implications, and suggest some last questions.

Recurrent Themes

A feminist approach to ethical issues in reproduction involves careful consideration of the consequences of the use of reproductive technology, particularly for women and children. It exhibits, for example, a concern for the effects of fetal sex preselection on the offspring produced and for the implications of surrogate motherhood for the women and children involved. Such concerns are often overlooked within much of the current nonfeminist and antifeminist literature.

The most obvious indication of this myopic tendency is a persistent and almost exclusive focus on the embryo/fetus. Processes such as fetal surgery and prenatal diagnosis serve to draw more and more attention to the status and well-being of the embryo/fetus,[1] the sheer existence of which is assumed to be morally valuable, and permit the treatment of the woman as no more than a sort of carrier or environment for it. They also set the stage for a potential conflict between the alleged rights of the embryo/fetus and those of the woman. For the pregnant woman, correct moral behaviour is then claimed to involve the sacrifice of her own well-being for the sake of the well-being of her embryo/fetus. Moreover the requirements of health and safety, primarily of the embryo/fetus but also of the woman herself, are assumed to be in conflict, actual or potential, with the psychological needs of the woman, which are therefore assumed to be of lesser importance.

In pondering the purportedly rival claims of pregnant woman and embryo/fetus, I suggested that we move beyond rights claims and instead contemplate the rights that are *not* possessed by the parties to the conflict: the woman (or anyone else) has no right to kill or to injure the embryo/fetus; and the embryo/fetus has no right to occupancy or use of its mother's (or any other woman's) body. The virtue of nonmaleficence should govern our relationships with the embryo/fetus, but reproduction ordinarily should not require sacrifices from women.

A feminist approach to reproductive ethics also leads us to reconsider the meanings of reproductive freedom and choice. The new reproductive technology has a paradoxical effect on reproductive freedom, particularly the reproductive freedom of women: on the one hand, it appears to enhance our capacity to make choices, but on the other hand, a closer examination suggests that there are many ways in which reproductive technology may serve to reduce the choices we can make.[2] For example, some prenatal diagnostic procedures, while appearing to extend women's choices in regard to their pregnancies, are now so routine that some women may not fully understand that they are entitled to refuse them. It is taken for granted that a pregnant woman will submit to an ultrasound test twice in her pregnancy and that, if she is thirty-five or over, she will undergo amniocentesis.[3]

It has been argued by feminist historians that "in most cultures of the world and throughout most of history it is women who have controlled their own reproductive function. That is, the management of reproduction has been restricted to women, and regarded as part of the feminine role."[4] But this system has gradually been usurped by a system of control "based on a profession of formally trained men,"[5] and such a system is enhanced and extended by the addition of complex and invasive reproductive procedures such as in vitro fertilization.

The social uses of these technologies typically stress conformity to the requirements of stereotypical womanhood—heterosexuality, marriage, motherhood—and to the personal attributes associated with that role: passivity, nurturance, desire for children. The imposition of these constraints does not enhance women's freedom as responsible moral agents but instead reinforces traditional limits. Thus as Rosalind Pollack Petchesky points out, an absolute or exclusive assertion of women's right to reproductive control and choice "can be turned back on us to reinforce the view of all reproductive activity as the special, biologically destined province of women."[6]

Furthermore it is essential to reevaluate what is *meant* by reproductive choice and freedom. Fetal sex preselection, for example, enables people (men in particular) to act upon their biases against females. The extension of misogyny to the point of human conception is not part of what we should mean by reproductive freedom. Another example is surrogate motherhood: not only is surrogacy not the kind of choice that should be socially valued; it is not a real reproductive choice for women at all.

Another recurrent theme found in a feminist approach to reproductive ethics concerns the tendency toward the commodification of reproduction—that is, the introduction of economic relationships into the social patterns of human reproduction. Human gametes and embryos are now or will soon be items that can be purchased from private or state-supported banks. Children are also commodified by reproductive technology, for it permits them to be treated as consumer goods that can be made to order through IVF, prenatal diagnosis, and fetal surgery, and purchased on the open market. Reproductive technology appears to permit us to raise higher and higher our standards for acceptable children.[7] In such a system both pronatalism and a profound dislike of children coexist: only certain kinds of offspring—those free of physical and mental disabilities, those of the right race or the chosen sex—are held to be of real value.

At the same time, reproductive technology permits men to become primarily the consumers of reproductive services and reproductive products. And it makes women into reproductive consumers as well—but, more directly and significantly, it makes women the suppliers of reproductive services and products through the donation or sale or eggs and embryos and the provision of gestational services for rent. Given the historical connection between the status of children and the value attributed to mothering, there is also a connection between the treatment of embryos and children as luxury items and the promotion of a role for women as reproductive entrepreneurs. Women can perform a "job" involving the lease of their uterus; they produce child-products for sale to wealthy men.

Another theme concerns the emphasis upon a genetic link with one's offspring. Much of the development of reproductive technology has been predicated upon an alleged concern for infertility, particularly infertility in women, which is depicted as a serious handicap deserving every possible treatment. At the same time, the growing commodification of children encourages an emphasis on acquiring one's own children, as personal property. The very genuine and legitimate desires of some women for the experiences of pregnancy and childbirth and caring for a newborn are misconstrued as a desire for a genetic link with one's children. It is not enough to appreciate and enjoy children for their own sake; one must come to possess one who is the product of one's own egg or sperm. Reproductive technology is claimed to offer the one opportunity for women and men with certain types of infertility to have offspring who are genetically linked to them. The implication is that social parenting is secondary in importance to the opportunity to reproduce oneself.

At the same time, of course, the technologies also permit the severing of the genetic tie. "The new techniques . . . not only serve to ensure and reserve lineage, but . . . also serve to confound and complicate it."[8] Thanks to new reproductive technology a baby could, potentially, have five different parents: its genetic mother and genetic father, who supply the ovum and the sperm; its carrying mother, who gestates the embryo produced by the union of ovum and sperm; and finally its social parents, the individuals who rear the child produced by the carrying mother.

A final theme that emerges from this investigation concerns the suspicion of and contempt for women's bodies, particularly women's procreative and sexual capacities, which pervades many of the social structures governing human reproduction. Fear of the female body, regarded as incompetent or dangerous, helps to produce alarm over supposedly widespread "prenatal abuse." It also accounts for an often punitive attitude toward the provision of abortion services: that women who seek abortions must instead pay for their sexual pleasures by undergoing an unwanted pregnancy. And the perceived need for massive technological intervention in conception, pregnancy, and childbirth is bolstered by the conviction that women's bodies are incompetent and inadequate, in need of a "technological fix" in order to function adequately.

Policy

I have shown that a feminist approach to reproductive ethics emphasizes women's own experiences, needs, and wants in reproduction—for example, women's experience of being pregnant and having a relationship to a fetus, women's attitudes toward fertility and infertility, and women's feelings about children and childbirth.

Yet this attention to women's actual experience as reproductive beings, and as both consumers and providers of reproductive products and services, can be coopted for sexist and androcentric purposes. Some writers have tended to use an alleged concern for women—and in particular, for what women want—to justify certain antifeminist policies. It is claimed, for example, that women want to be surrogates, want the "liberty" to sell their reproductive services. It is also claimed that women want access to in vitro fertilization, want desperately to be able to overcome their infertility with the help of artificial reproduction, and are therefore largely responsible for the proliferation of this technology.[9]

Should these supposed wants be taken at face value, in such a way that the women are held entirely responsible for the undesirable consequences of their supposed desire to sell or buy reproductive services and products? Or should the women be found guilty of "false consciousness," in that they do not know what is really good for them and their offspring? Both responses seem unjustified.

The first point to be made is that women are not to be blamed for having socially created desires—desires, for example, to become a mother no matter what the cost, or to sell their reproductive services as surrogate mothers. Instead we must fault the social circumstances responsible for the creation of these intensely felt needs and wants. Second, the undeniable fact that certain wants are socially created does not by itself entail a social obligation to fulfill them (although it may imply an obligation to avoid further contributing to them). The needs of individuals desperately seeking fetal sex preselection, in vitro fertilization, or the services of a surrogate need not outweigh the more general concern for the effects of these practices not only on the individuals who use them but more generally on attitudes toward women and children.

In chapter 8 I argued that access to reproductive technology is neither a right possessed by all human beings nor a privilege to be defended through rigorous screening of applicants. Women have a right not to reproduce, but there is no right to reproduce in the strong sense of an entitlement to all possible assistance to overcome infertility. Yet the absence of that right should not result and need not result in the control of women's reproductive capacities by men; and it need not imply that elaborate criteria of eligibility for access to technology are justified.

Unfortunately the existing social situation appears to require that access to the means of reproduction be structured as *either* a right *or* a privilege. In such a system we seem to have only a no-win choice between, on the one hand, permitting free access to reproductive technology, thereby exploiting children and using women's bodies as experimental material controlled mainly by male scientists, and, on the other hand, depriving some infertile women of what is apparently the only means by which they will be able to have children.[10]

It is safe to say that what I have described as nonfeminist or antifeminist approaches to reproductive ethics have implicitly or explicitly dominated and determined much of the social policy governing reproduction in Western society, at least until quite recently. They serve to legitimate a system of abortion regulation that is concerned almost exclusively with the alleged rights of the fetus; they make abortion a privilege for women rather than a service to which we are entitled. Moreover these approaches help to perpetuate the existing system of ad hoc reactions to infertility, with its emphasis on dramatic treatment and technological overcompensation rather than on prevention. They also permit the continued rapid, unchallenged, and unregulated growth of research in and marketing of reproductive technologies such as in vitro fertilization and embryo transfer, as well as fetal sex selection and preselection, but do not encourage us to ask who these services are really for, who benefits (or should be protected) from them, and whether they constitute a just allocation of medical funds, personnel, resources, and facilities. Finally, these approaches endorse the maintenance of a social system in which women's wants, needs, expectations, and experiences are overlooked or undervalued, and in which control of reproduction—in research, social policy, legislation, and provision of services—is primarily in male hands.

In powerful contrast, a feminist perspective on issues in reproductive ethics suggests, first, that we should reassess the criteria of eligibility that determine which women have access to which types of reproductive technology. And second, we should step back and reevaluate the social system itself. A feminist social policy for reproduction would include the following potentially revolutionary elements, many of which are already familiar and ongoing demands made by the women's movement:

(1) research into and development of safe, effective, reversible, low-cost contraceptive methods, and widespread dissemination of birth planning information;

(2) a focus on abortion as a service for women—that is, the adequate provision of abortion clinics where the service is medically sound and easily available early in pregnancy;

(3) the direction of medical resources to discovering and reducing the causes of infertility, and eliminating iatrogenic sources of infertility;

(4) withdrawal of any support for, research into or implementation of technology that increases or contributes to preferences for offspring of one sex rather than the other;

(5) the decriminalization of surrogate motherhood and the promotion of positive life choices for women who would otherwise be likely to sell their reproductive and sexual services;

(6) the prevention of the sale of reproductive products such as gametes and embryos, and discouragment of social conditions that tend to promote the commodification of reproduction;

(7) research into and development and availability of reproductive technology that genuinely reflects women's experiences, needs, and wants and that respects, not exploits, the interests of women and children;

(8) the reexamination of our attitudes toward and treatment of children, a process that would include the encouragement of general feelings of responsibility and care toward all children, the eradication of pronatalist pressures, and questioning of the alleged primacy of a genetic link to one's offspring;

(9) the promotion of safe pregnancies and joyous childbirth, whether in hospitals, clinics, or homes, along with financing paid maternity leave, and supporting all parents and caregivers in their efforts to provide the best for children; and

(10) encouraging many more feminists to become scientists, lawyers, politicians, and academics so that research into

and development and regulation of reproduction and reproductive technology can eventually break loose of its patriarchal and misogynist origins.

Last Questions

Under patriarchy women's sexual and reproductive capacities are manipulated, exploited, and appropriated; antifeminist and nonfeminist discussions of reproductive technology abundantly illustrate the patriarchal concern for male power and control over and property in female procreation. Yet there is a curious dichotomy in patriarchal attitudes toward this technology. On the one hand, some writers are concerned that men will be rendered superfluous by new technologies and policies for reproduction:

It's still true that love makes the world go round, that mama's little baby needs a daddy to get started. But there are suspicions it doesn't really have to be that way.

Nature keeps adding fuel to the question: "Who needs men?"[11]

They express the fear that men will have insufficient power over reproduction, or will lose that power entirely, through such means as the use by independent women of artificial insemination by donor and in vitro fertilization.[12] For example, one writer argues that although AID and IVF "permit women who want it the freedom to avoid men entirely," both processes still require men as sources of sperm. But using new techniques—"women reproducing without *any* contribution from men whatsoever"—"males [may] become a memory."[13] He concludes, "we men may not be entirely dispensable (yet), but it is surely only a matter of time."[14] This fear is also manifested in the obsession of some nonfeminist writers with the possibility that "career women" might hire surrogate mothers[15]—an event that has never yet occurred.

Furthermore, some male opponents of abortion seem to feel personally threatened by abortion: "To many men, each aborted pregnancy is the killing of a son—and he is the son killed. . . . *I* was once a fertilized egg; therefore to abort a fertilized egg is to kill *me*."[16] And female "sceptical feminist" Janet Radcliffe Richards is anxious that the provision of free state-run child care would have the result that "women could, if they wanted to, keep children to themselves and not share them with men, but that men (as well as other women who did not have children) would still have to pay for them through the state system."[17]

By contrast, some other nonfeminist and antifeminist writers seem to view reproductive technology as a golden opportunity for men to take over reproduction entirely[18] by controlling ovulation, conception, implantation, pregnancy, and birth through technological means, and by making reproductive products and services into marketable commodities. Surprisingly, even the current tendency toward more humane birthing may help to consolidate this gradual male appropriation of reproduction. Although "it is rare indeed for a woman to be permitted another woman of her own choosing to be with her in labor," "prepared childbirth methods frequently give [the father] an authoritarian role he did not have before. . . . Often he is cast in partnership with hospital personnel."[19] The new participation by fathers in childbirth, then, can be seen as a contemporary expression of the needs and wants of the "expectant father," who "envies the woman her starring role and wants to claim some of the attention showered on her; he wants his role in the creation of the child to be recognized."[20]

According to Pat Allen and Jalna Hanmer, the covert goal of reproductive engineers is to make women more like men by taking reproduction from us, or alternatively, to make women less like women.[21] But it seems at least as plausible to say that reproductive technology is tending toward making men more like women, at least in terms of reproductive capacities. For example, a recent popular science magazine carried a detailed article extolling the possibility of male pregnancy, which would involve implanting an embryo in a man's abdominal cavity where it would develop for nine months and be delivered by a type of cesarean section.[22]

Some nonfeminist writers are inclined to minimize the future significance of artificial reproduction, on the grounds that

> the traditional method . . . is cheap, can be performed at home, takes little time [*sic*!], training, or skill, and is a great deal of fun. It will remain the method of choice, and atypical reproduction will have little overall impact on the institutions of marriage or the family.[23]

Yet this view is inconsistent with the twentieth-century pattern according to which reproductive technologies such as prenatal diagnosis, fetal monitoring, and in vitro fertilization were first introduced for special use in a limited number of cases and then rapidly extended to a wide variety of circumstances.[24] Furthermore, these technologies can be seen as part of the much larger historical pattern of control, manipulation, and suppression of female sexuality and reproduction.[25]

A variety of possible future developments in reproductive technology are projected by proponents and critics alike. They include (1) cloning—asexual reproduction achieved by removing the nucleus of a fertilized egg and inserting a donor cell to produce an adult organism genetically identical to the donor;[26] (2) parthenogenesis, the production of an embryo from an ovum without fertilization by a sperm cell;[27] and (3) ectogenesis, the development of embryos using an artificial placenta or within an artificial uterus.[28]

There is ample historical evidence that new forms of technology, claimed to have the potential to free women from traditional roles, may actually contribute to the further reinforcement of patriarchal oppression, often expressed in new ways.[29] Indeed, some oppressive uses of the reproductive technology of the future have been enthusiastically recommended by nonfeminist writers. Joseph Fletcher, for example, envisages that cloning will produce "persons specially constituted genetically to survive long periods outside space capsules at great heights," control the sex of offspring, provide children for the infertile, "replicate healthy people to compensate for the spread of genetic diseases," and supply "top-grade soldiers and scientists." These goals are reminiscent of current preoccupations with producing perfect offspring free of disease and possessing special characteristics and talents, and helping the infertile by providing genetically related children. Fletcher also favors "making and using man-machine hybrids rather than genetically designed people for dull, unrewarding, or dangerous roles needed nonetheless for the community's welfare."[30] While giving lip service to the notion that these creatures would "be free to choose roles and functions other than the ones for which they had a special constitutional capability,"[31] Fletcher's proposal overlooks the idea that such beings should themselves be regarded as part of the moral community.[32]

All of these processes seem to provide the opportunity for further appropriation of reproduction by patriarchal science. According to one prediction, "reproduction will remain a cottage or craft industry until the artificial placenta is perfected. . . . [At that point] the way opens for factory techniques or 'baby farms' to become the mode of production. The elimination of women, or femicide becomes a possibility."[33] Support for this possibility can be found in descriptions of possible advantages of artificial placentae or uteri: the advancement of fetology; the complete and ultimate protection of the embryo/fetus from infection, radiation, and the effects of smoking, alcohol, drugs, or poor nutrition; and selective breeding of offspring.[34] The concern for "protecting" the fetus in "a perfect artificial environment of ectogenesis [rather] than in the natural intrauterine one"[35] appears to derive from the same distrust and fear of the female body that motivates the concern for "prenatal abuse." One nonfeminist writer favors the use of artificial wombs whenever there are "not enough uteri" (presumably he means women) available.[36] In general, with the development of ectogenesis, what IVF specialist Alan Trounson calls "the maternal component"[37] and what Bayles calls "the rather uncontrolled environment of the womb"[38] would just no longer be necessary.

The ambivalence of nonfeminist and antifeminist writers about the roles of men and women in reproduction, and the great potential of future developments in artificial reproduction to promote the further male appropriation of procreation, suggest important questions for feminists in our evaluation of new reproductive technology and the social practices governing them. Should men be encouraged to share to an ever greater extent in reproduction, or should the arena of reproduction be reserved as an area of expertise and authority for women only? Are new reproductive technologies a route to the further patriarchal control of women's reproductive capacities, or are they a means to women's liberation?[39]

Feminists have disagreed about the answers to these questions, and in my view it is not yet possible to discern who is correct. One response is given by Marge Piercy, who depicts in a positive fashion the total sharing of reproduction by men and women. In her feminist science fiction novel, *Woman on the Edge of Time*, Piercy describes a future in which embryos of various genetic backgrounds are deliberately bred, fetuses grow in "brooders," and men are "mothers" who are treated with hormones to enable them to breastfeed "their" children. One of the characters in the novel states,

> It was part of women's long revolution. When we were breaking all the old hierarchies. Finally there was that one thing we had to give up too, the only power we ever had, in return for no more power for anyone. The original production: the power to give birth. Cause as long as we were biologically enchained, we'd never be equal. And males never would be humanized to be loving and tender. So we all became mothers. Every child has three.[40]

By contrast, other feminists have advocated the reservation of reproduction and new reproductive technologies for women only. Adrienne Rich, for example, sees access to new forms of artificial reproduction as part of women's entitlement to complete reproductive choice:

> Ideally, of course, women would choose not only whether, when, and where to bear children, and the circumstances of labor, but also between biological and artificial reproduction. . . . The mother should be able to choose the means of conception (biological, artificial, or even parthenogenic), the place of birth, her own style of giving birth, and her birth attendants.[41]

And Sally Miller Gearhart advocates the development of ovular merging or egg fusion, "the mating of two eggs," to produce only female offspring, in order to help produce a female-positive world in which "species responsibility" is returned to all women (women monitor the reproduction of the species) and the value of female freedom, responsibility, and control of the body are the foundation of every culture.[42]

A possible resolution for the problem of women's and men's roles in reproduction is suggested by Kathleen McDonnell. She distinguishes between the "macro" level and the "personal" level in reproduction, and proposes that women resume control at the macro level while fostering involvement by men at the personal level:

> As women, we have to work together to end the "macro" male domination of reproduction. At the same time, we, women and men alike, can work to end the male alienation from reproduction on the personal level. This means substantive involvement of men in the work of reproduction—both of their own, biological children and in the more general nurturing skills that have heretofore been seen as exclusively "women's work". . . . Ending male alienation from reproduction also means having men take their full measure of responsibility in the work of *preventing* reproduction—in contraception, sterilization and abortion.[43]

A proposal such as this helps to point the way toward a reproductive ethic that is both caring and fair and hints at the substance of a new social policy for procreation.

Reproductive prostitution, egg farming, gynecide, and the misuse of eugenics; or egg fusion, parthenogenesis, and male mothers: feminists have foreseen several possible reproductive futures, both bad and good. But in any case, in a world where it is already possible to buy sperm, to rent a uterus, and to "pluck a fetus from its womb," it is difficult to accept uncritically the optimistic nonfeminist pronouncement that "on balance, human reproduction is better today than it has been, and with certain changes it can be a rewarding experience that has better chances than ever before of providing people with normal, wanted children—and only wanted children."[44] Nevertheless, the careful investigation by feminists of the social conditions of reproduction and the values, attitudes, and beliefs that sustain them make the attainment of that utopian state a little more likely.

Notes

Earlier versions of parts of this chapter appeared in *Women and Men: Interdisciplinary Readings on Gender*, ed. Greta Hoffman Nemiroff (Markham, Ontario: Fitzhenry and Whiteside, 1986), pp. 245–261, under the title, "Reproductive Technology and the Future of the Family"; and will appear in *Medicine, Ethics, and Law: Canada and Poland in Dialogue*, ed. Tomasz Dybowski, David J. Roy, Marek Safjan, and Jean-Louis Baudouin (forthcoming 1987), under the title "Ethical Issues of Modern Reproductive Technology." The material is used here with the permission of the editors of these books.

1 An interesting example of this is the paper by A. W. Liley, "The Foetus as a Personality," *Fetal Therapy* 1 (1986): 8–17, which purports to examine the psychology of the fetus—inevitably referred to by masculine pronouns.
2 Barbara Katz Rothman, "The Products of Conception: The Social Context of Reproductive Choices," *Journal of Medical Ethics* 11 (December 1985): 191–193. See also E. Peter Volpe, *Patient in the Womb* (Macon, Ga.: Mercer University Press, 1984), p. 134; Kathleen McDonnell, *Not an Easy Choice: A Feminist Re-Examines Abortion* (Toronto: Women's Press, 1984), pp. 70–79.
3 Abby Lippman, "Access to Prenatal Screening Services and Trials: Who Decides?" (Paper delivered at the Policy Workshop on Medical Control: Pregnancy Issues, Sixth National Biennial Conference of the National Association of Women and the Law, Ottawa, 22 February 1985), pp. 12–14.
4 Ann Oakley, "Wisewoman and Medicine Man: Changes in the Management of Childbirth," in *The Rights and Wrongs of Women*, ed. Juliet Mitchell and Ann Oakley (Harmondsworth: Penguin, 1976), p. 19.
5 Ibid., p. 18.
6 Rosalind Pollack Petchesky, *Abortion and Woman's Choice: The State, Sexuality, and Reproductive Freedom* (Boston: Northeastern University Press, 1985), p. 7.
7 Samuel Gorovitz, "On Surrogate Mothers," in *Difficult Decisions in Medical Ethics*, ed. Doreen Ganos, Rachel E. Lipson, Gwynned

Warren, and Barbara J. Weil (New York: Alan R. Liss, 1983), p. 148.

8 Leon R. Kass, "'Making Babies' Revisited," *The Public Interest* 54 (Winter 1979): 45.

9 Mary Margaret Steckle, letter, *Healthsharing* 7 (Winter 1985): 25.

10 Compare the disastrous social alternatives to providing in vitro fertilization envisaged by Paul Bravender-Coyle in "In Vitro-Fertilization and the Law in Australia," *Health Law in Canada* 6 (1986): 70–71.

11 Jack Miller, "Scientists Try to Create Life without Males," *The Toronto Star* (21 April 1985): F8.

12 See the discussion by Mary Anne Warren in *Gendercide: The Implications of Sex Selection* (Totowa, N.J.: Rowman & Allanheld, 1985), pp. 61–67.

13 Jeremy Cherfas, "No More Men," *Omni* 8 (December 1985): 28, Cherfas's emphasis.

14 Ibid.; compare Jeremy Cherfas and John Gribbin, *The Redundant Male: Is Sex Irrelevant in the Modern World?* (New York: Pantheon Books, 1984), pp. 60, 177–179.

15 E.g., Rodney Deitch, "Implications of In-vitro Fertilisation," *The Lancet* (10 April 1982): 864; and Iwan Davies, "Contracts to Bear Children," *Journal of Medical Ethics* 11 (June 1985): 61.

16 Andrea Dworkin, *Right-Wing Women* (New York: Perigee Books, 1983), p. 74, Dworkin's emphasis.

17 Janet Radcliffe Richards, *The Sceptical Feminist: A Philosophical Enquiry* (Harmondsworth: Penguin, 1980), p. 301.

18 See Warren, *Gendercide*, pp. 57–61.

19 Datha Clapper Brack, "Displaced—The Midwife by the Male Physician," in *Biological Woman—The Convenient Myth*, ed. Ruth Hubbard, Mary Sue Henifin, and Barbara Fried (Cambridge, Mass.: Schenkman, 1982), p. 221.

20 Coleman Romalis, "Taking Care of the Little Woman," in *Childbirth: Alternatives to Medical Control*, ed. Shelly Romalis (Austin: University of Texas Press, 1981), p. 95.

21 Jalna Hanmer and Pat Allen, "Reproductive Engineering: The Final Solution?" in *Alice Through the Microscope: The Power of Science over Women's Lives*, ed. The Brighton Women & Science Group (London: Virago, 1980), p. 211.

22 Dick Teresi and Kathleen McAuliffe, "Male Pregnancy," *Omni* 8 (December 1985): 51, 52, 54, 56, 118.

23 Samuel Gorovitz, "Engineering Human Reproduction: A Challenge to Public Policy," *Journal of Medicine and Philosophy* 10 (August 1985): 272.

24 Gena Corea, "Unnatural Selection," *The Progressive* 50 (January 1986): 22.

25 Hanmer and Allen, "Reproductive Engineering," pp. 222–226.

26 Michael D. Bayles, *Reproductive Ethics* (Englewood Cliffs, N.J.: Prentice-Hall, 1984), pp. 116–118; Jalna Hanmer, "Reproductive

Technology: The Future for Women?" in *Machina Ex Dea: Feminist Perspectives on Technology*, ed. Joan Rothschild (New York: Pergamon, 1983) p. 193; Hanmer and Allen, "Reproductive Engineering," pp. 218–219; Clifford Grobstein, *From Chance to Purpose: An Appraisal of External Human Fertilization* (Reading, Mass.: Addison-Wesley, 1981), pp. 125–130; Margot Joan Fromer, *Ethical Issues in Health Care* (St. Louis: C. V. Mosby, 1981), pp. 66–72.

27 Hanmer, "Reproductive Technology," p. 193; Hanmer and Allen, "Reproductive Engineering," pp. 219–221; Grobstein, *From Chance to Purpose*, pp. 130–132.

28 Hanmer and Allen, "Reproductive Engineering," pp. 221–222; Bayles, *Reproductive Ethics*, pp. 125–127.

29 Joan Rothschild, "Technology, Housework, and Women's Liberation: A Theoretical Analysis," in Rothschild, *Machina Ex Dea*, p. 79.

30 Joseph Fletcher, *Humanhood: Essays in Biomedical Ethics* (Buffalo: Prometheus Books, 1979), p. 85.

31 Ibid., pp. 85–86.

32 Bayles, *Reproductive Ethics*, p. 122.

33 Hanmer and Allen, "Reproductive Engineering," p. 212.

34 Fromer, *Ethical Issues*, p. 159.

35 William A. W. Walters, "Cloning, Ectogenesis, and Hybrids: Things to Come?" in *Test-Tube Babies: A Guide to Moral Questions, Present Techniques and Future Possibilities*, ed. William Walters and Peter Singer (Melbourne: University of Oxford Press, 1982), p. 117.

36 Ibid., p. 116.

37 Robert Weil, "Interview: Alan Trounson," *Omni* 8 (December 1985): 126.

38 Bayles, *Reproductive Ethics*, p. 125.

39 See Kathleen McDonnell, *Not an Easy Choice: A Feminist Re-Examines Abortion* (Toronto: Women's Press, 1984), pp. 113–123.

40 Marge Piercy, *Woman on the Edge of Time* (New York: Fawcett Crest, 1976), p. 105.

41 Adrienne Rich, "The Theft of Childbirth," in *Seizing Our Bodies: The Politics of Women's Health*, ed. Claudia Dreifus (New York: Random House Vintage Books, 1977), pp. 153, 1163.

42 Sally Miller Gearhart, "The Future—If There Is One—Is Female," in *Reweaving the Web of Life*, ed. Pam McAllister (Philadelphia: New Society Publishers, 1982), pp. 268–284.

43 McDonnell, *Not an Easy Choice*, p. 123, her emphasis.

44 Bayles, *Reproductive Ethics*, p. 130.

Bibliography

Abramowitz, Susan. "A Stalemate on Test-Tube Baby Research." *Hastings Center Report* 14 (February 1984): 5–9.

Acosta, Anibal, and Jairo E. Garcia. "Extracorporeal Fertilization and Embryo Transfer." In *Infertility: Diagnosis and Management*, edited by James Aiman, 215–230. New York: Springer-Verlag, 1984.

Albury, Rebecca. "Who Owns the Embryo?" In *Test-Tube Women: What Future for Motherhood?* edited by Rita Arditta, Renate Duelli Klein, and Shelley Minden, 54–67. London: Pandora Press, 1984.

Allgeier, Elizabeth Rice, and Naomi B. McCormick. "Introduction: The Intimate Relationship Between Gender Roles and Sexuality." In *Changing Boundaries: Gender Roles and Sexual Behavior*, pp. 1–14. Edited by Elizabeth Rice Allgeier and Naomi B. McCormick. Palo Alto, California: Mayfield Publishing Co., 1983.

Andrews, Lori B. "Ethical Considerations in In Vitro Fertilization and Embryo Transfer." In *Human In Vitro Fertilization and Embryo Transfer*, pp. 403–423. Edited by Don P. Wolf and Martin M. Quigley. New York: Plenum Press, 1984.

Andrews, Lori B. "Legal Issues Raised by In Vitro Fertilization and Embryo Transfer." In *Human In Vitro Fertilization and Embryo Transfer*, edited by Don P. Wolf and Martin M. Quigley, 11–36. New York: Plenum Press, 1984.

Andrews, Lori B. "My Body, My Property." *Hastings Center Report* 16 (October 1986): 28–38.

Annas, George J. "Artificial Insemination: Beyond the Best Interests of the Donor." *Hastings Center Report* 9 (August 1979): 14–15, 43.

Annas, George J. "Contracts to Bear a Child: Compassion or Commercialism?" *Hastings Center Report* 11 (April 1981): 23–24.

Annas, George J. "Forced Cesareans: The Most Unkindest Cut of All." *Hastings Center Report* 12 (June 1982): 16–17, 45.

Annas, George J. "Redefining Parenthood and Protecting Embryos: Why We Need New Laws." *Hastings Center Report* 14 (October 1984): 50–52.

Ardall, Pall. Review of *Ethics and Population*, edited by Michael D. Bayles. *Dialogue* 19 (1980): 163–171.

Arditti, Rita, Renate Duelli Klein, and Shelley Minden, eds. *Test-Tube Women: What Future for Motherhood?* London: Pandora Press, 1984.

Arms, Suzanne. *Immaculate Deception: A New Look at Women and Childbirth in America*. Boston: Houghton Mifflin, 1975.

Armstrong, Janice. "The Risks and Benefits of Home Birth." Unpublished paper, Toronto, Ontario, 1982.

Aubry, Richard H. "The American College of Obstetricians and Gynecologists: Standards for Safe Childbearing." In *21st Century Obstetrics Now!*, 2d ed., edited by Lee Stewart and David Stewart, 15–26. Marble Hill, Mo.: NAPSAC, 1977.

Bainbridge, Isabel. "With Child in Mind: The Experience of a Potential IVF Mother." In *Test-Tube Babies: A Guide to Moral Questions, Present Techniques and Future Possibilities*, edited by William Walters and Peter Singer, 119–127. Melbourne: Oxford University Press, 1982.

Barker, Diana Leonard, and Sheila Allen. *Sexual Divisions and Society: Process and Change*. London: Tavistock Publications, 1976.

Baron, Charles C. "Fetal Research: The Question in the States." *Hastings Center Report* 15 (April 1985): 12–16.

Bartky, Sandra Lee. "Toward a Phenomenology of Feminist Consciousness." In *Philosophy and Women*, edited by Sharon Bishop and Marjorie Weinzweig, 252–258. Belmont, Calif.: Wadsworth, 1979.

Baruch, Elaine Hoffman, and Amadeu F. D'Adamo Jr. "Resetting the Biological Clock: Women and the New Reproductive Technologies." *Dissent* (Summer 1985): 273–276.

Bayer, Ronald. "Women, Work, and Reproductive Hazards." *Hastings Center Report* 12 (October 1982): 14–19.

Bayles, Michael D. "Limits to a Right to Procreate." In *Having Children: Philosophical and Legal Reflections on Parenthood*, edited by Onora O'Neill and William Ruddick, 13–24. New York: Oxford University Press, 1979.

Bayles, Michael D. "No Easy Answers on Questions of Surrogate Mothers." *Toronto Star*, 7 July 1982, pp. B1, B7.

Bayles, Michael D. *Reproductive Ethics*. Englewood Cliffs, N.J.: Prentice-Hall, 1984.

Bean, Constance A. *Methods Of Childbirth*. Garden City, N.Y.: Doubleday, 1974.

Bean, Constance A. *Labor and Delivery: An Observer's Diary*. Garden City, N.Y.: Doubleday, 1977.

Beekman, Daniel. *The Mechanical Baby: A Popular History of the Theory and Practice of Child Raising*. Westport, Conn.: Lawrence Hill & Co., 1977.

Bennett, Neil G., ed. *Sex Selection of Children*. New York: Academic Press, 1983.

Bennett, Neil G., and Andrew Mason. "Decision Making and Sex Selection with Biased Technologies." In *Sex Selection of Children*, edited by Neil G. Bennett, 101–111. New York: Academic Press, 1983.

Berger, Merle J., and Donald J. Goldstein. "Infertility Related to Exposure to DES In Utero." In *Infertility: Medical, Emotional and Social Considerations*, edited by Miriam D. Mazor and Harriet F. Simons, 157–168. New York: Human Sciences Press, 1984.

216   *Bibliography*

Bernard, Jessie. *The Future Of Motherhood*. New York: Penguin Books, 1974.

"The Birth of a Feminist Sperm Bank." *Hastings Center Report* 13 (February 1983): 3–4.

Bishop, Sharon, and Marjorie Weinzweig. *Philosophy and Women*. Belmont, Calif.: Wadsworth, 1979.

Blakely, Mary Kay. "Surrogate Mothers: For Whom Are They Working?" *Ms.* (March 1983): 18, 20.

Block, Robert. "Paying a High Price for the Pill." *Maclean's*, 30 April 1984, p. 52.

Bok, Sissela, Bernard N. Nathanson, and LeRoy Walters. "Commentary: The Unwanted Child: Caring for the Fetus Born Alive after an Abortion." In *Cases in Bioethics*, edited by Carol Levine and Robert M. Veatch, 1–6. Hastings-on-Hudson, N.Y.: Hastings Center, 1982.

Boone, C. Keith. "New Conceptions of Artificial Reproduction." *Hastings Center Report* 14 (August 1984): 46–48.

Boston Women's Health Book Collective. *The New Our Bodies, Ourselves*, 3d ed. New York: Simon & Schuster, 1984.

Bouma, Gary D., and Wilma J. Bouma. *Fertility Control: Canada's Lively Social Problem*. Don Mills, Ontario: Longman Canada, 1975.

Brack, Datha Clapper. "Displaced—the Midwife by the Male Physician." In *Biological Woman—The Convenient Myth*, edited by Ruth Hubbard, Mary Sue Henifin, and Barbara Fried, 207–226. Cambridge, Mass.: Schenkman, 1982.

Brackbill, Yvonne, June Rice, and Diony Young. *Birth Trap: The Legal Low-Down on High-Tech Obstetrics*. St. Louis: C. V. Mosby, 1984.

Bradley, Robert A. *Husband-Coached Childbirth*. New York: Harper & Row, 1965.

Bravender-Coyle, Paul. "In Vitro-Fertilization and the Law in Australia." *Health Law in Canada* 6 (1986): 61–72.

The Brighton Women and Science Group. "Technology in the Lying-in-Room." In *Alice Through the Microscope: The Power Of Science over Women's Lives*, edited by The Brighton Women and Science Group, 165–186. London: Virago, 1980.

Brodribb, Somer. "Reproductive Technologies, Masculine Dominance and the Canadian State." In Occasional Papers in Social Policy Analysis, No. 5. Toronto: Ontario Institute for Studies in Education, 1984.

Brody, B[aruch] A. "Abortion and the Law." *Journal of Philosophy* 68 (June 1971): 357–369.

Brody, B[aruch] A. "The Morality of Abortion." In *Ethics and Public Policy*, edited by Tom L. Beauchamp and Terry P. Pinkard, 284–297. Englewood Cliffs, N.J.: Prentice-Hall, 1963.

Burcher, Betty. "Midwifery Update." *Healthsharing* (Fall 1982): 8–9.

Callahan, Daniel. "Ethics and Population Limitation." In *Ethics and Population*, edited by Michael D. Bayles, 19–40. Cambridge, Mass.: Schenkman, 1976.

Callahan, Daniel. "Abortion: A Matter of Conscience." In *Ethics for*

Modern Life, edited by Raziel Abelson and Marie-Louise Friquegnon, 117–132. New York: St. Martin's Press, 1982.

Callahan, Daniel. "How Technology Is Reframing the Abortion Debate." *Hastings Center Report* 16 (February 1986): 33–42.

Camenisch, Paul F. "Abortion: For the Fetus's Own Sake?" In *Medical Ethics and Human Life*, edited by John E. Thomas, 135–143. Toronto: Samuel Stevens, 1983.

Caplan, Arthur L., H. Tristram Engelhardt Jr., and James J. McCartney, eds. *Concepts of Health and Disease: Interdisciplinary Perspectives.* Reading, Mass.: Addison-Wesley, 1981.

Caplan, Melissa. "Sex Preselection Techniques: A Desirable, Morally Justifiable Innovation." Unpublished paper, Montreal, Quebec, 1983.

Carney, Thomas P. *Instant Evolution: We'd Better Get Good at It.* Notre Dame, Ind.: University of Notre Dame Press, 1980.

Carter, C. O., ed. *Developments in Human Reproduction and Their Eugenic, Ethical Implications.* London: Academic Press, 1983.

"Case Conference—Lesbian Couples: Should Help Extend to AID?" *Journal of Medical Ethics* 4 (1978): 91–95.

Cayley, David. "Being Born." CBC Transcript, Toronto, September 1983.

Chenier, Nancy Miller. *Reproductive Hazards at Work: Men, Women and the Fertility Gamble.* Ottawa: Canadian Advisory Council on the Status of Women, December 1982.

Cherfas, Jeremy, "No More Men." *Omni* (December 1985): 28.

Cherfas, Jeremy, and John Gribbin. *The Redundant Male: Is Sex Irrelevant in the Modern World?* New York: Pantheon Books, 1984.

Cherry, Sheldon H. *Understanding Pregnancy and Childbirth.* New York: Bantam Books, 1975.

Churchill, Larry R., and Jose Jorge Siman. "Abortion and the Rhetoric of Individual Rights." In *Medical Ethics and Human Life*, edited by John E. Thomas, Toronto: Samuel Stevens, 1983.

Clark, Adele. "Subtle Forms of Sterilization Abuse: A Reproductive Rights Analysis." In *Test-Tube Women: What Future for Motherhood?* edited by Rita Arditti, Renate Duelli Klein, and Shelley Minden, 188–212. London: Pandora Press, 1984.

Code, Lorraine. "Commentary on 'Surrogate Motherhood' by Christine Overall." Unpublished paper, Kingston, Ontario, February 1985.

Cohen, Carl. "Sex, Birth Control and Human Life." In *Philosophy and Sex*, edited by Robert Baker and Frederick Elliston, 158–165. Buffalo: Prometheus Books, 1975.

Cohen, Howard. "Abortion and the Quality of Life." In *Feminism and Philosophy*, edited by Mary Vetterling-Braggin, Frederick A. Elliston, and Jane English, 429–448. Totowa, N.J.: Littlefield, Adams & Co., 1978.

Collins, Anne. *The Big Evasion: Abortion, the Issue That Won't Go Away.* Toronto: Lester & Orpen Dennys, 1985.

Coman, Carolyn. "Trying (and Trying and Trying) to Get Pregnant." *Ms.* (May 1983): 21–24.

Corea, Gena [Genoveffa]. "Egg Snatchers." In *Test-Tube Women: What Future For Motherhood?* edited by Rita Arditti, Renate Duelli Klein, and Shelley Minden, 37–51. London: Pandora Press, 1984.

Corea, Gena [Genoveffa]. *The Mother Machine: Reproductive Technologies from Artificial Insemination to Artificial Wombs.* New York: Harper & Row, 1985.

Corea, Gena [Genoveffa]. "Unnatural Selection." *The Progressive* 50 (January 1986): 22–24.

Council for Science and Society. *Human Procreation: Ethical Aspects of the New Techniques.* Oxford: Oxford University Press, 1984.

Cragg, Wesley, ed. *Contemporary Moral Issues.* Toronto: McGraw-Hill Ryerson, 1983.

Culpepper, Emily Erwin, moderator. "Sex Preselection Discussion." In *The Custom-Made Child? Women-Centered Perspectives,* edited by Helen B. Holmes, Betty B. Hoskins, and Michael Gross, 215–224. Clifton, N.J.: Humana Press, 1981.

Daly, Mary. *Gyn/Ecology: The Metaethics of Radical Feminism.* Boston: Beacon Press, 1978.

Daniel, William J. "Sexual Ethics in Relation to IVF and ET: The Fitting Use of Human Reproductive Power." In *Test-Tube Babies: A Guide to Moral Questions, Present Techniques and Future Possibilities,* edited by William Walters and Peter Singer, 71–78. Melbourne: Oxford University Press, 1982.

Daniels, Charles B. "Abortion and Potential." *Dialogue* 18 (June 1979): 220–223.

David, Cynthia. "Midwifery: Women Helping Women." *Status of Women News* (Spring 1983): 10–12.

Davies, Iwan. "Contracts to Bear Children." *Journal of Medical Ethics* 11 (1985): 61–65.

Davies, Jackie. "Commentary on J. E. Bickenbach's 'The Empty Garage? Recent Feminist Critiques of Scientific Methodology.'" Paper presented at the Department of Philosophy Colloquium, Queen's University, Kingston, Ontario, 29 November 1984.

Deitch, Rodney. "Implications of In-Vitro Fertilisation." *Lancet* (10 April 1982): 864.

Dickason, Anne. "The Feminine as a Universal." In *"Femininity," "Masculinity,"* and *"Androgyny,"* edited by Mary Vetterling-Braggin, 10–30. Totowa, N.J.: Littlefield, Adams & Co., 1982.

Dickens, Bernard M. "Reproduction Law and Medical Consent." *University of Toronto Law Journal* 35 (Summer 1985): 255–286.

Dickens, Bernard M. "Social Dilemmas in Medical Ethics." *Columns* (Fall 1985): 8–9.

Dickin, Katherine L., and Bruce A. Ryan. "Sterilization and the Mentally Retarded." *Canada's Mental Health* (March 1983): 4–8.

Dick-Read, Grantly. *Childbirth without Fear.* New York: Harper & Row, 1970.

Direcks, Anita. "Has the DES Lesson Been Learned?" *DES Action Voice* 28 (Spring 1986): 1–2, 4.

"Discussion on the Ethics of Fertilization In Vitro." In *Human Conception In Vitro*, edited by R. G. Edwards and Jean M. Purdy, 359–370. London: Academic Press, 1982.

Dixon, Bernard. "Engineering Chimeras for Noah's Ark." *Hastings Center Report* 14 (April 1984): 10–12.

Doherty, Dennis J. "The Ethics of Reproductive Intervention." In *Infertility: Diagnosis and Management*, edited by James Aiman, 337–344. New York: Springer-Verlag, 1984.

Dore, Michele, and Diana Majury. "Update: On Abortion." *Status of Women News* (Spring 1983): 22–24.

Dranoff, Linda Silver. "Ask a Lawyer: My Wife Plans to Be a Surrogate Mother." *Chatelaine* (January 1982): 12.

Dreifus, Claudia, ed. *Seizing Our Bodies: The Politics of Women's Health*. New York: Random House, 1977.

Dworkin, Andrea. *Right-Wing Women*. New York: Perigee Books, 1983.

Dworkin, Ronald. *Taking Rights Seriously*. Cambridge, Mass.: Harvard University Press, 1977.

Edwards, Margot, and Penny Simkin. "Obstetric Tests and Technology: A Consumer's Guide." Seattle, Wash.: Pennypress, 1980.

Edwards, Margot, and Mary Waldorf. *Reclaiming Birth: History and Heroines of American Childbirth Reform*. Trumansburg, N.Y.: Crossing Press, 1984.

Edwards, R[obert] G. "Fertilization of Human Eggs In Vitro: Morals, Ethics and the Law." Introduction by Bentley Glass. *Quarterly Review of Biology* 50th Anniversary Special Issue 49 (1976): 367–391.

Edwards, R[obert] G. "The Case for Studying Human Embryos and Their Constituent Tissues In Vitro." In *Human Conception In Vitro*, edited by R. G. Edwards and Jean M. Purdy, 371–388. London: Academic Press, 1982.

Edwards, R[obert] G. "The Current Clinical and Ethical Situation of Human Conception In Vitro." In *Developments in Human Reproduction and Their Eugenic, Ethical Implications*, edited by C. O. Carter, 53–115. New York: Academic Press, 1983.

Edwards, R[obert] G. "Human Conception In Vitro: New Opportunities in Medicine and Research." In *In Vitro Fertilization and Embryo Transfer*, edited by Alan Trounson and Carl Wood, 217–250. Edinburgh: Churchill Livingstone, 1984.

Edwards, R[obert] G., and Ruth E. Fowler. "Human Embryos in the Laboratory." *Scientific American* 223 (December 1970): 2–12.

Edwards, Robert, and Patrick Steptoe. *A Matter of Life: The Story of a Medical Breakthrough*. London: Hutchinson & Co., 1980.

Ehrenreich, Barbara, and Deirdre English. *For Her Own Good: 150 Years of the Experts' Advice to Women*. Garden City, N.Y.: Anchor Books, 1978.

Eisen, Jill. "Drawing the Line: Reproductive Technology." Transcript of CBC *Ideas*, 17, 24 March 1986.

220   Bibliography

Eisenberg, John, and Paula Bourne. "Compulsory Sterilization." In *The Right to Live and Die*, 67–86. Toronto: Ontario Institute for Studies in Education, 1973.

Eisenstein, Zillah. *The Radical Future of Liberal Feminism*. New York: Longman, 1981.

Elkins, Valmai Howe. *The Rights of the Pregnant Parent*. Don Mills, Ontario: Waxwing Productions, 1976.

Elkins, Valmai Howe. *The Birth Report*. Toronto: Lester & Orpen Dennys, 1983.

Elshtain, Jean Bethke. "A Feminist Agenda on Reproductive Technology." *Hastings Center Report* 12 (February 1982): 40–43.

Englehardt, H. Tristram, Jr. "Viability and the Use of the Fetus." In *Ethics and Public Policy*, edited by Tom L. Beauchamp and Terry P. Pinkard, 297–310. Englewood Cliffs, N.J.: Prentice-Hall, 1980.

Engels, Frederick. "The Origin of the Family, Private Property and the State." In *Karl Marx and Frederick Engels: Selected Works*. 449–583. Moscow: Progress Publishers, 1970.

English, Jane. "Abortion: Introduction." In *Feminism and Philosophy*, edited by Mary Vetterling-Braggin, Frederick A. Elliston, and Jane English, 377–393. Totowa, N.J.: Littlefield, Adams & Co., 1978.

English, Jane. "Abortion and the Concept of a Person." In *Values in Conflict*, pp. 83–91. Edited by Burton M. Leiser. New York: Macmillan, 1981.

Etzioni, Amitai. "Sex Control, Science, and Society." *Science* 161 (September 1968): 1107–1112.

Evans, V. Jeffery. "Legal Aspects of Prenatal Sex Selection." In *Sex Selection of Children*, edited by Neil G. Bennett, 147–200. New York: Academic Press, 1983.

Federation of Feminist Women's Health Centers. *A New View of a Woman's Body*. New York: Simon & Schuster, 1981.

Feinberg, Joel. "Abortion." In *Matters of Life and Death: New Introductory Essays in Moral Philosophy*, edited by Tom Regan, 183–217. New York: Random House, 1981.

Ferguson, Evelyn E. "'The Real Cabbage Patch Kids': An Examination of the Canadian Private Adoption System." Occasional Papers in Social Policy Analysis, No. 2. Toronto: Ontario Institute for Studies in Education, 1984.

Fertility and Sterility 46 Supplement 1 (September 1986).

Firestone, Shulamith. *The Dialectic of Sex*. New York: William Morrow & Co., 1970.

Fletcher, John [C]. "Emerging Issues in Fetal Therapy." In *Research Ethics*, edited by Kare Berg and Knut Erik Tranoy, 293–318. New York: Alan R. Liss, 1983.

Fletcher, John [C]. "Ethics and Public Policy: Should Sex Choice Be Discouraged?" In *Sex Selection of Children*, edited by Neil G. Bennett, 213–252. New York: Academic Press, 1983.

Fletcher, John [C]. "Is Sex Selection Ethical?" In *Research Ethics*, edited by Kare Berg and Knut Eric Tranoy, 333–348. New York: Alan R. Liss, 1983.

Fletcher, John [C]., and Joseph D. Schulman. "Fetal Research: The State of the Question." *Hastings Center Report* 15 (April 1985): 6–12.

Fletcher, Joseph. *Humanhood: Essays in Biomedical Ethics*. Buffalo: Prometheus Books, 1979.

Foot, Philippa. "The Problem of Abortion and the Doctrine of the Double Effect." In *Moral Problems*, edited by James Rachels, 59–70. New York: Harper & Row, 1975.

Forer, Lucille, with Henry Still. *The Birth Order Factor*. New York: Pocket Books, 1977.

Francoeur, Robert T. *Utopian Motherhood: New Trends in Human Reproduction*. Garden City, N.Y.: Doubleday, 1970.

Franks, Darrell D. "Psychiatric Evaluation of Women in a Surrogate Mother Program." *American Journal of Psychiatry* 138 (October 1981): 1378–1379.

Freedman, Benjamin. "Status Report: Ethical Issues of Infertility Clinics." *Westminster Affairs: The Newsletter of the Westminster Institute for Ethics and Human Values* (April 1984): 3–6.

Freishtat, Harvey W. "Legal Implications of AID." In *Infertility: Medical, Emotional and Social Considerations*, edited by Miriam D. Mazor and Harriet F. Simons, 138–144. New York: Human Sciences Press, 1984.

Freitas, Robert A., Jr. "Fetal Adoption: A Technological Solution to the Problem of Abortion Ethics." *The Humanist* (May/June 1980): 22–23.

Frisch, Lawrence E. "On Licentious Licensing: A Reply to Hugh LaFollette." *Philosophy and Public Affairs* 11 (1981): 173–180.

Fromer, Margot Joan. *Ethical Issues in Health Care*. St. Louis: C. V. Mosby, 1981.

Frye, Marilyn. *The Politics of Reality: Essays in Feminist Theory*. Trumansburg, New York: Crossing Press, 1983.

Fuller, Elizabeth. *Having Your First Baby after Thirty*. New York: Dodd, Mead, 1983.

Gallagher, Janet. "The Fetus and the Law—Whose Life Is It Anyway?" *Ms.* (September 1984): 2–6.

Gearhart, Sally Miller. "The Future—If There Is One—Is Female." In *Reweaving the Web of Life*, edited by Pam McAllister, 268–284. Philadelphia: New Society Publishers, 1982.

Gimenez, Martha E. "Feminism, Pronatalism, and Motherhood." In *Mothering: Essays in Feminist Theory*, edited by Joyce Trebilcot, 287–314. Totowa, N.J.: Rowman & Allanheld, 1984.

Glass, Robert H., and Ronald J. Ericsson. *Getting Pregnant in the 1980s: New Advances in Infertility Treatment and Sex Preselection*. Berkeley: University of California Press, 1982.

Goodman, Madeleine J., and Lenn E. Goodman. "The Overselling Of Genetic Anxiety." *Hastings Center Report* 12 (October 1982): 20–27.

222   *Bibliography*

Gorney, Cynthia. "For Love and Money." *California Magazine*, October 1983, p. 88.

Gorovitz, Samuel. *Doctors' Dilemmas: Moral Conflict and Medical Care.* New York: Macmillan, 1982.

Gorovitz, Samuel. "On Surrogate Mothers." In *Difficult Decisions in Medical Ethics*, edited by Doreen Ganos, Rachel E. Lipson, Gwynedd Warren, and Barbara J. Weil, 145–154. New York: Alan R. Liss, 1983.

Gorovitz, Samuel. "Engineering Human Reproduction: A Challenge to Public Policy." *Journal of Medicine and Philosophy* 10 (August 1985): 267–274.

Gould, Carol C. *Beyond Domination: New Perspectives on Women and Philosophy.* Totowa, N.J.: Rowman & Allanheld, 1983.

Govier, Trudy. "What Should We Do about Future People?" In *Moral Issues*, edited by Jan Narveson, 399–413. Toronto: Oxford University Press, 1983.

Grady, Wayne. "The Abortionist." *Saturday Night*, July 1984, pp. 30–39.

Graham, Hilary, and Ann Oakley. "Competing Ideologies of Reproduction: Medical and Maternal Perspectives on Pregnancy." In *Women, Health and Reproduction*, edited by Helen Roberts, 50–74. London: Routledge & Kegan Paul, 1981.

Greenglass, Esther R. *After Abortion.* Don Mills, Ontario: Longman Canada, 1976.

Greer, Germaine. *Sex and Destiny: The Politics of Human Fertility.* London: Secker & Warburg, 1984.

Grim, Patrick. "Sex and Social Roles: How to Deal with the Data." In *"Feminity," "Masculinity," and "Androgyny,"* edited by Mary Vetterling-Braggin, 128–147. Totowa, N.J.: Littlefield, Adams & Co., 1982.

Grimsditch, Dianne. *Love Your Enemy? The Debate between Heterosexual Feminism and Political Lesbianism.* London: Onlywomen Press, 1981.

Grisez, Germaine. "Abortion: Ethical Arguments." In *Today's Moral Problems*, edited by Richard Wasserstrom, 83–104. New York: Macmillan, 1975.

Grobstein, Clifford. *From Chance to Purpose: An Appraisal of External Human Fertilization.* Reading, Mass.: Addison-Wesley, 1981.

Grobstein, Clifford. "The Moral Use of 'Spare' Embryos." *Hastings Center Report* 12 (June 1982): 5–6.

Grove, Sarah Jane. "Tempest in a Test Tube." *Toronto Star*, 30 March 1985, pp. L2, L4.

Guttentag, Marcia, and Paul F. Secord. *Too Many Women? The Sex Ratio Question.* Beverly Hills, Calif.: Sage Publications, 1983.

Guttmacher, Alan F. *Pregnancy, Birth and Family Planning.* New York: Viking, 1973.

Hafez, E. S. E. *Human Reproduction: Conception and Contraception.* 2d ed. Hagerstown: Harper & Row, 1980.

Haire, Doris. "The Cultural Warping of Childbirth." Seattle, Wash.:

International Childbirth Education Association, 1972.

Hall, Martha. "Rights and the Problem of Surrogate Parenting." *Philosophical Quarterly* 35 (October 1985): 414–424.

Hanmer, Jalna. "Sex Predetermination, Artificial Insemination and the Maintenance of Male-Dominated Culture." In *Women, Health and Reproduction*, edited by Helen Roberts, 163–190. London: Routledge & Kegan Paul, 1981.

Hanmer, Jalna. "Reproductive Technology: The Future for Women?" In *Machina Ex Dea: Feminist Perspectives on Technology*, edited by Joan Rothschild, 183–197. New York: Pergamon Press, 1983.

Hanmer, Jalna, and Pat Allen. "Reproductive Engineering: The Final Solution?" In *Alice Through the Microscope: The Power of Science over Women's Lives*, edited by the Brighton Women & Science Group, 208–227. London: Virago, 1980.

Harding, Sandra, and Merrill B. Hintikka, eds. *Discovering Reality: Feminist Perspectives on Epistemology, Metaphysics, Methodology, and Philosophy of Science*. Dordrecht, Holland: D. Reidel, 1983.

Hardwick, Peggy A. "Legal Issues in Reproduction." In *Infertility: Diagnosis and Management*, edited by James Aiman, 345–357. New York: Springer-Verlag, 1984.

Hare, R[ichard] M. "Abortion and the Golden Rule." In *Philosophy and Sex*, edited by Robert Baker and Frederick Elliston, 356–375. Buffalo: Prometheus Books, 1975.

Hare, R[ichard] M. "Survival of the Weakest." In *Moral Problems in Medicine*, edited by Samuel Gorovitz, 364–369. Englewood Cliffs, N.J.: Prentice-Hall, 1976.

Harrison, Beverly Wildung. *Our Right to Choose: Toward a New Ethic of Abortion*. Boston: Beacon Press, 1983.

Hazell, Lester Dessez. *Commonsense Childbirth*. New York: Berkley Windhover, 1976.

Hazell, Lester Dessez. "Spiritual and Ethical Aspects of Birth: Who Bears the Ultimate Responsibility?" In *21st Century Obstetrics Now!* 2d ed., edited by Lee Stewart and David Steward, 255–260. Marble Hill, Mo.: NAPSAC, 1977.

Hearn, Alison. "Infertility: A Choice Denied." *News/Nouvelles: Journal of Planned Parenthood Federation of Canada* 4 (September 1983): 8–9.

Henley, John A. "IVF and the Human Family: Possible and Likely Consequences." In *Test-Tube Babies: A Guide to Moral Questions, Present Techniques and Future Possibilities*, edited by William A. W. Walters and Peter Singer, 79–87. Melbourne: Oxford University Press, 1982.

Henshel (Ambert), Anne-Marie. *Sex Structure*. Don Mills, Ontario: Longman Canada, 1973.

Herbenick, Raymond M. "Remarks on Abortion, Abandonment, and Adoption Opportunities." *Philosophy and Public Affairs* 5 (Fall 1975): 98–104.

Hirsch, Bernard D. "Parenthood by Proxy." *Journal of the American Medical Association* 249 (22/29 April 1983): 2251–2252.

Hoff, Gerard Alan, and Lawrence J. Schneiderman. "Having Babies at Home: Is It Safe? Is It Ethical?" *Hastings Center Report* 15 (December 1985): 19–27.

Holmes, Helen B[equaert], Betty B. Hoskins, and Michael Gross, eds. *Birth Control and Controlling Birth: Women-Centered Perspectives.* Clifton, N.J.: Humana Press, 1980.

Holmes, Helen B[equaert], *The Custom-Made Child? Women-Centered Perspectives.* Clifton, N.J.: Humana Press, 1981.

Hoskins, Betty B., and Helen Bequaert Holmes. "Technology and Prenatal Femicide." In *Test-Tube Women: What Future for Motherhood?* edited by Rita Arditti, Renate Duelli Klein and Shelley Minden, 237–255. London: Pandora Press, 1984.

Hubbard, Ruth, Mary Sue Henifin, and Barbara Fried, eds. *Biological Woman—The Convenient Myth.* Cambridge, Mass.: Schenkman, 1982.

Hubbard, Ruth. "The Fetus as Patient." *Ms.* (October 1982): 28–32.

Hutchinson, D. S. "Utilitarianism and Children." *Canadian Journal of Philosophy* 12 (March 1982): 61–73.

"In Britain and Australia, New In Vitro Guidelines." *Hastings Center Report* 13 (February 1983): 2.

Ince, Susan, "Inside the Surrogate Industry." In *Test-Tube Women: What Future for Motherhood?* edited by Rita Arditti, Renate Duelli Klein, and Shelley Minden, 99–116. London: Pandora Press, 1984.

Jagger, Alison. "Abortion and a Woman's Right to Decide." In *Women and Philosophy,* edited by Carol C. Gould and Marx W. Wartofsky, 347–360. New York: Putnam's, 1976.

Jagger, Alison. "Political Philosophies of Women's Liberation." In *Philosophy and Women,* edited by Sharon Bishop and Marjorie Weinzweig, 258–265. Belmont, Calif.: Wadsworth, 1979.

Jagger, Alison. *Feminist Politics and Human Nature.* Totowa, N.J.: Rowman & Allanheld, 1983.

James, William H. "Timing of Fertilization and the Sex Ratio of Offspring." In *Sex Selection of Children,* edited by Neil G. Bennett, 73–99. New York: Academic Press, 1983.

Jansen, Robert P. S. "Sperm and Ova as Property." *Journal of Medical Ethics* 11 (September 1985): 123–126.

Jones, A. D., and C. Dougherty. "Childbirth in a Scientific and Industrial Society," In *Ethnography of Fertility and Birth,* edited by Carol P. MacCormack 269–290. London: Academic Press, 1982.

Jones, H. W., Jr. "The Ethics of In-Vitro Fertilization—1981." In *Human Conception In Vitor,* edited by R. G. Edwards and Jean M. Puddy, 351–357. London: Academic Press, 1982.

Kadushin, Alfred, and Judith A. Martin. *Child Abuse: An Interactional Event.* New York: Columbia University Press, 1981.

Karmel, Marjorie. *Thank You, Dr. Lamaze.* Garden City, N.Y.: Doubleday, 1965.

Kass, Leon R. "Babies by Means of In Vitro Fertilization: Unethical Experiments on the Unborn?" *New England Journal of Medicine* 285 (18 November 1971): 1174–1179.

Kass, Leon R. "Making Babies— The New Biology and the 'Old' Morality." *Public Interest* 26 (Winter 1972): 18–56.

Kass, Leon R. "'Making Babies' Revisited." *Public Interest* 54 (Winter 1979): 32–60.

Kaye, Marcia. "Worth Keeping." *Today Magazine*, 21 August 1982, pp. 6–8, 20.

Kazenel, Michael. "Alcohol and the Unborn: A Disastrous Mix." *Perspectives Sante/Future Health* (Automne 1981): 3–4.

Keane, Noel P. "Surrogate Motherhood: Past, Present and Future." In *Difficult Decisions in Medical Ethics*, edited by Doreen Ganos, Rachel E. Lipson, Gwynedd Warren, and Barbara J. Weil, 155–164. New York: Alan R. Liss, 1983.

Keller, Paul J. "Introduction." In *Female Infertility*, edited by Paul J. Keller, 1–5. New York: Karger, 1978.

Keolkar, Kathy. "Cesarean Birth—A Special Delivery." Seattle, Wash.: Pennypress, 1979.

Ketchum, Sara Ann. "The Moral Status of the Bodies of Persons." *Social Theory and Practice* 10 (Spring 1984): 25–38.

Ketchum, Sara Ann, and Christine Pierce. "Separatism and Sexual Relationships." In *Philosophy and Women*, edited by Sharon Bishop and Marjorie Weinzweig, 163–171. Belmont, Calif.: Wadsworth, 1979.

Keyserlingk, Edward W. "The Unborn Child's Right to Prenatal Care." Part 1. *Health Law in Canada* 3, no. 1 (1982): 10–21.

Keyserlingk, Edward W. "The Unborn Child's Right to Prenatal Care." Part 2. *Health Law in Canada* 3, no. 2 (1982): 31–41.

Keyserlingk, Edward W. "Clarifying the Right to Prenatal Care: A Reply to a Response." *Health Law in Canada* 4 (1983): 35–38.

Kitzinger, Sheila. *The Experience Of Childbirth*. Harmondsworth, England: Penguin, 1974.

Kitzinger, Sheila. *Giving Birth: The Parents' Emotions in Childbirth*. New York: Schocken Books, 1977.

Kitzinger, Sheila. *Women as Mothers*. Glasgow: Fontana Books, 1978.

Kitzinger, Sheila. *The Complete Book of Pregnancy and Childbirth*. New York: Alfred A. Knopf, 1980.

Kitzinger, Sheila. "The Social Context of Birth: Some Comparisons Between Childbirth in Jamaica and Britain." In *Ethnography of Fertility and Birth*, edited by Carol P. MacCormack, 181–203. London: Academic Press, 1982.

Klapholz, Henry. "The Electronic Fetal Monitor in Perinatology." In *Birth Control and Controlling Birth: Women-Centered Perspectives*, edited by Helen B. Holmes, Betty B. Hoskins, and Michael Gross, 167–173. Clifton, N.J.: Humana Press, 1980.

Knight, Norman. "Regulating Surrogate Births." *News/Nouvelles: Journal of Planned Parenthood Federation of Canada* 4 (September 1983): 13.

Knoppers, Bartha Maria. "Women and the Reproductive Technologies." In *Family Law in Canada: New Directions*, edited by Elizabeth

Sloss, 211–225. Ottawa: Canadian Advisory Council on the Status of Women, 1985.

Kolata, Gina [Bari]. "Early Warnings and Latest Cures For Infertility." *Ms.* (May 1979): 85–87.

Kolata, Gina [Bari]. "Beyond Amniocentesis: New Techniques in Fetal Testing." *Ms.* (December 1983): 91–92, 94.

Kremer, E. J., and E. A. Synan, eds. *Death before Birth: Canada and the Abortion Question.* Toronto: Griffin House, 1974.

Krimmel, Herbert T. "The Case against Surrogate Parenting." *Hastings Center Report* 13 (October 1983): 35–39.

Kuhse, Helga. "An Ethical Approach to IVF and ET: What Ethics Is All About." In *Test-Tube Babies: A Guide to Moral Questions, Present Techniques and Future Possibilities,* edited by William A. W. Walters and Peter Singer, 22–35. Melbourne: Oxford University Press, 1982.

Kuhse, Helga, and Peter Singer. "The Moral Status of the Embryo." In *Test-Tube Babies: A Guide to Moral Questions, Present Techniques and Future Possibilities,* edited by William A. W. Walters and Peter Singer, 57–63. Melbourne: Oxford University Press, 1982.

LaFollette, Hugh. "Licensing Parents." *Philosophy and Public Affairs* 9 (1980): 182–197.

LaFollette, Hugh. "A Reply to Frisch." *Philosophy and Public Affairs* 11 (1981): 181–183.

Lahey, Kathleen A. "Alternative Insemination: Facing the Conceivable Options." *Broadside* 8 (1986): 8–10.

Langham, Paul. "Between Abortion and Infanticide." *Southern Journal Of Philosophy* 17 (Winter 1979): 465–471.

Lappe, Marc, and Peter Steinfels. "Choosing the Sex of Our Children." *Hastings Center Report* 4 (February 1974): 1–4.

Lappe, Marc. "Risk-Taking for the Unborn." *Hastings Center Report* 2 (February 1972): 1–3.

Largey, Gale. "Reproductive Technologies: Sex Selection." In *Encyclopedia of Bioethics,* edited by Warren T. Reich, 1439–1444. New York: Free Press, 1978.

Larned, Deborah. "Cesarean Birth: Why They Are up 100 Percent." *Ms.* (October 1978): 24.

Laslie, Adele E. "Ethical Issues in Childbirth." *Journal of Medicine and Philosophy* 7 (1982): 179–195.

Laurance, Jeremy. "The Moral Pressure to Have Children." *New Society* 61 (5 August 1982): 216–218.

Lazare, Louise Cannon. "The Adoptive Parents' Experience: A Personal Narrative." In *Infertility: Medical, Emotional and Social Considerations,* edited by Miriam D. Mazor and Harriet F. Simons, 108–125. New York: Human Sciences Press, 1984.

Leal, H. Allan. "Vice Chairman's Dissent." In Ontario Law Reform Commission, *Report on Human Artificial Reproduction and Related Matters.* Ontario: Ministry of the Attorney General, 1985.

Leavitt, Judith Walzer. "Birthing and Anesthesia: The Debate over Twilight Sleep." *Signs* 6 (1980): 147–164.

Leboyer, Frederick. *Childbirth without Violence*. New York: Random House, 1975.

Leeton, John F., Alan O. Trounson, and Carl Wood. "IVF and ET: What It Is and How It Works." In *Test-Tube Babies: A Guide to Moral Questions, Present Techniques and Future Possibilities*, edited by William A. W. Walters and Peter Singer, 2–10. Melbourne: Oxford University Press, 1982.

Letters—"On Surrogate Mothers and 'Politically Correct' Sex." *Ms.* (June 1983): 5–6.

Levin, David S. "Abortion, Personhood and Vagueness." *Journal of Value Inquiry* 19 (1985): 197–209.

Levine, Carol, and Robert Veatch. Case: "The Unwanted Child: Caring for the Fetus Born Alive after an Abortion." In *Cases in Bioethics*, rev. ed., edited by Carol Levine and Robert M. Veatch, 1–6. Hastings-on-Hudson, N.Y.: The Hastings Center, 1984.

Levine, Helen. "The Power Politics of Motherhood." In *Perspectives on Women in the 1980s*, edited by Joan Turner and Lois Emery, 28–40. Winnipeg: University of Manitoba Press, 1983.

Levy, Steven R. "Abortion and Dissenting Parents: A Dialogue." *Ethics* 90 (January 1980): 162–163.

Liley, A. W. "The Foetus as a Personality." *Fetal Therapy* 1 (1986): 8–17.

Lippman, Abby. "Access to Prenatal Screening Services and Trials: Who Decides?" Paper presented at the Policy Workshop on Medical Control: Pregnancy Issues, Sixth National Biennial Conference of the National Association of Women and the Law, Ottawa, Ontario, 22 February 1985.

Long, Linda. "Artificially Assisted Conception." *Health Law in Canada* 5 (1985): 89–107.

MacCormack, C[arol] P. "Biological, Cultural and Social Adaptation in Human Fertility and Birth: A Synthesis." In *Ethnography of Fertility and Birth*, edited by Carol P. MacCormack, 1–23. London: Academic Press, 1982.

MacIntyre, Sally. "'Who Wants Babies?' The Social Construction of 'Instincts.'" In *Sexual Divisions and Society: Process and Change*, edited by Diana Leonard Barker and Sheila Allen, 150–173. London: Tavistock Publications, 1976.

Mackenzie, Thomas B., and Theodore C. Nagel. "Case Studies— When a Pregnant Woman Endangers Her Fetus." *Hastings Center Report* 16 (February 1986): 24–25.

MacKinnon, Catharine A. "Feminism, Marxism, Method, and the State: An Agenda for Theory." In *Feminist Theory: A Critique of Ideology*, edited by Nannerl O. Keohane, Michelle Z. Rosaldo, and Barbara C. Gelpi, 1–30. Chicago: University of Chicago Press, 1982.

Madison, Robert L. Foreword to *Having Your First Baby after Thirty*, by Elizabeth Fuller. New York: Dodd, Mead, 1983.

Mady, Theresa M. "Surrogate Mothers: The Legal Issues." *American Journal of Law and Medicine* 7 (Fall 1981): 323–352.

Mahowald, Mary B. "Concepts of Abortion and Their Relevance to the

Abortion Debate." *Southern Journal of Philosophy* 20 (Summer 1982): 195–208.

Mallovy, Naomi. "Survival of the Preselected." *Maclean's*, 10 November 1980, pp. 60, 62.

Marx, Karl. "Wage Labour and Capital." In *Karl Marx and Frederick Engels: Selected Works*, 64–93. Moscow: Progress Publishers, 1970.

Mazor, Miriam D. "Emotional Reactions to Infertility." In *Infertility: Medical, Emotional and Social Considerations*, edited by Miriam D. Mazor and Harriet F. Simons, 23–35. New York: Human Sciences Press, 1984.

McDonnell, Kathleen. *Not an Easy Choice: A Feminist Re-examines Abortion*. Toronto: Women's Press, 1984.

McKay, Shona. "A Media Judgement on Surrogate Birth." *Maclean's*, 14 February 1983, p. 41.

McQuaig, Linda. "Living without the Pill." *Maclean's*, 15 March 1982, pp. 40–45.

Meier, Richard L. "Sex Determination and Other Innovations." In *Population in Perspective*, edited by Louise B. Young, 406–412. New York: Oxford University Press, 1968.

Menning, Barbara [Eck]. "In Defense of In Vitro Fertilization." In *The Custom-Made Child? Women-Centered Perspectives*, edited by Helen B. Holmes, Betty B. Hoskins, and Michael Gross, 263–267. Clifton, N.J.: Humana Press, 1981.

Menning, Barbara [Eck]. "The Psychology of Infertility." In *Infertility: Diagnosis and Management*, edited by James Aiman, 17–29. New York: Springer-Verlag, 1984.

Menning, Barbara [Eck]. "RESOLVE: Counseling and Support for Infertile Couples." In *Infertility: Medical, Emotional and Social Considerations*, edited by Miriam D. Mazor and Harriet F. Simons, 53–60. New York: Human Sciences Press, 1984.

Midgley, Mary, and Judith Hughes. *Women's Choices: Philosophical Problems Facing Feminism*. London: Weidenfeld & Nicholson, 1983.

Miller, Jack. "Scientists Try to Create Life without Males." *Toronto Star*, 21 April 1985, p. F8.

Moen, Elizabeth W. "What Does 'Control over Our Bodies' Really Mean?" *International Journal of Women's Studies* 2 (March/April 1979): 129–143.

Morison, Robert S., and Sumner B. Twiss, Jr. "The Human Fetus as Useful Research Material." *Hastings Center Report* 3 (1973): 8–10.

Morreall, John. "Of Marsupials and Men: A Thought Experiment on Abortion." *Dialogos* 37 (1981): 7–18.

Moskop, John C. "Potential Persons and Murder: A Reply to John Woods." *Dialogue* 21 (1982): 307–315.

Munro, Margaret. "'Rent-a-Womb' Trade Thriving across Canada-U.S. Border." *Montreal Gazette*, 21 January 1985, p. D11.

Munroe, Robert B. "The Right to Be a Parent: A Legal Perspective." In *Medical Ethics and Human Life*, edited by John E. Thomas, 166–170. Toronto: Samuel Stevens, 1983.

Murphy, Julie. "Egg Farming and Women's Future." In *Test-Tube Women: What Future for Motherhood?*, edited by Rita Arditti, Renate Duelli Klein and Shelley Minden, 68–75. London: Pandora Press, 1984.

Murphy, Timothy F. "The Moral Signifiance of Spontaneous Abortion." *Journal of Medical Ethics* 11 (June 1985): 79–83.

Myrna, Frances. "The Right to Abortion." In *Ethics for Modern Life*, edited by Raziel Abelson and Marie-Louise Friquegnon, 103–116. New York: St. Martin's Press, 1982.

Narveson, Jan. "Tinkering and Abortion." *Dialogue* 17 (1978): 125–128.

Narveson, Jan. "Moral Problems of Population." In *Ethics and Population*, edited by Michael D. Bayles, 59–80. Cambridge, Mass.: Schenkman, 1976.

Nash, Susan E. Letter. *Ms.* (June 1983): 5.

Nentwig, M. Ruth. "Technical Aspects of Sex Preselection." In *The Custom-Made Child? Women-Centered Perspective*, edited by Helen B. Holmes, Betty B. Hoskins and Michael Gross, 181–186. Clifton, N.J.: Humana Press, 1981.

Nicholson, Susan T. "The Roman Catholic Doctrine of Therapeutic Abortion." In *Feminism and Philosophy*, edited by Mary Vetterling-Braggin, Frederick A. Elliston, and Jane English, 385–407. Totowa, N.J.: Littlefield, Adams & Co., 1978.

Noonan, John T., Jr. "An Almost Absolute Value in History." In *The Problem of Abortion*, edited by Joel Feinberg, 9–14. Belmont, Calif. Wadsworth Publishing Co., 1973.

Noonan, John T., Jr. "Against Abortion." In *Ethics for Modern Life*, edited by Raziel Abelson and Marie-Louise Friquegnon, 84–90. New York: St. Martin's Press, 1982.

"'No Problems' with Baby Girl Born during Abortion." *Montreal Gazette*, 23 March 1981, p. 2.

"Nothing Left to Chance in 'Rent-a-Womb' Agreements." *Toronto Star*, 13 January 1985, pp. H1, H4.

Oakley, Ann. "Wisewoman and Medicine Man: Changes in the Management of Childbirth." In *The Rights and Wrongs of Women*, edited by Juliet Mitchell and Ann Oakley, 17–58. Harmondsworth, England: Penguin Books, 1976.

Oakley, Ann. *Becoming a Mother*. New York: Schocken Books, 1980.

Oakley, Ann. *Women Confined: Towards a Sociology of Childbirth*. New York: Schocken Books, 1980.

O'Brien, Mary. *The Politics of Reproduction*. London: Routledge & Kegan Paul, 1981.

O'Donovan, Oliver. *Begotten or Made?* Oxford: Clarendon Press, 1984.

Ohlendorf, Pat. "Treating the Unborn Child as a Patient." *Maclean's*, 19 April 1982, pp. 47–49.

OMA Committee on Perinatal Care. "Ontario Medical Association Discussion Paper on Directions in Health Care Issues Relating to Childbirth." Toronto, Ontario, 1984.

O'Neill, Onora. "Begetting, Bearing and Rearing." In *Having Children: Philosophical and Legal Reflections on Parenthood*, edited by Onora O'Neill and William Ruddick, 25–38. New York: Oxford University Press, 1979.

O'Neill, Onora, and William Ruddick, eds. *Having Children: Philosophical and Legal Reflections on Parenthood*. New York: Oxford University Press, 1979.

Ontario Law Reform Commission. *Report on Human Artificial Reproduction and Related Matters* I and II. Toronto: Ministry of the Attorney General, 1985.

Ooms, Theodora, and Margaret O'Brien Steinfels. "AID and the Single Welfare Mother." *Hastings Center Report* 13 (February 1983): 22–23.

Oppenheimer, Jo. "Childbirth in Ontario: The Transition from Home to Hospital in the Early Twentieth Century." *Ontario History* 75 (March 1983): 36–60.

Overall, Christine. "Artificial Reproduction and the Meaning of infertility." *Queen's Quarterly* 92 (Autumn 1985): 482–488.

Overall, Christine. "New Reproductive Technology: Some Implications for the Abortion Issue." *Journal of Value Inquiry* 19 (1985): 279–292.

Overall, Christine. " 'Pluck a Fetus from Its Womb': A Critique of Current Attitudes toward the Embryo/Fetus." *University of Western Ontario Law Review* 24 (1986): 1–14.

Overall, Christine. "Reproductive Ethics: Feminist and Non-Feminist Approaches." *Canadian Journal of Women and the Law/revue juridique la femme et le droit* I, no. 2 (1986): 271–278.

Overall, Christine. "Reproductive Technology and the Future of the Family." In *Women and Men: Interdisciplinary Readings on Gender*, edited by Greta Hofmann Nemiroff, 245–261. Markham: Fitzhenry & Whiteside, 1987.

Overall, Christine. "Ethical Issues of Modern Reproductive Technology." In *Medicine, Ethics, and Law: Canada and Poland in Dialogue*, edited by Tomasz Dybowski, David J. Roy, Marek Safjan, and Jean-Louis Baudouin (forthcoming 1987).

Overall, Christine. "Sexuality, Parenting, and Reproductive Choices." *Resources For Feminist Research/Documentation sur la recherche féministe* 16 no. 2 (forthcoming 1987).

Overall, Christine. "Surrogate Motherhood," *Canadian Journal of Philosophy* (forthcoming 1987).

Parfit, Derek. "On Doing the Best for Our Children." In *Ethics and Population*, edited by Michael D. Bayles, 100–115. Cambridge, Mass.: Schenkman, 1976.

Parfit, Derek. "Rights, Interests, and Possible People." In *Moral Problems in Medicine*, edited by Samuel Gorovitz, 369–375. Englewood Cliffs, N.J.: Prentice-Hall, 1976.

Parker, Philip J. "Surrogate Motherhood: The Interaction of Litigation, Legislation and Psychiatry." *International Journal of Law and Psychiatry* 5 (1982): 341–354.

Parker, Philip J. "Motivation of Surrogate Mothers: Initial Findings." *American Journal of Psychiatry* 140 (January 1983): 117–118.

Parsons, Talcott. "Definitions of Health and Illness in the Light of American Values and Social Structure." In *Concepts of Health and Disease: Interdisciplinary Perspectives*, edited by Arthur L. Caplan, H. Tristram Engelhardt, Jr., and James J. McCartney, 57–81. Reading, Mass.: Addison-Wesley, 1981.

Patterson, Suzanne M. "Parenthood by Proxy: Legal Implications of Surrogate Birth." *Iowa Law Review* 385 (1982): 385–399.

Patychuk, Dianne. "Ultrasound: The First Wave." *Healthsharing* (Fall 1985): 25–28.

Paul, Ellen Frankel, and Jeffrey Paul. "Self-Ownership, Abortion and Infanticide." *Journal of Medical Ethics* 5 (1979): 133–138.

Pebley, Anne R., and Charles F. Westoff. "Women's Sex Preferences in the United States: 1970 to 1975." *Demography* 19 (May 1982): 177–189.

Peck, Ellen. *The Baby Trap*. New York: Pinnacle Books, 1972.

Peck, Ellen, and Judith Senderowitz. *Pronatalism: The Myth of Mom and Apple Pie*. New York: Thomas Y. Crowell, 1974.

Pelrine, Eleanor Wright. *Abortion in Canada*. Toronto: New Press, 1972.

Peplau, Lettitia Anne, and Steven L. Gordon. "The Intimate Relationships of Lesbians and Gay Men." In *Changing Boundaries: Gender Roles and Sexual Behavior*, edited by Elizabeth Rice Allgeier and Naomi B. McCormick, 226–244. Palo Alto, Calif.: Mayfield Publishing Co., 1983.

Petchesky, Roslind Pollack. *Abortion and Women's Choice: The State, Sexuality and Reproductive Freedom*. Reprint ed. Boston: Northeastern University Press, 1984.

Petchesky, Rosalind Pollack. "Reproductive Freedom: Beyond 'A Woman's Right to Choose.'" In *Women: Sex and Sexuality*, edited by Catharine R. Stimpson and Ethel Spector Person, 92–116. Chicago: University of Chicago Press, 1980.

Pfeffer, Naomi, and Anne Woollett. *The Experience of Infertility*. London: Virago, 1983.

Piercy, Marge. *Woman on the Edge of Time*. New York: Fawcett Crest, 1976.

Pogrebin, Letty Cottin. "Do Americans Hate Children? A Challenging Analysis of a National 'Phobia.'" *Ms.* (November 1983): 47–50, 126–127.

Pogrebin, Letty Cottin. *Family Politics: Love and Power on an Intimate Frontier*. New York: McGraw-Hill, 1983.

Postgate, John. "Bat's Chance in Hell." *New Scientist* 58 (5 April 1973): 12–16.

Powledge, Tabitha [M.]. "Prenatal Diagnosis—Now the Problems." *New Scientist* 69 (12 February 1976): 332–334.

Powledge, Tabitha [M.]. "Unnatural Selection: On Choosing Children's Sex." In *The Custom-Made Child? Women-Centered Perspectives*, edited by Helen B. Holmes, Betty B. Hoskins and Michael Gross, 193–199. Clifton, N.Y.: Humana Press, 1981.

Powledge, Tabitha [M.]. "Toward a Moral Policy for Sex Choice." In *Sex Selection of Children*, edited by Neil G. Bennett, 201–212. New York: Academic Press, 1983.

Powledge, Tabitha [M.]. "Windows on the Womb." *Psychology Today* 17 (May 1983): 37–42.

Prostitution in Canada. Ottawa: Canadian Advisory Council on the Status of Women, March 1984.

Ramsey, Paul. "The Morality of Abortion." In *Moral Problems*, edited by James Rachels, 37–58. New York: Harper & Row, 1975.

Rapp, Rayna. "The Ethics of Choice." *Ms.* (April 1984): 97–100.

Rassaby, Alan A. "Surrogate Motherhood: The Position and Problems of Substitutes." In *Test-Tube Babies: A Guide to Moral Questions, Present Techniques and Future Possibilities*, edited by William A. W. Walters and Peter Singer, 97–109. Melbourne: Oxford University Press, 1982.

Raymond, Janice G. "Sex Preselection: A Response." In *The Custom-Made Child? Women-Centered Perspectives*, edited by Helen B. Holmes, Betty B. Hoskins, and Michael Gross, 209–212. Clifton, N.J.: Humana Press, 1981.

Reich, Warren T., ed. *Encyclopedia of Bioethics*. New York: Collier-Macmillan, 1978.

Rent, Clyda S., and George S. Rent. "More on Offspring-Sex Preference: A Comment on Nancy E. Williamson's 'Sex Preference, Sex Control, and the Status of Women.'" *Signs* 3 (Winter 1977): 505–513.

Rich, Adrienne. "The Theft of Childbirth." In *Seizing Our Bodies: The Politics of Women's Health*, edited by Claudia Dreifus, 146–163. New York: Vintage Books, 1977.

Rich, Adrienne. "Compulsory Heterosexuality and Lesbian Existence." In *Women: Sex and Sexuality*, edited by Catharine R. Stimpson and Ethel Spector Person, 62–91. Chicago: University of Chicago Press, 1980.

Richards, Janet Radcliffe. *The Sceptical Feminist: A Philosophical Enquiry*. Harmondsworth, England: Penguin Books, 1980.

Rindfuss, Ronald R., Judith L. Ladinsky, Elizabeth Coppock, Victor W. Marshall, and A. S. Macpherson. "Convenience and the Occurrence of Births: Induction of Labor in the United States and Canada." In *Women and Health: The Politics of Sex in Medicine*, edited by Elizabeth Fee, 37–58. Farmingdale, N.Y.: Baywood Publishing Co., 1982.

Rivers, Caryl. "Cloning: A Generation Made to Order." *Ms.* (June 1976): 51.

Rivers, Caryl. "Genetic Engineers: Now That They've Gone Too Far, Can They Stop?" *Ms.* (June 1976): 49.

Roberts, Helen, ed. *Women, Health and Reproduction*. London: Routledge & Kegan Paul, 1981.

Robertson, John A. "Procreative Liberty and the Control of Conception, Pregnancy, and Childbirth." *Virgina Law Review* 69 (April 1983): 405–464.

Robertson, John A. "Surrogate Mothers: Not So Novel after All." *Hastings Center Report* 13 (October 1983): 28–34.

Robertson, John A. "John Robertson Replies." *Hastings Center Report* 14 (June 1984): 43.

Robertson, John A. "Embryo Research." *University of Western Ontario Law Review* 24 (1986): 15–37.

Rodgers-Magnet, Sanda. "Foetal Rights and Maternal Rights: Is There a Conflict?" Paper presented at the 6th National Biennial Conference of the National Association of Women and the Law, Ottawa, Ontario, 22 February 1985.

Roggencamp, Viola. "Abortion of a Special Kind: Male Sex Selection in India." In *Test-Tube Women: What Future for Motherhood?* edited by Rita Arditti, Renate Duelli Klein, and Shelley Minden, 266–277. London: Pandora Press, 1984.

Romalis, Coleman. "Taking Care of the Little Woman." In *Childbirth: Alternatives to Medical Control*, edited by Shelly Romalis, 92–121. Austin: University of Texas Press, 1981.

Romalis, Shelly. "Natural Childbirth and the Reluctant Physician." In *Childbirth: Alternatives to Medical Control*, edited by Shelly Romalis, 63–91. Austin: University of Texas Press, 1981.

Rose, Hilary, and Jalna Hanmer. "Women's Liberation: Reproduction and the Technological Fix." In *Sexual Divisions and Society: Process and Change*, edited by Diana Leonard Barker and Sheila Allen, 199–223. London: Tavistock Publications, 1976.

Rose, Hilary, and Jalna Hanmer. "Women's Liberation: Reproduction and the Technological Fix." In *Ideology of/in the Natural Sciences*, edited by Hilary Rose and Steven Rose, 117–135. Cambridge, Mass.: Schenkman, 1980.

Ross, Steven L. "Abortion and the Death of the Fetus." *Philosophy and Public Affairs* 11 (1982): 232–245.

Rothman, Barbara Katz. "Awake and Aware, or False Consciousness." In *Childbirth: Alternatives to Medical Control*, edited by Shelly Romalis, 150–180. Austin: University of Texas Press. 1981.

Rothman, Barbara Katz. "How Science Is Redefining Parenthood." *Ms.* (July/August 1982): 154–156, 158.

Rothman, Barbara Katz. "The Meanings of Choice in Reproductive Technology." In *Test-Tube Women: What Future for Motherhood?* edited by Rita Arditti, Renate Duelli Klein, and Shelley Minden, 23–33. London: Pandora Press, 1984.

Rothman, Barbara Katz. *Giving Birth: Alternatives in Childbirth*. Harmondsworth, England: Penguin Books, 1984.

Rothman, Barbara Katz. "The Products of Conception: The Social Context of Reproductive Choices." *Journal of Medical Ethics* 11 (1985): 188–193.

Rothman, Barbara Katz. "Case Studies—When a Pregnant Woman Endangers Her Fetus." *Hastings Center Report* 16 (February 1986): 24–25.

Rothman, Barbara Katz. *The Tentative Pregnancy: Prenatal Diagnosis and the Future of Motherhood*. New York: Viking/Penguin, 1986.

Rothschild, Joan, ed. *Machina Ex Dea: Feminist Perspectives on Technology*. New York: Pergamon Press, 1983.

Rothschild, Joan. "Technology, Housework, and Women's Liberation: A Theoretical Analysis." In *Machina Ex Dea: Feminist Perspectives on Technology*, edited by Joan Rothschild, 79–93. New York: Pergamon Press, 1983.

Rowland, Robyn. "Reproductive Technologies: The Final Solution to the Woman Question?" In *Test-Tube Women: What Future for Motherhood?* edited by Rita Arditti, Renate Duelli Klein, and Shelley Minden, 356–369. London: Pandora Press, 1984.

Rowland, Robyn. "Social Implications of Reproductive Technology." *International Review of Natural Family Planning* 8 (1984): 189–205.

Ruddick, William, and William Wilcox. "Operating on the Fetus." *Hastings Center Report* 12 (October 1982): 10–14.

Ruse, Michael. "Are Homosexuals Sick?" In *Concepts of Health and Disease: Interdisciplinary Perspectives*, edited by Arthur L. Caplan, H. Tristram Engelhardt, Jr., and James J. McCartney, 693–723. Reading, Mass.: Addison-Wesley, 1981.

Sandelowski, Margarete. *Pain, Pleasure, and American Childbirth*. Westport, Conn.: Greenwood Press, 1984.

Sayers, Janet. *Biological Politics: Feminist and Anti-Feminist Perspectives*. London: Tavistock Publications, 1982.

Scarf, Maggie. "The Fetus as Guinea Pig." *New York Times*, reprint ed., 1975.

Scarlett, B. F. "The Moral Status of Embryos." *Journal of Medical Ethics* 2 (1984): 79–81.

Schedler, George, and Matthew J. Kelly. "Abortion and Tinkering." *Dialogue* 17 (1978): 122–125.

Seaman, Barbara, and Gideon Seaman. *Women and the Crisis in Sex Hormones*. New York: Rawson Associates, 1977.

Shaw, Margery W. "Conditional Prospective Rights of the Fetus." *Journal of Legal Medicine* 5 (1984): 63–116.

Shorter, Edward. *A History of Women's Bodies*. New York: Basic Books, 1982.

Simons, Harriet F. "Infertility: Implications for Policy Formulation." In *Infertility: Medical, Emotional and Social Considerations*, edited by Miriam D. Mazor and Harriet F. Simons, 61–70. New York: Human Sciences Press, 1984.

Singer, Peter. "A Utilitarian Population Principle." In *Ethics and Population*, edited by Michael D. Bayles, 81–99. Cambridge, Mass.: Schenkman, 1976.

Singer, Peter, and Helga Kuhse. "Response." *Journal of Medical Ethics* 2 (1984): 80–81.

Singer, Peter, and Deane Wells. *The Reproduction Revolution: New Ways of Making Babies*. Oxford: Oxford University Press, 1984.

Smith, Janet Farrell. "Parenting and Property." In *Mothering: Essays in Feminist Theory*, edited by Joyce Trebilcot, 199–212. Totowa, N.J.: Rowman & Allanheld, 1983.

Smith, Janet Farrell. "Rights-Conflict, Pregnancy, and Abortion." In *Beyond Domination: New Perspectives on Women and Philosophy*, edited by Carol C. Gould, 265–273. Totowa, N.J.: Rowman & Allanheld, 1983.

Snowden, R., and G. D. Mitchell. *The Artificial Family: A Consideration of Artificial Insemination by Donor*. London: Unwin Paperbacks, 1983.

Snowden, R., G. D. Mitchell, and E. M. Snowden. *Artificial Reproduction: A Social Investigation*. London: George Allen & Unwin, 1983.

Somerville, Margaret A. "Reflections on Canadian Abortion Law: Evacuation and Destruction—Two Separate Issues." *University of Toronto Law Journal* 31 (1981): 1–26.

Somerville, Margaret A. "Birth Technology, Parenting and 'Deviance.'" *International Journal of Law and Psychiatry* 5 (1982): 123–153.

Spender, Dale, ed. *Men's Studies Modified*. Oxford: Pergamon Press, 1981.

Steckle, Mary Margaret. Letter. *Healthsharing* (Winter 1985): 25.

Steinbacher, Roberta. "Futuristic Implications of Sex Preselection." In *The Custom-Made Child? Women-Centered Perspectives*, edited by Helen B. Holmes, Betty B. Hoskins, and Michael Gross, 187–191. Clifton, N.J.: Humana Press, 1981.

Stewart, David, and Lewis E. Mehl. "A Rebuttal to Negative Home Birth Statistics Cited by ACOG." In *21st Century Obstetrics Now!* 2d ed., edited by Lee Stewart and David Stewart, 27–32. Marble Hill, Mo.: NAPSAC, 1977.

Strong, Carson. "The Tiniest Newborns." *Hastings Center Report* 13 (February 1983): 14–19.

Sumner, L. W. "Toward a Credible View of Abortion." *Canadian Journal of Philosophy* 4 (September 1974): 163–181.

Taymor, Melvin L. *Infertility*. New York: Grune & Stratton, 1978.

Teichman, Jenny. *Illegitimacy: A Philosophical Examination*. Oxford: Basil Blackwell, 1982.

Teper, Sue, and E. Malcolm Symonds. "Artificial Insemination by Donor: Problems and Perspectives." In *Developments in Human Reproduction and Their Eugenic, Ethical Implications*, edited by C. O. Carter, 19–52. London: Academic Press, 1983.

Teresi, Dick, and Kathleen McAuliffe. "Male Pregnancy." *Omni* (December 1985): 51.

Tew, Marjorie. "The Case against Hospital Deliveries: The Statistical Evidence." In *The Place of Birth*, edited by Sheila Kitzinger and J. A. Davis, 55–65. Oxford: Oxford University Press, 1978.

Thomas, David. *The Experience of Handicap*. London: Methuen, 1982.

Thomson, Judith Jarvis. "A Defense of Abortion." *Philosophy and Public Affairs* 1 (Fall 1971): 47–66. Reprinted in *Moral Problems*, edited by James Rachels, 89–106. New York: Harper & Row, 1975.

Thompson, Paul. "Childbirth in North America: Parental Autonomy and the Welfare of the Fetus." Unpublished paper, Toronto, Ontario, 1984.

Thompson, Paul. "Home Birth: Consumer Choice and Restriction of Physician Autonomy." *Journal of Business Ethics* 6 (1987): 75–81.

Thompson, Paul. "Home Birth: Safety and Values." Unpublished paper, Toronto, Ontario, 1986.

Tooley, Michael. "A Defense of Abortion and Infanticide." In *The Problem of Abortion*, edited by Joel Feinberg, 120–134. Belmont, Calif.: Wadsworth Publishing Co., 1973.

Tooley, Michael. "Abortion and Infanticide." In *Values in Conflict*, edited by Burton M. Leiser, 59–83. New York: Macmillan, 1981.

Trebilcot, Joyce, ed. *Mothering: Essays in Feminist Theory*. Totowa, N.J.: Rowman & Allanheld, 1983.

Tucker, William. "In Vitro Veritas." *New Republic*, 28 October 1981, pp. 14–16.

Veevers, Jean E. *Childless by Choice*. Toronto: Butterworths, 1980.

Verny, Thomas, with John Kelly. *The Secret Life of the Unborn Child*. New York: Summit Books, 1981.

Volpe, E[rminio] Peter. *Patient in the Womb*. Macon, Ga.: Mercer University Press, 1984.

Walsh, Vivien. "Contraception: The Growth of a Technology." In *Alice Through the Microscope: The Power Of Science over Women's Lives*, edited by The Brighton Women & Science Group, 182–207. London: Virago, 1980.

Walters, LeRoy. "Human In Vitro Fertilization: A Review of the Ethical Literature." *Hastings Center Report* 9 (August 1979): 23–43.

Walters, William A. W. "Cloning, Ectogenesis, and Hybrids: Things to Come?" In *Test-Tube Babies: A Guide to Moral Questions, Present Techniques and Future Possibilities*, edited by William [A. W.] Walters and Peter Singer, 110–118. Melbourne: Oxford University Press, 1982.

Walters, William [A. W.], and Peter Singer, eds. *Test-Tube Babies: A Guide to Moral Questions, Present Techniques and Future Possibilities*. Melbourne: Oxford University Press, 1982.

Walters, William [A. W.], and Peter Singer, eds. "Conclusions—And Costs." In *Test-Tube Babies: A Guide to Moral Questions, Present Techniques and Future Possibilities*, edited by William [A. W.] Walters and Peter Singer, 128–141. Melbourne: Oxford University Press, 1982.

Warnock, Mary. *A Question of Life: The Warnock Report on Human Fertilisation and Embryology*. Oxford: Basil Blackwell, 1985.

Warren, Mary Anne. "On the Moral and Legal Status of Abortion." In *Today's Moral Problems*, edited by Richard Wasserstrom, 120–136. New York: Macmillan, 1975.

Warren, Mary Anne. *Gendercide: The Implications of Sex Selection*. Totowa, N.J.: Rowman & Allanheld, 1985.

Warren, Mary Anne, Daniel Maguire, and Carol Levine. "Can the

Fetus Be an Organ Farm?" *Hastings Center Report* 8 (October 1978): 23–25.

Watters, W[endell] W., M. Cohen, D. Carr, and J. Askwith. "Response to Edward W. Keyserlingk's Article: The Unborn Child's Right to Prenatal Care." *Health Law in Canada* 4 (1983): 32–34.

Weil, Robert. "Interview: Alan Trounson." *Omni* (December 1985): 82–88, 124–128.

Wellman, Carl. "Abortion." In *Morals and Ethics*, 157–187. Glenview, Ill.: Scott, Foresman, 1975.

Wertheimer, Roger. "Understanding the Abortion Argument." *Philosophy and Public Affairs* 1 (Fall 1971): 67–95. Reprinted in *Moral Problems*, edited by James Rachels, 71–88. New York: Harper & Row, 1975.

Wertz, Dorothy C. "Man-Midwifery and the Rise of Technology." In *Birth Control and Controlling Birth: Women-Centered Perspectives*, edited by Helen B. Holmes, Betty B. Hoskins, and Michael Gross, 147–166. Clifton, N.J.: Humana Press. 1980.

Wertz, Richard W., and Dorothy C. Wertz. *Lying-In: A History of Childbirth in America*. New York: Schocken Books, 1977.

Westoff, Charles F., and Ronald R. Rindfuss. "Sex Preselection in the United States: Some Implications." *Science* 184 (10 May 1974): 633–636.

Whelan, Elizabeth M. *A Baby? . . . Maybe*. Minneapolis: Bobbs-Merrill, 1975.

Whelan, Elizabeth M. *Boy or Girl?* New York: Simon & Schuster, 1977.

Whitbeck, Caroline. "The Moral Implications of Regarding Women as People: New Perspectives on Pregnancy and Personhood." In *Abortion and the Status of the Fetus*, edited by William B. Bondeson, H. Tristram Engelhardt, Jr., Stuart F. Spicker, and Daniel H. Winship, 247–272. Dordrecht, Holland: D. Reidel, 1983.

Whitbeck, Caroline. "The Maternal Instinct." In *Mothering: Essays in Feminist Theory*, edited by Joyce Trebilcot, 185–198. Totowa, N.J.: Rowman & Allanheld. 1984.

Wikler, Daniel I. "Ought We to Try to Save Aborted Fetuses?" *Ethics* 90 (October 1978): 58–65.

Williams, Linda S. "But What Will They Mean for Women? Feminist Concerns about the New Reproductive Technologies." Ottawa: CRIAW/ICREF Feminist Perspectives Feministes, 1986.

Williams, Linda S. "Who Qualifies for In Vitro Fertilization? A Sociological Examination of the Stated Admittance Criteria of Three Ontario IVF Programs." Paper presented at the 21st annual meeting of the Canadian Sociology and Anthropology Association, Winnipeg, Manitoba, 7 June 1986.

Williamson, Nancy E. "Sex Preferences, Sex Control, and the Status of Women." *Signs* 1 (1976): 847–862.

Williamson, Nancy E. *Sons or Daughters: A Cross-Cultural Survey of Parental Preferences*. Beverly Hills, Calif.: Sage Publications, 1976.

Williamson, Nancy E. "Parental Sex Preferences and Sex Selection." In *Sex Selection of Children*, edited by Neil G. Bennett, 129–145. New York: Academic Press, 1983.

Winslade, William J. "Surrogate Mothers: Private Right or Public Wrong?" *Journal of Medical Ethics* 7 (1981): 153–154.

Wood, Carl, and John Kerin. "Ethics." In *Clinical In Vitro Fertilization*, edited by Carl Wood and Alan [O.] Trounson, 177–188. Berlin: Springer-Verlag, 1984.

Wood, Carl, and Ann Westmore. *Test-Tube Conception*. Englewood Clifts, N.J.: Prentice-Hall, 1984.

Young, Ernle W. D. "Caring for Disabled Infants." *Hastings Center Report* 13 (August 1983): 15–18.

Young, Louise B. *Population in Perspective*. New York: Oxford University Press, 1968.

Zahn, Gordon C. "A Religious Pacifist Looks at Abortion." In *Personal and Social Ethics: Moral Problems with Integrated Theory*, edited by Vincent Barry, 225–231. Belmont, Calif.: Wadsworth Publishing Co., 1978.

Index

Diethylstilbestrol: and infertility, 139
Dworkin, Andrea, 118, 119, 127;
  and surrogate motherhood, 118

ectogenesis, 85 n.8, 207, 208
Edwards, Robert, 137, 145, 146, 147,
  149, 157, 158
Egg banks, 74
Egg donation, 151
Egg farming, 210
Eisenstein, Zillah, 5
Embryo(s), 75, 170, 199, 204, 207;
  adoption, 70, 83, 84; banks, 48, 70;
  donation, 48; experimentation on,
  56; farming of, 47; freezing of, 47,
  78; "orphan", 78; as personal
  property, 86 n.22; production of,
  69; sale of, 51, 52; "stockpiling",
  52; surplus, 73; transfer, 7, 19, 47,
  50, 60, 135 n.68, 169, 171, 203; *see
  also* Right to destroy embryos
Embryo/fetus, 40–61, 85 n.1, 111,
  143, 144, 198; alleged rights of, 69,
  77; attitudes toward, 70; buying or
  selling of, 53; as consumer good,
  49; as consumer product, 50;
  death of, 68, 69, 70, 73, 77;
  defense of 43; ensoulment of, 41;
  experimentation on, 46, 47; and
  Hypocratic injunction, 58; in
  utero, 70, 79; killing of, 81;
  location of, 76; moral obligations
  to, 58; moral status of, 41, 80;
  mother as danger to, 55; and no
  right to kill, 84, 90, 198; and no
  right to occupancy of uterus, 84,
  90, 91, 198; and nonmaleficence,
  58, 59, 80, 198; ontological
  assumptions about, 59–61; and
  personhood, 41, 62 n.2; and
  pregnant woman, 89; primary
  danger to, 55; and "procreative
  autonomy", 50; as product, 49,
  58; as property, 50; protection of,
  208; responsibility toward, 80;
  right to care, 43; right to destroy,
  75; and right to kill, 75, 78, 79, 80,
  82; right to life, 42, 69, 71, 77, 78,
  81; and right to occupancy of
  uterus, 77–79, 82, 83; rights of, 42,
  69, 71, 198; as scientific
  experiment, 50, 58, 61; threat to,
  89; treatment of, 41–48, 49, 54, 56,

57, 68, 70; and women's bodies,
  54, 55; as work of art, 50, 61; *see
  also* Embryo; Fetus
Endometriosis: and infertility, 140
Engelhardt, H. Tristram, Jr., 82, 83
Episiotomy, 89, 92
Essentialist view, 25
Etzioni, Amitai, 30
Eugenics, 1, 197, 210
"Expectant father", 206
External fertilization, 75

"Family, The", 7, 174
Fatherhood, social, 150
Feinberg, Joel, 74, 75
"Femicide", 208
Feminist perspective, 12, 41, 105,
  203; and childbirth, 10; defined,
  2–4
Fertility, 131; lack of, 139
Fetal advocates, 96, 97
Fetal distress, 93
Fetal heart monitor, 92, 93
Fetal monitoring, 44, 101, 124, 207
Fetal rights, 77, 95, 203
Fetal sex preselection, 1, 17–35, 47,
  54, 197, 199, 202, 203; Michael D.
  Bayles, 19–21, 23; harmful
  consequences of, 30–35; and
  postconception sex selection, 18;
  and sexism, 20–22; and sexual
  similarity or complementarity, 27,
  35; social policy for, 28–35;
  techniques for, 18, 19; Mary Anne
  Warren, 21–23
Fetal sex selection, 203; antifeminist
  and nonfeminist approaches to, 8,
  feminist approaches to, 11
Fetal surgery, 43, 45, 48, 50, 54, 60,
  79, 198, 200
Fetal survival: outside uterus, 83
Fetal viability, 83; *see also* Viability
Fetology, 208
Fetoscopy, 44
Fetus, 40, 62 n.3; and Canadian
  Criminal Code, 42; declared legal
  person, 42; identity of, 155; as
  patient, 43, 96; right to diagnosis,
  43; and Section 7 of Charter of
  Rights, 42; psychology of, 211 n.1;
  welfare of, 93
Fetus/newborn, 96
Firestone, Shulamith, 10

About the Author

Christine Overall studied at the University of Toronto, where she received her Ph.D. in philosophy in 1980. From 1975 to 1984 she taught philosophy and women's studies at Marianopolis College in Montreal, Quebec. She is now Associate Professor of Philosophy and Queen's National Scholar at Queen's University, Kingston, Ontario. Her published papers, in the areas of philosophy of religion, feminist theory, and biomedical ethics, have appeared in such journals as *Religious Studies*, *The Southern Journal of Philosophy*, and *The University of Western Ontario Law Review*. She is currently working on a study of sexuality in the context of feminist theory. She is married and the mother of two children.